The Social Conscience of
Latin American Writing

Texas Pan American Series

THE SOCIAL CONSCIENCE
of Latin American Writing

Naomi Lindstrom

University of Texas Press
Austin

Requests for permission to reproduce material from this work
should be sent to Permissions, University of Texas Press, Box 7819,
Austin, TX 78713-7819.

∞ The paper used in this publication meets the minimum
requirements of American National Standard for Information
Sciences—Permanence of Paper for Printed Library Materials,
ANSI Z39.48-1984.

Lindstrom, Naomi, 1950–
    The social conscience of Latin American writing / Naomi Lindstrom.
        p.   cm. — (Texas Pan American series)
    Includes bibliographical references and index.
    ISBN 0-292-74698-9 (cloth : alk. paper). — ISBN 0-292-74699-7
(pbk. : alk. paper)
    1. Latin American literature—History and criticism.   2. Latin
American literature—20th century—History and criticism.
3. Literature and society—Latin America.   4. Postmodernism
(Literature)—Latin America.   I. Title.   II. Series.
PQ7081.L49   1998
860.9'98—DC21   97-30035

to Michael Lindstrom

Contents

Acknowledgments

Research for this book was carried out with the support of a Faculty Research Assignment from the University Research Institute of the University of Texas at Austin. Also contributing was a Faculty Research Award given by the Institute of Latin American Studies with the assistance of the Houston Endowment Fund. I would also like to thank both my parents for lending their sociological perspective to the project and David William Foster for reading and commenting on the manuscript.

The Social Conscience of
Latin American Writing

Introduction

This study has as its purpose to present and discuss five concepts useful to readers who would like to approach Latin American literature in a more analytic spirit. It is not primarily a book to assist those wishing to specialize in the more technical aspects of literary criticism. It is for those who are interested in Latin America as a region and in the literature it has produced, readers who would like to acquire a set of concepts that can be utilized to read this literature critically. Another presupposition is that readers will be interested in Latin American literature principally because it is from Latin America, and also, but only secondarily, because of its formal characteristics. They will have a concern with the social and historical dynamic that has made the region's literature unique, such as the effects of conquest, colonization, and subsequent difficult relations with economically and politically stronger powers. Care has been exercised to make the book accessible to readers who do not read Spanish.

Following these assumptions, the emphasis in this study will not be on developing in full the intricacies of the analytical concepts set forth. The point is to show why the concepts are important and useful in the actual reading of Latin American literature. While many of the issues discussed here are applicable to virtually any literature, one goal of the book is to focus attention on the ways in which literature has assumed distinctive forms in Latin America because of the historical dynamic that has produced it. Both the unique characteristics of Latin America's literary history and the features of individual literary texts will be important in this regard.

In accord with the aim of engaging a general, well-educated readership with a Latin-Americanist interest, little space goes to issues that would principally attract professional literary specialists. There are few references to the academic questions of Latin American literary studies that might strike nonspecialists as hair-splitting. For example, debates over the most accurate starting date for Latin American literature will not be discussed. Nor will such related questions as exactly which works and traditions constitute *Latin American literature* and whether the term itself should be questioned and possibly replaced. For the purposes of this book, Latin American writing is literature originating in Brazil and the Spanish-speaking New World countries. (Mexican-American or Chicano literature lies virtually beyond the scope of this discussion.) The use of a single term for writings from such diverse countries is justified by long-standing practice. Also bypassed is the potentially all-consuming search for precise definitions of terms often applied to Latin American writing, such as *modernismo, magical realism, neobaroque, indigenist novel, the marvelous real, neofantastic,* and *new novel.*

The two terms that do figure prominently in this study—*documentary literature,* or *testimonio* as this type of writing is often known in Spanish, and *postmodernism*—will not be seen primarily as terms requiring precise definition but more as concepts at the center of discussion. Documentary literature is here considered important because it accords the status of author, or at least identified speaking subject, to members of less literate groups. Postmodernism will probably never be unambiguously defined. Though unwieldy, it cannot be disregarded. Discussion of this concept's relation to Latin American cultures has become widespread, generating so many articles and books that only a sampling can be surveyed here. For the purposes of this study, the debate concerning postmodernism in Latin American societies merits attention both because it has involved many Latin American intellectuals, including distinguished innovators, and because the discussion illustrates clearly the struggle to adapt terms and concepts of largely U.S. and European origin.

Throughout this book, the specialized terminology of literary critics is used as sparingly as possible. The goals of this book do not include the resolution of long-running debates over Latin American literature; indeed, the issues treated are most likely perennial problems that will be developed but never solved. Nor is the point to unveil radically different analyses of these problems. Rather, this book seeks to familiarize readers with the main arguments currently being put forward and to allow them to follow the discussion. The chapters of this book are intended to survey the critical discourse that has arisen around these questions. It is first and foremost an overview.

After this introduction, each chapter of the book will present one issue currently important in the analysis of Latin American literature. These problems, such as the disproportionate dependency of one region upon others and the notion of a postmodern society, generally have their origins in the social sciences or in social criticism. Each chapter begins with an orienting discussion of the general issue under examination. Then the discussion turns to the transformations the concept has undergone to apply to literature from Latin American countries. In some cases, ideas have originated among intellectuals based in Latin America. In others, a tendency that first became evident in European or U.S. thought has been reworked to have relevance to Latin American societies. Ideas from the social sciences and cultural criticism have necessarily undergone reworking to be of use in literary studies.

While the primary focus of each chapter is a concept, the chapters at times include discussion, sometimes quite brief and other times more extensive, of works of Latin American literature. These are intended not to be fully developed textual analyses but rather to illustrate the application of the concept. Special attention will go to analytical problems that bring to the fore characteristics of writing from Latin American countries, the relations between this literature and social history, and the special considerations involved in the analysis of Latin American literature. Features that demand attention from students of this literature will receive exceptional emphasis throughout the book. This is not a book dedicated to covering the major movements in literary theory and criticism. The emphasis is not on presenting literary-critical thought as such but on the application of concepts to the discussion of Latin American literature.

One such far-reaching concern is the irregular synchronization between Latin America's literary history—with its succession of schools, tendencies, and movements—and that of Europe. The categories that literary historians have devised to describe European literature correspond sufficiently to Latin American literature to be applicable, but differences stand out clearly. For example, to say *romanticism* with reference to Latin American literature is not the same as to apply the term to European writing. Latin American romanticism runs on its own timetable, persisting, in various forms, well beyond the nineteenth century. Moreover, in Latin American writing, the manifestations of romanticism often commingle with those of realism, naturalism, and Spanish American *modernismo*, producing heterogeneous literary variants that have no equivalent in European literature. In Europe, the baroque manner in art, architecture, and writing is generally associated with a particular era (largely the seventeenth century) so that one can speak either of the baroque style or the period of the baroque. The baroque also flourished energetically in seventeenth-century Latin America. What is distinctive about Latin America is that unmistakable signs of the baroque continue to appear to the present day, although their form undergoes continuous renovation. The enduring presence of this mode gives rise to the often voiced suggestion that a baroque tendency is inherent in Latin American expression.

Clearly, Latin America's historical development, including its troubled and unequal relations with Spain, other Western European powers, the United States, and multinational corporations, has resulted in an erratic pattern of development and modernization. The uneven rate at which progress has occurred in Latin America affects literature as much as other activities. Latin American literature stands out simultaneously because of anachronisms, such as the persistence of stylistic conventions long after they have been discarded in Europe, and because of groundbreaking innovations in literary language, narrative construction, and treatment of subject matter. The irregular rate of development is especially evident during campaigns to modernize Latin America. For example, during the 1870s, 1880s, and 1890s, Latin America rapidly strengthened its ties with the industrialized nations. The region became much more a part of the world system of international exchange, including not just intensified trade relations but also a more rapid communication of artistic trends from area to area. Many technological advances occurred, while Latin American literature produced the determinedly up-to-date modernist movement. At the same time, though, other sectors of Latin American life and letters appeared scarcely affected by the struggle to attain modernity.

A related preoccupation is the tension between the effort on the part of Latin American intellectuals to internationalize and modernize culture by following patterns first established by Europe and the United States, and the drive to draw fully upon the unique regional and ethnic cultural resources of the New World. Angel Rama (1926–1983) hypothesizes that the originality of Latin American literature arises from a struggle between these two simultaneous tendencies. The effort by cosmopolitan intellectuals to bring Latin America up to an international ideal of modernity co-occurs with the insistence, most clearly exemplified by back-to-the-roots cultural nationalists, on a "more vigorous and persistent source of nourishment: the cultural uniqueness developed within" Latin America.[1] Rama disparages a single-minded devotion to being at the world forefront of narrative innovation if it entails a disregard for the home region's unique features. At the same time, though, he sees a puristic dedication to regionalist writing, ignoring the twentieth-century transformations in the writing of fiction, as "a defensive backtracking" that "doesn't solve any problems."[2] Rama singles out for approval those regionalist writers who were able to benefit from the changes that recent decades have brought about in the construction of narrative. He cites with some pleasure the Brazilian thinker Gilberto Freyre (1900–1987), author of the influential *Regionalist Manifesto* of 1926, who upon later reflection described what he had sought as "a movement as modernist as it was traditionalist and regionalist, revolutionizing the norms of Brazilian art."[3]

Many Latin American writers and artists have been zealous in their pursuit of a cosmopolitan ideal of modernity. Indeed, their extreme dedication to being up-to-date by international standards often seems to be the factor that sets them apart from European and U.S. contemporaries. At the same time, there has always been a sharp awareness of the special repertory of references, themes, beliefs, and expressive traditions found exclusively in Latin America. This consciousness is most readily evident when authors deal with the non-European currents in Latin American society. Indigenous cultures—both the high civilizations of the Aztec, Maya, and Inca empires, and current-day native groups—have long proven both attractive and problematic as a source for Spanish- and Portuguese-language literature. Latin America presents numerous cases of mixed groups, such as *mestizos;* the African-Latin syntheses of the Caribbean and Brazil; and populations combining African, native, and European backgrounds. The existence of these hybrid cultures is one of the clearest signs of Latin America's originality, and writers have turned to them as markers of the region's distinct identity as well as for their intrinsic fascination.

Whatever the sources of the ideas and terms, this book presents them in the context of the study of literature. An examination of Latin American literature that draws elements from dependency theory, generated in the 1960s by political economists, cannot truthfully be called an economic or political-science reading. An analysis of a literary work that utilizes ideas generated in the social sciences can only loosely be called a sociological or anthropological reading of that work. Stanley Fish, remarking on the changes that ideas undergo in moving from field to field, once suggested "the impossibility of the interdisciplinary project."[4] This study is inter-disciplinary in its sources, but it has an undeniable primary loyalty to lit-erary studies. It is less important to use a term or concept exactly as social scientists do than to take part in the discussion of issues in literature. Though the textual analyses presented must make sense first and foremost as literary commentary, the book owes a strong debt to sources outside literary criticism, especially to the traditions of sociological and anthropo-logical thought.

A word is in order concerning the selection of the works used as exem-plary texts. Some works of poetry are mentioned, but the texts from which actual quotations are taken are all prose narrative, including autobiogra-phies and eyewitness accounts of historical events. The principal reason for this choice is that, on the whole, readers not specialized in literature, espe-cially those utilizing translations, have been most likely to turn to fiction. While outstanding poets, such as Pablo Neruda and Octavio Paz, have en-joyed international respect, it is prose writers whose actual works (or, in some cases, their cinematic adaptations) have come in for discussion by a public well beyond the literary world. Translations of poetry, especially in brief excerpts, frequently fail to convey why the original is considered sig-nificant. Since all quotations in this study are in English, the greater trans-latability of prose was a consideration. Finally, the uniformity provided by selecting all prose texts permits comparative cross-references between one chapter and another.

While literary works from all periods since the Spanish and Portuguese conquest are used as examples, the lengthier analyses, including quotations, are from twentieth-century works. Again, the goal has been to select works that have become available to a wide, international public and to cite only from those texts whose special features will be readily apparent in English translation.

This book owes a great deal to the thought of Angel Rama, as well as to other critics who have studied Latin American literature in its social context: Noé Jitrik, Joseph Sommers, Jean Franco, as well as to such stu-dents of society as Néstor García Canclini. It has also made use of read-ings of Latin American literature carried out by less overtly social critics who nonetheless have a good eye for literature's historical context, such as John S. Brushwood and Seymour Menton.

The organization of the book, as noted, involves a series of chapters, each presenting one concept and its application in the discussion of Latin

American literature. What follows is a brief description of the issues presented in the various chapters.

In this overview, one major focus is the adjustments that concepts require to keep pace with the times. Perhaps the most striking example is that of dependency theory, examined in Chapter One. As formulated in the 1960s, the theory has become outdated. Accelerated global movement of capital, goods, and people, the rise of transnational firms, and the internal problems of economically strong nations have complicated the opposition between the powerful metropolis and exploited periphery, upon which the original theory was constructed. In addition, as soon as the theory became widespread, observers began to object to its oversimplification of what would later be known as the world system. While dependency theory was attracting negative criticism, it could not be abandoned because it dealt with issues still of great concern. Even those who viewed the theory itself as a relic of the 1960s continued to use its central terms and ideas. Concepts of dependency and autonomy have had to become more sophisticated in response to both critical objections and increasingly complex global interrelations.

In addition, the application of elements of dependency theory to the analysis of literature presents an unusual case of interdisciplinary transfer since the study of the economy is so unlike the study of literature. Concepts of dependency sprang up in a mode of analysis unlike anything employed by literary critics; to become part of literary studies, they had to develop into forms often very unlike their original ones.

Some of the analysis in this chapter will be not so much of individual works but rather of long-standing problems in the history of Latin American literature. Although dependency is really a long-term, almost intractable problem that affects all of Latin America's cultural development, it is still possible to analyze its manifestations in a particular text. The 1968 novel *Betrayed by Rita Hayworth* by the Argentine Manuel Puig lends itself to such discussion. Because *Rita Hayworth* clearly brings out the issues discussed in Chapter One, this novel comes in for more extended analysis than any other literary text discussed in this book.

As dissatisfaction with dependency theory continued, despite continual refinements, the concept of *transculturation* has provided a somewhat different way of focusing on the relations between the cultures of dominant groups and those of less powerful regions and peoples. *Transculturation*, a term and concept originated by the Cuban anthropologist Fernando Ortiz and since adapted to literary studies, will be discussed at the end of the chapter on dependency and autonomy. While it is not in any direct line of descent from dependency theory, it is one manifestation of an undiminished concern with Latin America's place among the world's societies and cultures.

Chapter Two, on postmodernism, begins with a general introduction to this phenomenon. By its very nature, postmodernism will probably never be characterized with any precision. In the present survey, the emphasis is on features of postmodernism that have most excited debate. Chapter Two provides more coverage to European and U.S. scholars than the other chapters because the term *postmodernism* was undeniably developed outside Latin America. Indeed, the foreign origin of the word and concept has been an issue in Latin American discussion of postmodernism.

Then the chapter turns to the discussion of the application of the term and concept *postmodernism* to Latin American culture. The use of postmodernism has been controversial, in great part because it is such a clear case of a term developed to describe U.S. and Western European social changes transferred to another set of realities. There has been much doubt as to the applicability of the term. Some scholars argue that Latin American societies have never experienced any thorough, overall modernization and therefore cannot be postmodern in the usual sense. Many observers believe that the region has always exhibited what appear to be postmodern features. Some of those involved in the debate reject the term as an ill-fitting foreign imposition. Still, the discussion of postmodernism inevitably has spread through Latin America. Its importance in the discussion of late-twentieth-century culture has been so great that the term cannot be artificially excluded from the critical examination of Latin American societies. Yet, scholars continue to question its relevance and to make adjustments in the concept of the postmodern to suit Latin American societies.

The examples discussed in Chapter Two are, on the one hand, works of Spanish American and Brazilian essayists who have debated the application of the term and concept and, on the other, creative writing. Selected Latin American prose fiction of the period from the 1970s forward is considered as presenting a case of postmodernism.

Chapter Three treats the issues raised by documentary narratives authored by members of native groups. Testimonial or documentary literature is one category in which Latin American writers have produced notable innovations. Not only have significant texts appeared and excited discussion, but the very category of documentary literature has provoked a good deal of analysis and debate, both among writers themselves and among academic literary critics. The growth of documentary literature is at times seen as necessitating a vigorous effort of redefinition, including a rethinking of the boundaries of creative writing itself. In this chapter, though, the search for a definition of the phenomenon will not be pursued in any exhaustive manner. While documentary literature involves many types of authors and speakers, this book focuses specifically on the place that Spanish American and Brazilian literature accords to information coming from speakers who are from less literate ethnic subpopulations. Part of this chapter is a general overview of the lengthy transition from the custom of regarding Indians, African-Hispanics, and persons of mixed ancestry as informants or sources to the present practice of assigning author or at least senior-collaborator status to the poorer and ethnically distinctive narrators and autobiographers. Several texts come in for consideration in this chapter, but especially the 1966 *Biografía de un cimarrón* (translated as *Autobiography of a Runaway Slave*) by the Cuban Miguel Barnet, who worked with the ex-slave Esteban Montejo, and *Me llamo Rigoberta Menchú* (*I, Rigoberta Menchú: An Indian Woman in Guatemala*) by Elizabeth Burgos Debray with Rigoberta Menchú (1959), the latter the winner of the 1992 Nobel Peace Prize.

According to long-standing convention, the sole credited author of ethnographic or regionalist narratives was generally a highly educated person responsible for gathering the material and seeing it through the publication process. The author often had gathered information by speaking with informants from indigenous groups or isolated communities. The concept of the native informant is most closely associated with anthropology and with the study of living Amerindian languages, which outsiders cannot master without assistance from native speakers. Yet writers of *indigenista* or Indian-themed novels have also often emphasized to their public the confidential relations that they had established with members of native communities. Having drawn out from real-life Indians their experiences and cultural information gave these writers a special entitlement to treat indigenous life in fiction. Clearly, by the late twentieth century the public was eager to read the first-person accounts, as little mediated as possible, of people who would not ordinarily publish their life stories. Many readers are looking for a positive answer to the question Gayatri Chakravorty Spivak poses in the title of her much-cited essay "Can the Subaltern Speak?" which is hardly sanguine on the point.[5] Identifying Indians as authors appeals to the current-day campaign to recognize the creative and inventive talents of native peoples and other disadvantaged populations. Yet the image of the Indian-authored text is complicated by the assistance, of some sort, needed by nearly all Indians, so far, who have published in Spanish or Portuguese. Someone more at home in the mainstream culture assumes responsibility for the actual writing of the text in Spanish or Portuguese, using as a basis conversations or tape-recorded reminiscences. The collaborator who is sophisticated in the dominant culture may well be the one to shape the narrative according to the conventions of the autobiography or the eyewitness report and to add such elements as chapter titles, epigraphs, glossaries of words in the native language, and notes explaining folkways unfamiliar to outsiders.

In Chapter Four, whose topic is the relations between Latin American literary intellectuals and the mass media, a central problem is how to think critically about modern mass culture and its effects on both society and art. Many Latin American scholars and social critics have published examinations of twentieth-century commercial pop culture, and an effort to survey all of their writing on the topic would result in, at the least, a book. This chapter is specifically on literary intellectuals and how they have reacted to, and become involved with, mass media and cultures. This chapter is not primarily concerned with researchers' theories and findings about popular and mass culture, although there is mention of the Frankfurt School and alternatives to it as well as the innovative analyses of Ariel Dorfman. The chapter concentrates not on research but on creative responses to the rise of commercial popular culture. Some literary creators have sought to join the makers of mass culture, hoping to bring about renovation from within. Others use their essays and creative writings to deliver a critique of mass culture and its passive consumers. The example examined in most detail is that of the Argentine novelist and essayist Julio Cortázar, who maintained a sanguine belief that mass culture could be refashioned to increase awareness of social forces.

Chapter Five treats the related topics of women's writing from Latin America and critical efforts to examine gender issues in Latin American literature. It is inevitable that, in the construction of a gender-studies approach to Latin American writing, there will be some use of elements from European and U.S. feminism. At the same time, many scholars are eager to point out the differences between the Latin American nations and the areas in which present-day feminism was formulated. Considerable discussion has gone to ways in which international feminist thought may be transformed and adapted for Latin American literature. Clearly, critics of Latin American literature have another source to tap besides feminist theory: Latin American literature itself, especially imaginative writing and essays by women.

While many works by Latin American women writers have been translated into English, especially in recent years, it is still difficult for English-language readers to glimpse the full historical range of literature by women authors from the region. For this reason, as well as because of the importance of Latin American women's writing in the shaping of a feminist criticism applicable to it, the chapter includes a brief survey of this literature.

The development of a criticism centered on issues of gender first manifested itself in feminist criticism. Other related investigative fields began to establish themselves later. The most important of these other types of gender-based research is gay and lesbian studies. While the chapter on gender issues is predominantly occupied with the study of women's writing and feminism in literary criticism, its final section follows the more recent development of gay and lesbian studies as applied to Latin American writing. While this newer field as yet has produced much less criticism than the better-established feminist approach, it is one of the most quickly expanding areas in the study of Latin American literature and culture.

The choice of critical sources to quote reflects, beyond the inherent relevance of the material cited, two criteria. On the one hand, a major point of the book is to present critical thought as elaborated by Latin American intellectuals. This goal makes it desirable to cite the work of authors from Latin American countries. At the same time, this book is meant to accommodate readers not able to read Spanish; there should be at least some sources that this audience can use to pursue further reading. The ideal citation is one from a Latin American author's work for which a published English translation already exists. When this ideal solution is not possible, the citations either come from Spanish-language materials or from works by European and U.S. researchers that summarize or continue the ideas of Latin American thinkers. All English versions of Spanish and Portuguese citations for which no translator is credited are my own.

1 Autonomy and Dependency in Latin American Writing

The Spanish and Portuguese conquest of the New World marked, among other things, the beginning of Latin American intellectuals' efforts to think clearly about problems of cultural autonomy, whether for a specific country or regionwide. Latin America's unequal relations with Europe and, later, the United States and transnational firms have been an important theme of discussion. As the Independence wars receded in time, it became clear that disadvantageous economic and cultural relations would persist well beyond the abolition of colonial rule. (In most cases, declarations of independence were issued in the early years of the nineteenth century, with Cuba and Puerto Rico lagging behind; the latter has never attained autonomous status.) The end of official colonial rule, rather than equalize relations between the highly powerful nations and Latin America, has brought more subtle means of continuing the formers' advantage. Accordingly, it becomes a more complex task to identify and analyze the means by which stronger nations maintain inequality.

Dependency is the term and concept that has come into use to refer to the less-developed nations' inability to set their own course, whether in economic or cultural matters. The intensity of fairly recent debate can give the illusion that dependency and its inverse, autonomy, are concepts first theorized in the mid–twentieth century. Yet references to Latin America's disadvantage in international relations have a lengthy history in general intellectual discussion. The Independence-era thinker who most thoroughly explored the aftereffects of colonialism, Andrés Bello, published an essay under the still-current title "The Cultural Autonomy of America." Bello understood an inequality much discussed today: creators and thinkers from centers of economic and political power enjoy a disproportionate chance of exercising worldwide influence. Access to major publications and influential critics brings recognizable benefits. Talented creators based in less dominant countries may find it difficult to find a public even locally. To lessen the magnified attraction of metropolitan culture, Bello urged local publics to recognize their region's distinctive subject matters and cultural production as worthy of notice.

Since the Independence era, unequal cultural relations have regularly been examined. Sometimes the discussion is detached and analytical, while in other cases social critics and creative people come under polemical fire for their *europeísmo*. Intellectuals living and working in Latin American countries are among those likely to be adversely affected by the imbalance of influence between more- and less-powerful areas. Although it cannot be clearly demonstrated, many observers believe that the prestige of writers is often inflated when their home countries or cities are predominant in the world economy, politics, and technical expertise. The inequality of cultural interrelations has been a virtually unavoidable topic in Latin American intellectual life. While the issue most often arises in the discussion of international relations, inequities within Latin America or within a single country also deserve notice. For example, it has long been apparent that writers living in such capitals of publishing and literary activity as Mexico City and Buenos Aires enjoy an advantage over those located where editorial resources are scarce and there is relatively little organized literary life.

As well as being a longtime theme of discussion, the concept of international and interregional inequalities was formally elaborated during the 1960s and 1970s in dependency theory, to be discussed shortly. Dependency theory arose among political economists examining the impasse faced by poorer nations in their interchange, especially trade relations, with economically powerful ones. It helps explain how nations that have enjoyed decades of political independence and have been the site of expertly designed development programs cannot become equal trading partners with the long-industrialized countries and, despite what seem to be rapid advances, lag behind them technologically.

Some concepts elaborated by dependency theorists have moved from the field of economics into the general intellectual environment, becoming part of the public discussion of social and cultural issues. The theoretically formalized concept of dependency then merges with the more general notion of powerful countries' advantage that has long been a theme of Latin American nonspecialist intellectuals. The theory has spread to communications studies, cultural studies, and literary criticism. Obviously, literary studies little resemble economics, and a theory formulated for the latter cannot be used in its original form by the former. The discussion of dependency theory will emphasize the changes that this current of thought has undergone in its journey between dissimilar fields.[1]

Since its formulation in the 1960s, the political-economic theory has been questioned and forced to adapt to changing times. Not only did theorists need to account for complexities initially obscured by overgeneralization, but further modifications were required by changing world conditions. These include the rise of transnational firms, which makes the locus of economic power and the globalization of culture more difficult to identify. There is a clearer recognition that such countries as the United States, despite the power they can still wield in the international marketplace, contain regions so impoverished as to resemble an internal third world. Conversely, in economically disadvantaged regions particular groups may attain a position of superior strength. Inequalities among nations and regions have certainly not disappeared or lost their significance. But it has become more difficult to identify which entities are at the center of economic power and which are on the periphery.

The final portion of the chapter examines a further development in critical thought concerning the relations between dominant and disadvantaged cultures. This is the term and concept of *transculturation*. Transculturation is not, strictly speaking, an outgrowth or descendant of dependency theory. Still, it can be viewed as a further effort to deal with the concerns with which dependency theorists struggled. One of the weaknesses of early cultural dependency theory was an assumption that disadvantaged countries or peoples were defenseless against the onslaught of cultural patterns and products from dominant nations. The concept of transculturation was developed to take into account the resilience often exhibited in the cultural sphere by nations and peoples lacking political and economic power. When a dominant culture invades or is forced upon a disadvantaged group, the latter is frequently ingenious in adapting the new culture and combining it with its long-standing patterns.

All the issues involved have a long history of discussion. While dependency was not formally theorized until the 1960s, the problem of achieving and maintaining autonomy is a constant in the history of Latin America. Before examining the theory as such, it is worth taking a brief retrospective look at the history of the asymmetrical relations between Latin American countries and more powerful entities, as well as the struggle to achieve a measure of autonomy despite this inherent imbalance.

During the conquest, the Europeans had as their explicit assignment to claim the land for Spain and Portugal and to convert the inhabitants to Christianity. However, these announced purposes were accompanied by other, secondary missions dealing with the Europeanization of the New World's culture. One could compose a lengthy list of the features of European culture that the colonizers sought to substitute for native ones. It would include the typically Mediterranean urban layout, Roman law, the Gregorian calendar, numerous items of dress and diet, and folkways. The campaign to introduce new items into the region's cultural repertory was more successful than the attempt to delete existing ones. Although the goal was to catholicize and Latinize the new subject populations, these populations instead became more heterogeneous in composition and culture. But from the point of view of readers and writers of literature, the greatest area of change was one in which Europeanization was exceptionally thorough. Spanish and Portuguese emerged as virtually the sole vehicles of written communication. Latin American writing takes place, with few exceptions, in one or the other of these languages.

It will be remembered that, before the conquest, native writing systems flourished in the Aztec empire and throughout Mesoamerica. In addition, the governance of the vast Inca empire relied on a notational system involving knots of different types. The native writing and record-keeping systems did not immediately vanish with the Spanish and Portuguese conquest. Indeed, the Europeans at times encouraged native writing insofar as it encoded information needed for administrative purposes. Martin Lienhard notes several instances in which the Spaniards received from their new subjects communications either in native systems or a combination of these forms with graphics.[2] Nonetheless, the use of indigenous writing began to die out with colonization. Lienhard observes that the reason for its demise was not the Europeans' effort to suppress it. Instead, native writing was not maintained because there were no longer enough people left who used it as part of normal communicative practices. Lienhard observes that native writing systems were emptied of meaning when they lost their link to the spoken communication of communities and so became "orphans of voice."[3]

Pedro Henríquez Ureña, considering the circumstances described above, sets out some cautionary words to anyone hoping for the emergence of a completely original literary expression in Latin America. While fascinated by these Utopians, Henríquez Ureña reminds them of the sobering fact that they must write in languages brought by the conquerors.[4] The exceptions, such as texts produced by Maya-language writers' workshops or transcriptions of Guaraní narratives (in both cases, written out phonetically in Roman alphabet), necessarily have a limited audience. Angel Rama notes that, following the 1920s–1930s surge of interest in native American Indian affairs, "several books . . . were published in native American languages by people who were *mestizado* Indians," that is, Indians who had gained entry into mainstream culture. Not only did the instances of such neo-native writing remain virtually unknown, but Rama considers that these efforts were not "radically Indian."[5]

In Henríquez Ureña's analysis, nonliterary arts could potentially achieve a greater liberation from Spanish and Portuguese influence because they do not rely on a European cultural form for their very medium.[6] Henríquez Ureña does not view these circumstances as reason to despair of attaining a distinctive expressive tradition in Latin American writing. Rather, the situation should infuse Latin American literary culture with an awareness that the autonomy this writing achieves will always be a relative and complicated one.

Students and critics of society have adopted various frames of reference to describe and theorize about Latin America's relations with economically and politically advantaged nations. During the last decades of colonial rule, Enlightenment thought and rhetoric concerning the people's right to self-governance were prominent among Latin American intellectuals, as was the case in the United States. However, participants in the discussion of the New World's need for independence went well beyond the terms of French-derived Enlightenment rationalism. This is nowhere more the case than when the problem at hand was not political independence as such but the attainment of a degree of autonomy in expressive and cultural patterns and independence of outlook.

Not long after Spanish and Portuguese rule spread in the New World, at least some colonists of European ancestry and upbringing began to realize that their vision and language were diverging from those found in the Old World. Populations sprang up that, while speaking Spanish and Portuguese and forming part of colonial society, were unlike the first-generation colonizers in their identities, beliefs, and outlook. Increasing proportions of New World inhabitants were either of European descent but American-born (the *criollos*) or had mixed Indian and European ancestry (the *mestizos*). These groups had an obvious motivation to promote political independence, especially since the Spanish reserved posts of authority for the European-born. At the same time, they were rapidly moving away from the Iberian standard in their culture. Juan José Arrom has examined the history of the term *criollo*, which was applied to a wide spectrum of traits considered peculiar to the Spanish-speaking New World. *Criollo* could designate exceptional sharpness of wit, a talent for mockery, an informal style of interaction, or an attitude of resentment toward crown and church authorities. Whatever it designated, the spread of the term signaled an awareness that those born in the New World, regardless of ancestry or citizenship, were developing a certain autonomy of outlook that preceded outright calls for the end of colonial rule.[7]

The distinctive outlook of New World dwellers manifested itself in various ways. Printed expression was under the control of crown authorities; in a famous ruling, novels were forbidden, out of suspicion that they could overstimulate and confuse the imaginations of the New World's excitable population. Nonetheless, certain documents that have somehow survived from the colonial era attest to a continuing drive to maintain a degree of independence from European rule. Researchers have been attracted to the *Nueva corónica y buen gobierno* (New chronicle and good governance), a 1189-page petition addressed to the king of Spain. While there is debate over its true authorship, it is attributed to Felipe Guaman Poma de Ayala (c. 1526–after 1613), an Andean Indian. This petition, completed around 1615, was archived upon arrival and only came to light in 1908. Obviously struggling with his Spanish, Guaman Poma attempts to bring to the king's attention the damage wreaked by the conquest; he believes this destruction to be, in some respects, reversible. He proposes that the Spaniards restore, at least in part, the Inca empire's original system of government. Students of this exceptional text have been fascinated by the petitioner's laborious and highly original use of European-style writing and illustrations to present the case for the Quechua-speaking population, its rights, and its culture.[8] Lienhard emphasizes the advance in autonomy represented by the letters of Guaman Poma and a similar Indian petitioner: "For the first time, here, the bearers of collective conscience and memory stop being 'native informants' or composers of European-style reports to become the authors . . . of a text that is fully their own, the makers of a radically new literary practice."[9]

Jean Franco draws attention to the importance of oral interaction as an outlet for potentially risky attitudes. She notes that native peoples used oral transmission not only to preserve the community's special knowledge but also "to maintain a consciousness of their past and build up resentment and subversion over long periods."[10] Talk as a conduit for anti-establishment attitudes was also important for *criollos*. In the latter case, what was unsafe to print could be uttered, especially mockery of and expressions of disrespect toward viceregal and church authorities.

Talk from the past is difficult to study. But certain literary texts that mimic oral expression give evidence of the distinctive outlook spreading in the colonies and encourage the inhabitants of the New World to focus their attention away from Europe. One of the best-known is Concolorcorvo's (real name Alonso Carrió de la Vandera) *Lazarillo de ciegos caminantes desde Buenos Aires hasta Lima* (Guide for blind travelers from Buenos Aires to Lima), published about 1775. The *Lazarillo* was published not only under a pseudonym but also with the date and place of publication falsified to shield the author and printer from repercussions.

Purportedly a descriptive guidebook, the *Lazarillo* features two travelers, one of them an Indian, who accompany one another from Buenos Aires to Lima. They spend their time observing the local scene and talking to one another and to people along the route. The *Lazarillo* aims its satire chiefly at figures of authority, uneducated and superstitious common folk, and pretentious or snobbish characters. It also encourages dwellers to focus their attention on the continent they inhabit and accord it due importance. Among the targets of its satire is the colonist who, believing that significance resides in the Old World, fails to acquire a knowledge of the surrounding land. This wrong-headed man is afflicted with what would, in later decades, be known as a Eurocentric vision or cultural dependency.

Though the *Lazarillo* is manifestly concerned with identifying distinctive features of the New World, many colonial-era texts less deliberately reveal Latin America's growing dissimilarity to Spain and Portugal. Franco has suggested that the Latin American writer's situation in the periphery necessarily left its mark on all of literary production. In her judgment, "some mysterious oddness marks even the work of those writers who labor most strenuously to enter into the paradise of universal culture," such as the baroque poet Sor Juana Inés de la Cruz.[11] Because of their colonial situation, the early Latin American writers inescapably exhibit features unknown in European literature. Anxiety lest they be perceived as behind the times, as dwellers in a cultural backwater, may have motivated colonial writers to display their erudition and sophistication to an unusual degree, producing results unlike anything seen in European literature.[12] Octavio Paz, referring primarily to a later era, has also suggested that Latin American writers, when they are most seized with a desire to keep pace with European trends, generate unanticipated, and distinctively Latin American, variations.[13]

While a work like the *Lazarillo* anticipates the movement for independence, much Latin American writing of the early nineteenth century takes as its topic not only the end of colonial rule but the difficulties of creating an autonomous New World in the wake of official decolonization. During this period both literary writers and speechmakers developed concepts, metaphors, images, and cultural allusions to help the now-independent Latin Americans see their lands as endowed with special properties, qualities, and opportunities lacking in Europe.

Hopes were running high to unite the former colonies, or large areas of Latin America, into vast confederations. Consequently, Independence rhetoric stressed features that made all the areas of Latin America similar to one another and unlike the European powers. Prime among these was the common, uniting mission of building a new society to supersede the corrupt, exhausted civilizations of Europe. Some Spanish American authors link the glory of the great indigenous empires to the exciting fresh start offered by independence, contrasting both these high points with the depths of oppression represented by colonial rule.[14] Enrique Anderson Imbert notes the appearance of idealized figures of the Indian in the work of Independence-era intellectuals who displayed little concern for here-and-now native peoples. "The men of [José Joaquín Olmedo's] generation (both Creoles and Spaniards) had worked up a sentimental Indianism which served to condemn the cruelties of the conquest and, while they were at it, agitate against political absolutism."[15] *A la agricultura de la Zona Tórrida* (On the agriculture of the torrid zone), the lengthy 1826 poem by the Venezuelan-Chilean Andrés Bello (1781–1865), uses the conventions of pastoral poetry to promote the belief that the New World has an agricultural mission that will distinguish it from the commercial and urban decadence into which Europe has fallen. This poem, in looking forward to the period after the Independence wars, emphasizes the New World's linguistic divergence from Europe by employing native words for life forms found exclusively in the Americas. Like Bello's work, poems and speeches on independence themes often attribute purity and freshness to the New World.

Henríquez Ureña, whose research reveals a fascination with Utopian ideas, has identified several that flourished following independence, designed to bolster cultural autonomy. Many hoped to see the Spanish spoken in the Americas diverge from the peninsular standard. Pursuing this idea further, certain thinkers proposed that the Spanish-speaking New World should make a fresh linguistic start with a new language that could no longer be called Spanish. Henríquez Ureña calls this proposal for securing autonomy a "mad hope." Yet the conception of this project proves how strongly language is perceived as uniting Latin America, for good or ill, with the Iberian peninsula.[16]

After independence, it became increasingly apparent that colonial rule and its associated mercantile system for restricting colonies' trade relations were by no means the only methods of maintaining an advantage over less developed and established countries. During the 1870s, 1880s, and 1890s, Latin American economies became much more heavily engaged with those of the most industrialized nations. A pattern was set in which Europe and, increasingly, the United States looked to Latin America as a source of commodities. One result was that the industrialized nations buying raw materials and exporting manufactured goods established trade relations that inherently favored them. Latin American economies became so tightly connected with foreign ones that worldwide depressions or fluctuations in the foreign demand for commodities could provoke economic slumps at home. Another outcome was the rise to prosperity of a new Latin American elite specializing in finance, trade, and supplying products in demand abroad. These merchants and traders, motivated not only by their fresh prosperity but by the contemporary vogue for elaborate ornamentation and household decoration, were responsible for the construction of noted architectural showpieces and for the importation and display of objets d'art and other status-bearing items. Closer European and U.S. contact made Latin Americans more eager to be up-to-date, and there were many projects to speed up technical progress.

As Paz, Rama, and others have observed, it was during this same period that Spanish American literature produced the movement known as *modernismo*, which also involved a campaign for internationalization and modernization, although on the esthetic front.[17] For some time, studies of *modernismo* tended to focus attention on the modernists' innovations in poetic form and the esthetic and spiritual principles that motivated their work. Joseph Sommers has reprehended the preoccupation of U.S. critics with "questions of formal innovation and topics of literary escapism" in

Latin American *modernismo*, to the exclusion of its place in overall social changes and the cultural criticism present in much modernist writing. For Sommers, this focus "has tended, directly or indirectly, to reinforce the asymmetrical relations, whether economic, political, or cultural, between the United States and Latin America." [18] Even if this is the case, one should remember that many modernist poets actively cultivated an image of themselves as detached esthetes.

Since the late 1960s, however, *modernismo* has attracted critics concerned with Latin America's unequal situation vis-à-vis Europe. Modernist poets exhibited, in both explicit and covert ways, an extreme awareness of these difficult relations. *Modernismo* presents a number of contradictions and paradoxes that have allowed critics to sharpen their understanding of relations between sectors of the world.

Modernismo is frequently pointed out as the first literary movement to originate in Spanish America and subsequently to influence Spanish peninsular writers. This honor would seem to make *modernismo* a sign of Latin America's growing cultural independence. Yet modernist writers are also often criticized for an imitative attachment to foreign, especially French, literary trends. Paz, in his 1965 *Cuadrivio* (portions of which appear in English in *The Siren and the Seashell*), examines this seeming paradox. In his assessment, generally favorable to the modernists, the outstanding originality that *modernismo* achieved at its best was driven, in large part, by fear of not participating in the contemporary era. Paz has noted that the name *modernista* betrays an anxiety that one must struggle to gain access to modernity and is in danger of falling behind the times. The *modernistas'* deliberate campaign to become modern contrasts with the self-assured attitude of Western European urban intellectuals. For the latter, modernity naturally included, and was partly defined by, their work. Paz describes the Latin American intellectual as motivated by the conviction that "history . . . belongs to others," but that it is something that, with struggle and experimentation, "one somehow makes one's own." [19]

Rama applies the notion of dependency theory in discussing the paradox that the scramble after European innovations made Spanish American *modernismo* unique. He locates the originality of *modernismo* in its unprecedented fusion of literary tendencies considered mutually antagonistic in Europe—Parnassianism and symbolism together with movements long established in Latin America, realism and romanticism. For Rama, this heterogeneity "is the consequence of a colonized way of functioning. . . . It is distinguished by the anxious drive for novelty as it is dictated by the imperial centers and a corresponding resistance to abandon values already acquired, trying out sometimes eccentric combinations that have given rise to original inventions."[20]

Students of *modernismo* have also found absorbing the *modernistas*' ambivalent relations with Latin America's new development and prosperity. One does not need to look very hard at *modernista* writing to identify a stream of negative criticism directed against industrialists, merchants, financiers, and entrepreneurs. The most famous such text is probably the very short story "El rey burgués" (The bourgeois king) by the Nicaraguan-born Rubén Darío, which creates an opposition between the poet and the acquisitive, materialistic nouveau riche. Many other *modernista* texts similarly cast the innovative writer as being above the material concerns that are coming to dominate the contemporary scene. The preoccupation with technological advances, material gains, and finance receives a negative portrayal in a great many texts from this movement.

The recent tendency in research on *modernismo* has been to remind readers that, however strong the creator's desire to devote all energies to belles lettres, no one can opt out of the economy. Rama drove this point home in his very brief 1967 *Los poetas modernistas en el mercado económico* (Modernist poets in the economic marketplace), later included in his 1970 *Rubén Darío y el modernismo* (*Circunstancias socioeconómicas de un arte americano*) (Rubén Darío and modernism [socioeconomic circumstances of an American art]). This study details the ways in which modernist poets acquired the money for their personal living expenses and the publication of their experimental poetry and prose.[21] Some modernists earned their living in ways that had no relation to their writing and that were perceived as intruding upon it. Others, though, marketed their writing by different routes. Many practiced journalism, which was then rapidly evolving from reflective essays to a mass-media style, with a rapid succession of up-to-date, catchy items. Some modernists found sponsors to underwrite their creative publications. Whatever their means of financing their poetic labors, the modernists had no choice but to participate in the economic market. As Rama notes, the late-nineteenth-century marketplace afforded a place for modernist poets, as well as "many ex-poets," as members of the liberal professions, public servants, and clerks and bureaucrats.[22] Yet "In the last decades of the nineteenth century and the beginning of the twentieth, in that strictly *modernista* period that comes to an end in 1910, it is not only evident that there is no place for the poet in the utilitarian society that has been created; rather, this society, as it is bound by the rule of economy and the rational use of all its elements for the productive goals it sets itself, must destroy the dignity the aristocracy formerly gave the poet and revile him as a dangerous growth on society." [23]

It was during the late nineteenth century that fairly substantial Latin American elites enjoyed the possibility of importing luxury goods, especially for decoration and adornment. While mocking the acquisitive zeal of the newly prosperous, the modernist poets exhibited a fascination of their own with beautiful, exotic items. The modernists viewed their esthetic appreciation of beautiful objects as very different from the bourgeoisie's effort to win status as the possessors of costly showpieces. Yet the shared obsession with the display of material splendor is another indication that the modernists were participating in, as well as criticizing, Latin America's new experience of prosperity and economic internationalization.

The twentieth century added further complexities to the relations between Latin America and advantaged countries, among whom the United States came to assume increasing prominence. Industrial manufacturing capacity in itself was no longer able to determine a nation's economic strength and influence. Research and development was now focused upon innovations in communications technologies and mass media, which came to include radio, film, and television, and marketing and advertising techniques. These changes produced concern among many observers that foreign firms, attaining a dominant place in media and popular culture, would displace Latin American forms of culture and communications. After all, the new media were designed to be persuasive and attractive. It was easy for audiences to be drawn to innovative cultural products expertly designed in the United States and Europe. Imported technical novelties had the potential to outdazzle forms of culture originating closer to home. A much-discussed case is the widespread fascination with satellite news, expensively produced and metropolitan in outlook and emphasis, which often pulled viewers away from local reporting.

During the 1960s, the emergence of dependency theory helped bring together the concerns outlined above. Dependency theory arose as a response to the shortcomings of contemporary concepts of economic development. To assist the newly emerged countries and other disadvantaged nations and to dissuade them from aligning themselves with socialist countries, economic planners urged the implementation of development programs. A recognizable set of ideas and beliefs supported these campaigns to modernize poorer regions. These notions are sometimes referred to as development theory, using the term most favored by planners of the aid programs, or as modernization theory.

To summarize crudely the ideas associated with *development*, economists who rallied around this concept viewed poverty as the result of insufficient technical development. The remedy was an infusion of foreign aid, expert advisers, and investment in order to construct communications and transportation networks, manufacturing operations, water distribution systems, and other improvements. After building up their infrastructures to a certain point, the developing economies would be able to "take off" and join the ranks of the developed countries.

This vision of the future came into focus during the Cold War and necessarily entered into competition with the socialism that was the other principal option for emerging nations. Inevitably, concepts of development thought were tinged with a Cold War outlook. While this discussion is of Latin America, it is worth remembering that many development programs were designed for Africa, where Soviet and U.S. advisors were also seeking to bring newly independent nations into their respective camps. As well as reflecting the competition between Soviet and U.S. interests, development theory was marked by the confidence in planning, technical expertise, and trained consultants that typified the sanguine early 1960s. In this climate, it was not unusual for experts to predict the worldwide eradication of poverty. Such projects as the "Green Revolution," to be realized through hybrid strains, and the Aswan Dam were publicized as triumphs of progress.

A flaw in this outlook was suggested by the failure of the developing nations to reach the take-off point, despite years of aid, investment, and advising. They continued to be not merely less developed but also disadvantaged in trade. An alternate way of looking at the situation was that those wielding the greatest economic power—whether the old-line colonial rulers, military and technological superpowers, or multinational firms—formed a *metropolis* or *core* able to set the world's economic agenda. Those nations that had never achieved this central place remained in the periphery, at an inherent and perennial disadvantage in trade relations and unable to determine their own economic programs. Theotônio dos Santos defines the key concept of dependency theory: "Dependency is a situation in which a certain group of countries finds its economy affected by the development and expansion of another economy to which its own is subjugated. The relation of interdependence between two or more economies, and between them and world commerce, takes the form of dependency when some countries (the dominant ones) can expand and further themselves, while other countries (the dependent ones) can only act as a reflex to that expansion, which can act positively or negatively on their immediate development."[24]

Dependency theory continued a line of thought going back to Lenin's 1916 *Imperialism: The Highest Stage of Capitalism*, which postulated that as capitalist society exhausts internal avenues for investment, it must take capital abroad. Yet the theory was designed especially to account for the persistent inequalities of the latter half of the twentieth century.[25] Latin American political economists were extremely prominent in the elaboration of dependency theory: Oscar Braun, Osvaldo Sunkel, Francisco C. Weffort, Fernando Enrique Cardoso, Fernando Tenjo, Marcos Kaplan, Theotônio dos Santos, and others. Though the dependency theorist with the greatest name recognition is a European, André Gunder Frank, he often analyzed Latin American cases and worked with scholars from the region. These circumstances suggest not only that dependency theory applied well to Latin America's economic conditions, but also that the theory prolonged, in a more formalized way, a discussion that had long been part of Latin American intellectual life. Confirming a close tie between dependency theory and generally held beliefs about interregional inequalities, terms and ideas from dependency theory quickly came into use among nonspecialists. For example, creative people working in Latin America had often expressed a sense of being far from such art-world capitals as Paris and New York, where innovations were rapidly publicized and international reputations were made; their situation was now summed up as being *in the periphery.*

Dependency theory was no sooner formulated than it drew objections for its overly schematic description of the relation between metropolitan centers and nations in the periphery. One of the most frequent criticisms was that relations of dominance and dependency existed not only between nations or regions but within a single country or world area. Such great centers as Buenos Aires, Lima, Mexico City, and Rio de Janeiro had been resented, well before the rise of dependency theory, for their ability to control national economic life and to exploit the rest of their countries. Many efforts were made to add such complexities into the initially too-stark characterizations that theorists had made.

Since the 1960s–1970s heyday of dependency theory, some of the conditions that it arose to explain have changed. The principal transformations have resulted from the speeded-up global flow of capital. This tendency is manifested in such well-publicized phenomena as international debt crises and the rise of transnational corporations, whose capital and products cannot be associated with one nation. The countries that, during the prosperous 1960s, appeared to control the world economy via their advantaged position and expertise have since revealed vulnerabilities. The failure of announced economic plans, especially those devised for Latin American countries by advisers (both U.S. and Latin American) trained at U.S. universities, has eroded confidence in the efficacy of expert consultants and planners. The U.S. domestic economy, once perceived as stable in contrast to the volatile economies of less powerful countries, surprised its longtime analysts with erratic changes and previously unimaginable rates of inflation. Other economies admired for their efficient productivity and steadiness, such as that of Japan, also displayed weaknesses. Economic superpowers no longer seemed so extremely different from the periphery. Throughout the 1980s and into the 1990s, not only was it less clear who exercised dominance over the world economy, but it was uncertain how responsive the economy was to systematic planning. Accordingly, there was a diminished belief that a concerted effort was working to maintain peripheral nations in poverty. The end of the Cold War removed an important stimulus to both development programs and dependency theory's critique of them.

One could cite many other factors that have complicated the bipolar scheme of metropolis and periphery mapped out by early theorists of dependency. Among these are the accelerated international movement of goods, people, and cultural tendencies, and the increased economic importance of the Mexican-U.S. border region, resulting in such new developments as the often-studied *maquiladoras* or assembly plants that have industrialized the Mexican side of the border. Also deserving of mention is the expansion throughout Latin America of informal (not officially recorded) economic activities. One of these, the production and international distribution of cocaine, also illustrates an area in which Latin American exporters enjoy an advantage over U.S. trading partners.

Many researchers of interregional relations now rely on the more recently developed world systems or global systems theory. This form of analysis differs from dependency theory in shifting attention toward the global movement of labor and wage levels, and away from the international flow of capital, a characteristic focus of dependency theory. World systems analysts, rather than divide the world starkly into core and periphery, recognize a semi-periphery of areas that are neither dominant nor among the most deprived areas. Followers of this trend of thought identify, within the world system, larger aggregates than individual nations; Latin America would be one such supranational area.

The point of these observations is not that dependency theory has become obsolete, but rather that its original formulations require some transformation to correspond to the more heterogeneous, fragmented, and international present-day situation. Although the words *dependency theory* may seem to refer to a phenomenon of the 1960s and 1970s, the theory cannot yet be discarded because of the persistence of the inequalities which it seeks to take into account. Even scholars who regard dependency theory as an outdated tendency often use many of its characteristic terms and concepts, such as *peripheral* and *metropolitan*. Emile McAnany, using the phrase *cultural imperialism model* to refer to concepts of dependency in communications, summarizes the persistence of a central problem: "There is a strong sense that although the cultural imperialism model may have been critiqued by many of its own creators, the concern about transnational cultures has not been dropped from the discourse. In fact, the most recent [scholarship on these issues] still places transnational political and cultural issues at the heart of the problem of mass media, only now in more sophisticated form."[26]

Dependency theory came into being in response to perceived failures in the concepts of development and modernization and the programs that they justified. But it was also clear that this way of looking at interregional relations could help students of culture think about certain long-standing problems. As Robert Buckman has put it, cultural dependency appears "nebulous" in contrast to the economic reliance of one nation upon another, easily confirmed through such indices as debt.[27] Still, the general idea helps account for some often-observed occurrences.

One example is the pattern described above, in which Latin American writers striving to follow European trends sometimes produced unexpectedly novel results (although many efforts never went beyond imitation). Another is the persistent lack of synchronization between European esthetic movements and their Latin American counterparts. To apply to these cultural questions, dependency thought had far to travel. It appears likely that, for the most part, concepts of dependency spread from economics to the discussion of communications, popular culture, and the media before influencing students of literature. The mass media, constantly calling attention to themselves, made metropolitan pre-eminence in the culture industries difficult to ignore. Intellectuals such as the Brazilians Celso Furtado, Silviano Santiago, and Ruy Mauro Marini brought ideas from dependency theory to the public discussion of cultural problems and policy. As dependency theory spread to the academic study of communications, Herbert I. Schiller's 1969 *Mass Communications and American Empire* helped establish its place.[28] Schiller's title sums up the concept that the media and advertising are among the new strategies of influence that have succeeded colonial rule.

An exceptionally influential work, the 1971 *Para leer al Pato Donald* (*How to Read Donald Duck: Imperialist Ideology in the Disney Comic*), was co-authored by the Chilean literary critic and writer Ariel Dorfman and the Belgian-born communications researcher Armand Mattelart. Their interdisciplinary collaboration transmitted ideas from dependency theory into cultural analysis. The two had given stories from Donald Duck comics the detailed content analysis usually reserved for literary works. The resulting study showed that Donald Duck and his nephews traveled to less developed countries when unable to raise money at home, a pattern reminiscent of Lenin's tenet summarized above about the last stages of capitalism. The wily ducks' adventures abroad often consisted of despoiling innocent natives ignorant of the value of their homelands' resources. Dorfman went on to treat a variety of mass-culture works as texts to be analyzed in detail. While much of the research done by communications specialists is not likely to grip a literary audience, Dorfman's content analyses fascinated students of literature.[29]

Latin American literary critics who study international cultural exchange often cite readings in communication studies and exhibit concern over mass media as well as over elite literature. Fábio Lucas, for example, in order to see how dependency is manifested in the Brazilian avant-garde, first portrays the general impact of the culture industry. Lucas identifies the phenomenon that has probably most disturbed students of cultural dependency: "an effect of *internationalization* of cultural material, whereby local or national culture is devalued and the superiority of the foreign culture affirmed. In this way, the inferiority complex of the periphery is reinforced."[30]

How do literary critics go about applying the insights of dependency theory in their studies? Some of the effects of Latin America's unequal relations with powerful nations are not easy to specify or analyze. Critics have asserted that a knowledgeable and experienced reader can recognize, perhaps without being able to say why, that a given text originated in the New World. As Henríquez Ureña summed up, "In literature, everyone feels [the difference]."[31] It seems reasonable that the region's distinctive historical dynamic leaves a perceptible effect on its literature, and that readers should sense "some mysterious oddness," in Jean Franco's telling phrase. Yet this difference is difficult to specify. Detailed analysis of individual literary works cannot reveal much about cultural dependency unless it is an overt theme of the texts.[32]

Perhaps for this reason, literary critics researching dependency and autonomy are unlikely to rely exclusively on analyses of particular texts, the typical method of studying changes in literary form, language, and style.[33] Instead, the analysis may include the careers of authors, the way the work done by writers was regarded and rewarded, important publication outlets and their financing, and the composition and tastes of the public for literature and journalism.

Certain periods of Latin American literature are especially fertile for this type of analysis because they reveal moments of change in relations with metropolitan culture. The most obvious example is the study of *modernismo* in its simultaneous drive toward imitation and toward American originality. Another, to some degree similar, moment occurs in the 1920s and 1930s. Avant-gardes arose in Latin American literary capitals, some of them closely patterned on European examples. Yet contemporary groups of intellectuals, dissatisfied with an undifferentiated, international style of modernity, were calling upon writers to work with regional themes and language.[34] The avant-gardists, with their striving for internationalization and modernization, widened the divisions that *modernismo* had opened.

Literary relations with the economically powerful nations again became an issue during the 1960s and 1970s, as Latin American writing, especially innovatively constructed fiction including magical realism, began to achieve international success in translation. Critics were commenting upon the evolution of living writers, often resulting in a more polemical type of critique. An example is Hernán Vidal's brief but much-discussed 1975 *Literatura hispanoamericana e ideología liberal: surgimiento y crisis, una problemática en torno a la narrativa del Boom* (Spanish American literature and liberal ideology: emergence and crisis, problems concerning the Boom narrative). Here the noted Chilean critic links the triumph of technically innovative Latin American fiction with the desire to compete in a world obsessed with technical advancements and breakthroughs. Like many observers, Vidal concludes that the desire to win a place in lucrative foreign literary markets influences Latin American writers. The international fascination with experimentally constructed fiction from Latin America is disadvantageous to the regional-realist tradition that has often allowed literature to disseminate social criticism.[35]

The international success of Latin American writing, while bringing obvious benefits, has raised concerns, particularly when writers, who should ideally be the critical questioners of a society, undergo what Vidal summarizes as "the absorption into the international market" of in-demand public intellectuals.[36] Joseph Sommers raises these issues concerning the Peruvian Mario Vargas Llosa, finding in his fiction from 1963 to 1973 an increasing frivolity toward society's problems: "There is a shift toward a conception of the novel as entertainment instead of a challenge."[37] This period of transition, Sommers observes, coincides with the transformation of certain Latin American writers, including Vargas Llosa, into international celebrities: "Translations were frequent, expanding the reading public and royalties. Residences or long stays in Europe . . . were a common thing. Film contracts, though not so common, were still a factor in publication plans." For Sommers, writers' "flood of" exposure to international publics, including "interviews, television appearances, banquets for literary prizes, invitations to lecture at universities," erodes the critical capacity they could exercise before they assumed public roles as media figures.[38]

The critical analyses cited above are from the 1970s, when dependency theory was still a novelty to many scholars who were not economists or political scientists. Later, as aspects of the theory spread through the general intellectual environment, it would be unusual for a literary researcher to call such explicit attention to his or her use of these ideas. Nonetheless, literary critics have continued to employ notions from dependency theory, whose central terms, such as *metropolis/periphery*, still appear regularly in the titles of critical monographs and collections of essays on Latin American literature. Through their choice of terms, authors express an enduring sense that Latin American societies are on the *periphery*, *margin*, or *edge* of the economic and cultural activity of the long-established centers.[39]

All the above examples of the discussion of cultural autonomy come from such forms of communication as the research essay and debate in intellectual journals and reviews. But the same concerns are also perceptible in creative writing. As Franco notes, all literary works from Latin America are in some sense marked by the distinctive historical dynamic of a less-powerful part of the world. Beyond this general difference, though, certain texts make a thematic point of the disproportionate cultural influence of powerful nations.

Manuel Puig (1932–1990), whose career as a novelist began with *Betrayed by Rita Hayworth* (1968), draws attention through his creative writing to the concerns outlined above. In real life, Puig had reason to be exceptionally aware of the influence of imported popular culture. He often spoke of the influence of the many English-language movies he had seen as a child. He had many links to the film industry, having been a student-trainee at the Cinecittà studios, having held assistant director jobs, and at various times having tried his hand at screenwriting.[40] Puig has said that he began *Betrayed* as a screenplay.[41] His work offers a critique of commercial mass culture and the dominant role the U.S. culture industry has exercised in it.

Puig's novels are not unilaterally condemnatory of mass-media productions, though they frequently mimic them for comic effect. Rather they manifest a passionate ambivalence. In *Betrayed*, Puig evokes the often sumptuously produced, melodramatic movies of the 1930s and 1940s, with their power to construct a universe of glamor and pull readers into it. Although Puig developed a critical awareness of these movies and their enraptured audiences, he continued to find them more complex and stimulating than realist films.[42] The attention of literary critics has often gone to the frequent mention Puig's characters make of their moviegoing and reading. Pamela Bacarisse, who has studied these references in detail, correlates the spectacle and excitement offered by mass culture with the lack of stimulation or novelty that torments many of Puig's dissatisfied characters.[43]

The young protagonist of *Betrayed* lives in Coronel Vallejos, a cover name for the author's hometown of General Villegas. It is a drab location, remote from the capital. The townspeople exhibit scant interest in creating a cultural life that would reflect their specific circumstances and experiences. They passively receive, without adapting or transforming them, the productions that come to them from more advantaged areas, whether the United States, Europe, or Buenos Aires. The central character's imagination is in thrall to the movies, and he uses the plots and characters of films to define himself. His experiences as a filmgoer are rendered with a certain admiration for the evocative power of the romantic and spectacular films of the late 1930s and early 1940s. Though Toto is impressed by his diet of films, readers quickly recognize that the movie theater in his town only occasionally offers classics of U.S. sound film. Many of the novel's chapters are marked by dates, so it is easy to see that movies arrive in Coronel Vallejos years after their date of release. The isolated provincial town appears to be a dumping ground for foreign films that would be rejected as out-of-date or poorly made by audiences with more moviegoing choices available to them.

Betrayed by Rita Hayworth reminds readers of many forms of cultural dependency. An especially prominent theme is the reliance of small, isolated communities on large cities, especially the great literary and artistic capitals that dominate many Latin American nations. While this form of dependency is internal to Argentina, *Betrayed* also treats the influence of European culture, which carries a high prestige, and the lower-status products of the U.S. culture industry.

A more pervasive and general dependency, a broader category than the above, affects the town. It consists of a belief that culture is manufactured in the entertainment industry or, in its elite forms, the fine-arts establishment. In this vision, ordinary members of society simply consume the products of these industries, without modifying them in accord with their local circumstances, which many of them regard with contempt. The townspeople have the uncreative, imitative habit alluded to by such terms as "following the dictates of fashion."

One chapter transcribes part of a personal and intellectual journal maintained by Herminia. She is a spokesperson for the belief that the national capital is the center of European-style enlightened culture and that the provinces represent a deterioration from this ideal. Originally from Buenos Aires, Herminia associates herself with cosmopolitan values as opposed to her provincial environment. As a classically trained pianist and music teacher, she feels distinguished from her neighbors by her intellectual life and the high art she reproduces. In some passages of her notebook, Herminia identifies the capital with a purely elite culture and the provincial environment with such popular forms as recordings of tangos. Herminia, in a literal way, depends on the metropolitan center. She feels her cultural life has been frustrated when she is interrupted while listening to an opera broadcast by radio from Buenos Aires.

Herminia shares with one of her fellow townspeople, the young protagonist Toto, the idealized vision of a cosmopolitan, elite, and highly intellectual culture. Both Herminia and Toto are disaffected by the common life of the town and eager to believe that they maintain higher values than their neighbors. The novel accords sympathetic treatment to these characters who, feeling isolated and understimulated, console themselves by holding to treasured beliefs. Yet it also mocks some of their notions of culture. Despite their elitist outlook, both Herminia and Toto in practice share many of the same entertainments as the other townspeople. They both read, write, and spend time considering intellectual problems, but they also frequent the town's moviehouse and participate in the gossip that is one of the major local recreations.

Moreover, despite their striving for a high seriousness, they are passive recipients of cultural products that arrive from elsewhere. These characters judge their surroundings to be devoid of all cultural significance. It would not occur to them to attempt a creative transformation of material from outside the community to generate a new hybrid variant incorporating more local material. From their point of view, worthy culture is necessarily created far from their town. Beyond being consumers, both Toto and Herminia reproduce cultural products that they admire. Toto is developing his skill in the retelling of films, while Herminia sustains musical high culture by giving piano lessons to young people.

Both characters betray a sense of something lacking in their prestigious activities. Herminia is dissatisfied with the results of her efforts to make a respected space for European art music in the town. She is embittered by the thought that pianistic skills do not raise her students' status among the townspeople. Herminia has just learned that a young woman with no elite cultural accomplishments to bring to the marriage has made an outstanding match. She is indignant that the bride was not chosen from among the "better women" in town, "who could grace the home with music."[44]

Moreover, Herminia gradually reveals that she is deriving little satisfaction from the elite art and intellectual activity she outwardly values and cultivates. As a performer and teacher, she reproduces a fixed repertory, to which no new element may be added; she performs and teaches only celebrated compositions of the romantic era. She refuses to listen to twentieth-century music even when Toto brings it to her house. Her limitation to an already-completed musical period suggests the museum-like preservation of treasures from the past, into which no new features may be incorporated.

Later she admits that her enthusiasm for music is not as strong as her father's was. Shortly afterward she confesses in her journal: "Even though it's something you shouldn't say, I hate the piano" (295). Although she disparages the townspeople for their popular tastes and provincial outlook, she also expresses a desire to live as they do. In her perception, her elite culture and capacity for reflection deprive her of the primitive companionship enjoyed by townspeople united by the commonalities of low culture, sexual attraction, and everyday concerns.

Toto and Herminia are drawn together by their alienation from the town's values and their identification with an intellectual, urban, and international ideal, but Toto does not express Herminia's extreme dissatisfaction. Yet the title *Betrayed by Rita Hayworth*, derived from Toto's meditations on his filmgoing, gives an early hint that this protagonist is not entirely well-served by his consumption of U.S. popular film.

Toto, who in the novel grows from a newborn to an adolescent, derives many of his beliefs from his mother, Mita, with whom he spends much time. Mita, a voracious reader who "has the look of a woman who has studied," ascribes cultural and intellectual life to major centers (54). The vision of Mita and her family of origin extends the metropolis beyond the nation's capital to include the nearby small city of La Plata, their home. According to her family of origin, Mita could be pursuing a career in pharmacology at that city's university; instead, she is in danger of remaining in the small town, consigned to obscurity as a dispensing pharmacist. Mita typifies many Puig characters who perceive themselves as geographically removed from life's opportunities.

Toto, absorbing this outlook, gives special significance to his visits to La Plata and to Buenos Aires itself. Toto has recognized that the distribution of cultural products favors residents of urban centers. As a small child, he notes that "In La Plata they show new movies and the cakes are taller than in Vallejos" (93). Toto gains an early awareness of the high prestige of Buenos Aires and European art culture. Reminiscing about meeting a new friend, he remembers "I got the chance to tell him that I was in Buenos Aires and I saw live theater" (90). Further embellishing his cosmopolitan image, he said "In Buenos Aires I went to the theater at night. . . . I saw *The Merchant of Venice*" (91). The latter detail is not literally true; as outsiders briefly visiting the city, Mita and Toto could not wait for tickets to the heavily booked production of *Merchant*. However, Toto's claim shows his desire to be associated with a theatrical production that not only emblem-izes the classics of Europe (Shakespeare) but also the metropolitan chic of Buenos Aires (the most sought-after play; going out at night in the city).

Mita communicates to Toto an elite, predominantly European ideal of art, both through judgmental comments and through such shared activities as relating the plots of Shakespeare's plays. But in their everyday lives they content themselves with less prestigious diversions of largely U.S. origin. Together they watch movies and then recreate in drawings the characters and costumes. Some of these motion pictures contain an element of the prized European classics; *Romeo and Juliet* seems to have particularly im-pressed Mita. But most are more popular and are either from the United States or American in style.

Mother and son both select as the film they would most like to see again *The Great Ziegfeld.* The biography of the innovative showman Florenz Ziegfeld, renowned for its opulent costumes and dance productions, stands out among the numerous Depression-era films set in the entertainment industry. It received Academy Awards for Best Motion Picture and Best Dance Design of 1936. Mita's admiration for *Ziegfeld,* and her special praise for its lavish costumes and elaborate music-and-dance productions, is in tune with contemporary critics' opinion. At the same time, it is revealing that Mita, generally regarded as an intellectual, would select a U.S. enter-tainment movie over a European art film.

Mita's interior monologue, which occupies a chapter of the novel, shows that her cultural repertory is heterogeneous, including Argentine, Mexican, U.S., and European as well as elite and popular elements. Mita's family and friends have previously expressed admiration for her as a serious reader. In her monologue, she reveals reading preferences that are less urbane than one might expect. They include some lighter, popularized material and newspapers as well as original works of literature. Mita's attraction to ro-mantic narratives and her propensity for identifying with characters are likely to strike readers as old-fashioned and provincial.[45]

Toto devotes considerable time to the mental and verbal reconstruction of movies he has seen. An elaborate example is an essay "The Film I Liked Best Last Year," which Toto writes for a competition. Transcribed as a chapter in the novel, the essay recreates a romanticized film biography. The movie, unnamed in the essay but clearly *The Great Waltz* of 1938, already takes considerable liberties with historical events; Toto adds further em-bellishments and variations, producing what René Alberto Campos calls "a reading/rewriting of the film."[46] The plot has a bittersweet ending but presents two tales of success. In the course of its narrative, the waltz wins acceptance in respectable society and Johann Strauss attains the respect and acclaim of Vienna. (The hero appears to be a composite of Johann Strauss the elder and younger; like the elder, he begins as an outsider promoting a suspect musical genre, yet the film attributes to him the younger Strauss's better-known compositions.) The essay reveals many aspects of Toto's outlook, including his vacillating sexual identity. As Campos notes, Toto's manner of recounting the movie focuses attention on psychological issues.[47]

When one reads the essay, not for evidence of adolescent psychology or Toto's sexuality but for signs of cultural dependency, a complicated pattern appears. Toto is enraptured by Hollywood-style movies, and in that sense can be called dependent on U.S. popular culture. However, his essay is dedicated to a film that, although classified among the large-scale MGM musicals, is an American film with many European elements. The director (Julien Duvivier) was European, as were the principal actors (Luise Rainer, Fernand Gravet, and Miliza Korjus) and the setting. Though it won an Academy Award for its cinematography and received some favorable reviews, *The Great Waltz* did not enjoy the popular success of many contemporary musical films. It was perceived as somewhat intense and brooding for its lightweight genre. Most European of all, the plot depends on the concept of Vienna as a great focal point for Continental culture, a metropolis where careers are made and artistic influence is exercised.

Toto's essay reveals his identification with a protagonist who, like him, is a provincial outsider to the centers of cultural prestige and influence. Toto is absorbed by the story of how Strauss, a dance-hall violinist and the promoter of a low-prestige musical genre, wins over, both musically and amorously, a soprano from the Russian imperial opera. Arriving from St. Petersburg, the singer is attracted to the dance hall by the pleasurable sound of waltzes and spontaneously takes up the music sheets and begins to sing the lyrics. Toto appears fascinated that the movie's protagonist, though a celebrated figure in European musical history, comes from a village even less promising than Coronel Vallejos. The essay dwells on the squalor of the peasant hut shown as Strauss's original home. (The attribution of a provincial origin is an invention to dramatize the hero's triumph; the historical Strauss family was, of course, Viennese.)

Toto is also eager to point out a major theme of the film: Strauss gains entry into the prestigious circles of an important European capital by renovating a musical genre originally associated with disreputable neighborhoods. The mainstream success of the waltz was a triumph of mass taste, since waltz music and waltzing were opposed by established arbiters of both cultural fashions and morals. The coming together of elite and popular forms clearly strikes a chord in Toto, whose allegiance is divided. On the one hand, he idealizes the European high culture; for example, he creates an image of the soprano in a vast concert hall. At the same time, his essay glorifies two popular genres, film and the waltz, accessible even in the global periphery. The essay appears to be trying to reconcile an urban, European, and high-art ideal with the actual cultural life Toto is able to lead in a small town on the pampas. The waltz is a suitable meeting ground. Though the waltz is popular in origin, over the years the celebrated Strauss waltzes have achieved the ambiguous status of "light classics" and become familiar even to publics whose knowledge of art music is slight. This genre represents the main portion of concert music to which Toto has ready access in his peripheral isolation, though he wages an uphill struggle to become an aficionado of demanding twentieth-century music.

A more widespread type of dependency is epitomized by Mita's friend, Choli. Choli is set in contrast with the studious Mita. The former focuses her attention on physical appearances and may strike readers as vulgar. One chapter of the novel consists of a conversation between the two, though readers are only provided with Choli's side of the exchange. Choli, unlike Herminia, Toto, and Mita, has not mastered any prestigious body of cultural information. A traveling representative for a cosmetics manufacturer, she does possess a specialized knowledge concerning female dress and grooming, drawn in part from observing popular movies and photographs of actresses. While the previously discussed characters often follow the lead of European culture, Choli and the company she represents exhibit a reliance on U.S. examples. The firm employing her, though its head appears to be an Argentine, goes by the name Hollywood Cosméticos. The head of the company has instructed Choli to emulate the aloof style of one of her U.S. counterparts who, on a visit, impressed the Argentine manager with what he perceived as prestigiously Anglo-Saxon curtness. Choli prides herself on resembling an American. A tall woman, she has furthered her Anglo appearance by lightening her hair color. Following the manager's suggestion, she shows little warmth or deference to customers. At the same time, though, Choli follows popular Argentine entertainment, focusing on the style of female celebrities.

Choli most likely appears to readers as a typical slave of fashion, and not even a very high level of fashion. From her perspective, though, the glamorous persona she now cultivates is an expression of her liberation. Choli is the relieved widow of a traditional Mediterranean-style husband. (Another major theme of the novel is the critique of machismo.) Zealous about preserving his wife from other men's desires, he had forbidden her to wear her hair loose or use cosmetics. As Choli surveys her past, her current life appears as "the freedom I possess" (63).

Choli's glamor, which is low in prestige but easily appreciated, exemplifies a concept that appears frequently in the novel. U.S. culture and its Argentine derivatives are perceived as exciting, glamorous, sexually attractive, and requiring little effort to enjoy; in addition, U.S.-style diversions are abundant even in remote towns. European culture and its Argentine correlates bring high prestige but are seen as difficult to enjoy. Except in cities, access to European imports is infrequent, while U.S. culture is omnipresent; moreover, European culture is perceived as less gratifying and pleasurable than that of the U.S. Toto's cousin Héctor becomes involved in a boarding-house dispute over whether U.S. or French movies should be viewed. Héctor defends watching American movies. He cites Ann Sheridan as an exemplary star, in contrast to the unattractive actresses of French film. His adversary, a Spanish immigrant, believes that "French films are the only ones for intelligent people" (172). He disparages Sheridan as exercising a crude sex appeal. Staunchly linking Europe with high culture and the United States with mindless mass entertainment, he asserts: "American actresses couldn't act because they had no culture" (172). A notable feature of this polemic is that neither debater appears to consider the possibility of watching Argentine movies.

Few literary works are like *Betrayed by Rita Hayworth* in making an overt theme of the lack of cultural autonomy or creativity. Puig is exceptional among creative writers in his preoccupation with his characters as consumers of culture and especially of imported cultural items. In most cases, it would be difficult to isolate a single work of literature and analyze it for signs of dependency or autonomy. Critics with this concern need to examine entire literary tendencies and movements in their search to identify significant patterns.

Transculturation is a concept that has been useful in adding complexity to the picture painted by dependency theory. As has been noted, one of the deficiencies of dependency theory is its lack of recognition of the creativity of many cultures even when the members of those cultures have been enslaved, colonized, or bombarded with foreign cultural products. Though overrun by dominant cultures, the members of these cultures have ingenious means of adapting. The idea arose in the social sciences and crossed over to literary studies. The concept of transculturation originates with the outstandingly inventive Cuban anthropologist Fernando Ortiz (1881–1969). Presented through his famous book-length essay of 1940, *Contrapunteo cubano del tabaco y el azúcar* (*Cuban Counterpoint: Tobacco and Sugar*), Ortiz's term suggests a dynamic, two-way exchange between cultures, even when one of the cultures represents the dominant group and the other the subjugated population.

Useful in describing Cuba's cultural mixture, and by extension the situation found in all Latin American societies, *transculturation* takes into account certain factors omitted by *acculturation*. The term *acculturation* had been introduced to move away from the implication of *assimilation*—that individuals were eventually absorbed into a new culture, losing their original culture. (It should be noted that, for U.S. readers, the meaning that Ortiz gives *acculturation* is quite close to the sense they associate with *assimilation*.) Still, Ortiz found *acculturation* inadequate to describe, for example, the situation of peoples devising their way of life and outlook while living between two cultures, such as Africans brought to Cuba as slaves. His objection was that such populations did not simply suffer the death of certain portions of their old culture, which were then replaced by elements of a new culture such as the Hispanic one of the Caribbean. For Ortiz, such a vision failed to do justice to the liveliness of an original culture even after the encounter with a new culture. He wanted to focus greater attention on a more complex interaction between the old and the new, dominant culture. Sectors of the old culture are necessarily lost, but other elements become a continuing and still-evolving part of the individual's or community's attitudes and behavior. In transculturation, no matter how rapid and thorough the acquisition of new characteristics, these superimposed features commingle with the original source culture, affecting it but also being transformed by it. Importantly, during this process of exchange, the dominant culture also undergoes transformation, acquiring features of the subjugated culture.

Quite reasonably for a student of the Caribbean, whose highly original African-Hispanic culture has won wide admiration as an example of cultural innovation, Ortiz took a keen interest in hybrid forms. His term *neoculturation*, stemming from the same line of thought that produced *transculturation*, draws attention to the much-noted uniqueness of Latin American cultural forms born of the encounter between cultures.

Though a social scientist generated the term and concept, some forty years later the Uruguayan literary critic Angel Rama felt the need to adjust and rework it to apply it to the analysis of literary writing. This transformation is found in Rama's 1982 *Transculturación narrativa en América Latina* (Narrative transculturation in Latin America). Rama recognized that Ortiz had been striving to show cultural contact as a more interactive process, and especially to recognize the creativity that even enslaved or subjugated peoples exhibit in working out their cultural situation. In adapting Ortiz's term, Rama sought to strengthen the idea that individuals participate in the changes that their culture undergoes. He strove to recognize even more clearly that members of a culture in transition make active, creative choices. For example, while Ortiz observes that the original culture is partially lost during transculturation, Rama notes that people creatively select which elements of their culture will be retained and which abandoned. They are also able to exercise a degree of choice concerning which aspects of the new culture they will adopt; the fusion of the original and old cultures then involves further options.

Beyond refining *transculturation* to emphasize the active decision-making of the members of a culture, Rama needed to make the word and idea part of literary studies. He plainly states: "When the description of transculturation formulated by Fernando Ortiz is applied to literary works, it's time for some obligatory corrective adjustments."[48] As Rama notes, those who are carrying out transculturation, such as novelists bringing modern techniques to regionalist fiction, are not simply living out the cultural situation of their place and time, but making choices. The process of selecting from a "rich spectrum of components coming from outside" one's original culture and making creative decisions is especially evident in the creation of literary work. The writing of literature entails "the criteria of choice-making and those of invention";[49] more deliberate choices come into play. This indisputably successful transfer of ideas across disciplines is one factor making transculturation especially worthy of lengthier examination.

Rama's *Transculturación narrativa* is among the most frequently cited works of literary and cultural criticism from Latin America. In addition to direct allusions to and quotations from the study, many literary critics now use the term as Rama did, without needing to remind readers who adapted the word and concept to the study of literature. Despite the rapid spread of *transculturation*, there has yet to be another study as detailed and reflective as Rama's, which would move the concept further into literary studies. In this sense, even though the word has attained a certain currency, the concept of transculturation has yet to be fully developed as part of Latin American literary studies.

2 Postmodernism in Latin American Literary Culture

The term and concept *postmodernism* have become inescapable in the discussion of twentieth-century culture. The general intellectual public, in many cases, first began to use the term to designate a playful, eclectic manner in architecture, which won attention during the 1970s. Used in this way, *postmodern* possesses a fairly clear meaning as a term for the period style that follows *modern*. Scholars refined the term, especially Charles Jencks in such studies as *The Language of Post Modern Architecture* (orig. 1977; 5th rev. ed. 1988). However, one does not require the guidance of such scholarly works to recognize examples of postmodern architecture.

The postmodernist style stands in contrast to the austerity of the modernists. The revival of external ornamentation and the mimicry (often called citation or pastiche) of features from different periods, styles, and elite and popular sources marked postmodernist buildings. Postmodern architecture became known through such memorable examples as the architect Frank Gehry's house in Santa Monica and the Pompidou Center in Paris.

As the idea of postmodernism has spread to a number of fields, its architectural manifestations have remained the best agreed upon. Fredric Jameson summarizes why analyses of postmodernism often start with architecture: "It is in the realm of architecture . . . that modifications in aesthetic production are most dramatically visible, and that their theoretical problems have been most centrally raised and articulated."[1] For these reasons, this chapter opens with postmodernist architecture and proceeds through the 1970s spread of *postmodern* to other phenomena. European and Anglo-American thinkers deserve attention since they were chronologically first to develop the current-day term, if not necessarily the phenomena it describes. The chapter then presents its central problem: adapting *postmodern* to the study of Latin American writing. Many scholars research postmodernism, and any summary necessarily omits some of them. The discussion in this chapter seeks, not to name all students and practitioners of Latin American postmodernism, but to bring out the principal issues involved when the term *postmodernism* is applied to Latin American cultures, including literature.

Viewers often perceive the postmodernist manner as a relaxation of the austerity aspired to in the International style, exemplified by the work of Le Corbusier, Mies van der Rohe, and others; the functionalist architecture of Brasília, for example, is an extension of this manner. Those who admire postmodernist architecture are apt to speak of modernist buildings as cold and uninviting; their stark lines provide few details for the eye to linger over and enjoy. There is a strong association of the modernist style with dehumanization, to use the term Ortega y Gasset established. Aware that plainer structures are cheaper, observers often link the glass and steel boxes of modern architecture with the drive for cost-efficiency.

In contrast, postmodernist design seems to offer comfort and amusement to the observer. Its varied and at times witty details give viewers visual stimulation, unlike the more cerebral notion of beauty provided by severe modernist structures. With its diverting embellishments, the postmodern manner often wins the appreciation of a broader public than modernism can reach. Confirming the belief that postmodernism is crowd-pleasing, the Disney firm, devoted to popular entertainments, has commissioned structures in this style. A persistent criticism of postmodernist architecture is that, in making buildings diverting and nostalgic, it evades the central challenge of modernism. Dedicated to moving art forward, modernists needed to generate striking innovations rather than rely on already-developed conventions.

Despite the strong tie between modern art and architecture and dehumanization, postmodern style is not necessarily perceived as rehumanizing. Detractors see its appeal as shallow and trivial. Jameson, who sees the postmodern as the cultural manifestation of late capitalism, identifies "the waning of affect in postmodern culture."[2] He clarifies: "This is not to say that the cultural products of the postmodern era are utterly devoid of feeling, but rather that such feelings . . . are now free-floating and impersonal."[3]

Whether seen as self-indulgent or as playfully creative, architectural postmodernism stands out as a deliberate shift in esthetics. In literature, critics and other commentators generally use *postmodernist* for a wider diversity of creators. Students of literature who research postmodernism are almost invariably concerned with larger social and cultural changes in the late twentieth century. As a consequence, essays on postmodern literature generally establish a broad context for the discussion; the study of specific features of particular texts is less prominent.

Few literary authors have sought to develop a postmodern mode of writing, although many writers set themselves in opposition to literary modernism, which they perceive as elitist, cold, overconcerned with form, and inadequate to the expression of emotional experience. Marcel Cornis-Pope, researching the term, finds that as early as 1946, Randall Jarrell characterized Robert Lowell's *Lord Weary's Castle* as *postmodern.*[4] This term, used to designate a current in poetry, does not correspond exactly to the word *postmodernism* that caught on among literary scholars in the late 1970s. The literary postmodernism of the second half of the 1940s and the 1950s was "a post-World-War-II international poetry movement," arising among poets (parallel to similar tendencies among painters), rather than a concept developed by literary critics and theorists.[5] In great measure, it referred to actual poetic techniques that resulted in a departure from modernism.[6] Cornis-Pope provides the link between postmodernist poetry and the later, more theoretically grounded, postmodernism when he associates the former with an increasingly widespread dissatisfaction with modernism.[7] In literature, as in other areas, *postmodernism* has, gradually since the late 1970s, come to be used equally by scholars and by the educated nonspecialists, as Santiago Colás notes, "unlike, by the way, so many of the more specialized terms of our profession."[8]

As the term *postmodern* moves outside architecture, it becomes less evident which phenomena should receive the appellation. In some cases, new developments have attracted the label *postmodern*, although there had in all likelihood been no conscious effort to develop a postmodern style or attitude. There is an abandonment of long-standing hierarchies of taste, and the audience for cultural entertainment is no longer clearly divided into general, elite, and specialized publics. Néstor García Canclini, the Argentine-Mexican social anthropologist, is one of the scholars who has most drawn the attention of readers to the breakdown of generally accepted categories. Though he is most closely identified with anthropology, García Canclini makes frequent reference to the sociological vision of recent changes in society as well as beliefs harbored by the general public. He is equally well known for questioning accepted notions of popular culture and for his accounts of the fate of cultures in the postmodern era. He sums up: "High, popular, and elite are no longer to be found in their familiar places. The traditional and the modern are mixed together all the time." [9]

The word *postmodern* has been applied to such matters as intellectuals' unashamed fascination with very popular music and movies. The convergence of elite and mass culture was a break with modernism. Modernists had on occasion avowed a debt to folk art, a celebrated case being the avant-garde vogue for African sculpture and design. Yet high modernism defined itself in opposition to mass culture, seen as a supplier of facile satisfactions. Mass-cultural items that exercised a surprising fascination upon educated publics had previously been called kitsch, camp, cult, retro style, and nostalgia. They now could be called signs of postmodernism, with its mixture of past and present styles and elite and popular culture.

Frequently, the notions of increased vacuity, complacency, and hedonistic self-indulgence became attached to postmodernism. It suggested a purposeless society of consumers. Members of postmodernist society seemed easy prey to fads, manias, and obsessions. The term at times implies an absorption in sensational innovations and abandonment of responsibility for the general well-being. Jameson posits a diminished awareness of one's location in history as one of the prime features of postmodernism. In his analysis, "the random cannibalization of all the styles of the past" inculcates in the public an indifference toward history as a progression driven by identifiable forces.[10] Colás summarizes Jameson's argument: "Since we cannot recall the past out of which our present was shaped, we lose our sense of the present as changeable. We therefore weaken our capacity to formulate projects for new futures. We are left immobile as political subjects."[11]

Postmodern could refer to cultural consumers' intense, fascinated relation to new technologies of the late twentieth century, although technological advances are not in themselves postmodern. It could imply dependence on technological assistance to carry on cultural life, or a conflict-filled, self-conscious relation with new media.[12]

The application of the term *postmodern* to the effects of technical innovations developed since the Second World War reflects a belief that postmodernity is a period in social and economic history. Such an understanding of postmodernism is fairly close to the social studies' use of *postmodernism* as a descriptive period term, and is congruent with other terms that social scientists have used for the second half of the twentieth century.

Postmodernism has a lengthy history in the study of society; as early as 1959, C. Wright Mills suggested that "a postmodern period" was following "the Modern Age."[13]

If the present era constitutes postmodernism, then innovations now taking place in communications and the arts are almost necessarily postmodern ones. In this approach to the term, whether in architecture, the visual arts, or the social sciences in their more descriptive aspects, characterization proceeds largely through exemplification. The economic and political products of postmodernism, and their effects on society, are noted.

If postmodernism referred simply to matters of style, or if it were purely a category for post–World War II changes in society, it would not provoke the vigorous debate it has. Social scientists with a more theoretical, critical, and at times polemical approach have seen postmodernism as an outlook on social organization and relations held by the members of a society. This more abstract concept of postmodernism is difficult to characterize by means of examples and must be theorized more than illustrated. During the latter part of the 1970s, these more theoretical concepts of postmodern society touched off a general controversy.

The sociological theorist Jürgen Habermas in his *Legitimationsprobleme im Spätkapitalismus* (1973; English *Legitimation Crisis*, 1975) distinguishes the postmodern era by adverse changes in society's ability to place knowledge in a larger framework, share information and beliefs, and function ethically. Habermas, an heir of the Frankfurt School (to be discussed in Chapter Four, on popular culture studies), sees postmodernism as inhibiting the effort to increase communicative competence that allows a society collectively to reach rational ethical decisions. The know-how of technical specialists, daunting to outsiders, creates almost autonomous realms of expertise, not coordinated with the general norms of the society.[14] This theorist is unequivocally a critical observer of the postmodern society. Although Habermas contributes to theory about postmodernism, in no sense could his own thought and writing be considered postmodernist. He would like to see the tide turn toward a society united in a rational exchange over optimal ethical judgments.

On the other hand, the writing of such philosophers as Jean-François Lyotard and Jean Baudrillard is often perceived as itself constituting postmodernist philosophy, rather than a philosophical critique of the postmodern age and its culture. Lyotard, in particular, with his playful and sometimes contradictory manner of exposition, maintains ambiguity as to whether he is analyzing postmodernism, or whether he has entered post-modernism and is writing as a postmodern philosopher.

Lyotard gained wide attention with the publication of his 1979 *La Condition postmoderne: rapport sur le savoir* (*The Postmodern Condition: A Report on Knowledge*, 1984). This work, although issued to a general intellectual public by the Paris-based Editions de Minuit, originated as a commissioned report to the Council of Universities in Quebec. While it treats many themes, its official topic is a change in the status that society accords to knowledge.[15]

Postmodern society has little faith in the great missions assigned to non-applied knowledge, research, and teaching. Information becomes fragmented. Its value is assessed by its usefulness in accomplishing the task at hand. Especially in technical fields such as electrical engineering, where new applications of research can bring rapid profits, the specialist's information is apt to be seen as a marketable asset rather than as a contribution to society or the scholarly community. The same type of analysis can be applied to art and design. It might be claimed that the postmodern establishes its terrain, not necessarily in relation to the history of ideas, but often in relation to the market.

Lyotard derides, as an idealistic liberalism, Habermas's eagerness to see members of society reason together. In contrast to Habermas, who expresses straightforwardly what he wants for society, Lyotard is often playfully reticent or ironic, withholding his beliefs. He does, however, energetically condemn aspects of the present era, particularly the meager autonomy accorded university faculty despite much-publicized reforms of the late 1960s and early 1970s. Lyotard's complaint that knowledge is often valued by its current market value would seem to mark him as a critic of postmodernism. Yet he appears to find the era stretching from the Enlightenment through twentieth-century experimentalism as ridiculous and pretentious with its ambitious projects for humankind. His mocking, idiosyncratic style at times conceals the judgment he may be passing on the transition from the modern era to the postmodern age.

Baudrillard appears to take a more critical and less playful approach toward postmodernism than does the unpredictable Lyotard. In Baudrillard's analysis, postmodern society features an accelerated rate of change. Members of this fast-paced society come to expect and crave novelty. The postmodern public is overstimulated with items of information, much of it in the form of images; Baudrillard often focuses attention on new techniques for generating and transmitting images. In an environment of constant change, an onslaught of information, and proliferating images, the public is likely to lose sight of the distinction between naturally occurring realities and simulations. The latter is Baudrillard's term for the artificially constructed realities supplied by film, video, advertising, and computer graphics and models. A widely experienced example of this phenomenon occurs when filmed dramatizations of historical events are shown frequently, and at times excerpted for use in documentaries or news reports. At a rational level, viewers know that they are watching simulations of events. Nonetheless, they come to feel that these simulations are their own memories of events they have witnessed in person. Critics of postmodern society who speak of image addiction and of the interchangeability of reality and simulation are likely to be drawing upon the work of Baudrillard.[16]

In architecture and graphic design postmodernism may be primarily a style; in social theory it represents a shift in society's outlook. When *postmodernism* is applied to literature, and also when it refers to Latin American culture, it grows less clear which phenomena and problems are under consideration. Soon after talk of *postmodernism* became widespread, in the 1980s, it was sometimes claimed that the term and concept had scant relevance to Latin America, since not all portions of this large and variegated region had been modernized. If the postmodern meant postindustrial, then certain areas of Latin America, in which much labor was unmechanized, could not easily be viewed as part of the postmodern era. (One should note that even long-industrialized countries may include impoverished regions in which the benefits of modernization are difficult to discern.) García Canclini sums up the automatic response of many: "Why should we bother worrying about postmodernity, when on our continent modern advances have not completely reached everyone?"[17]

Many existing characterizations of postmodernism overlooked the altered trade and cultural relations that came with the transnationalization of capital and increased international movement of people, goods, and cultural tendencies. Previously it had seemed easy to single out the economic superpowers of the First World as the locus of control. Now the ownership and management of major economic entities were becoming decentralized and losing national identity. Latin American countries, historically among those nations disadvantaged in international commerce, were vulnerable to shifts in world economic relations. Their situation could not be fully described without reference to the economic and cultural globalization of the postindustrial age. These and other issues underlay the question that the literary critic George Yúdice voiced in the title and opening line of a much-noted essay: "Can one speak of postmodernity in Latin America?" [18]

In addition, many observers felt that postmodern culture, which encouraged participants to take pleasure in a cornucopia of consumer delights, was inherently disadvantageous to all but the wealthiest countries. Yúdice asserts: "First world postmodernism feeds off and is at the expense of an occluded third world warrant." [19] Postmodernism, associated with a dulled sense of social responsibility, would to some extent free stronger nations and corporations of scruples over the exploitation of poorer areas. (It should be noted, though, that such a concern has seldom spread beyond a limited number of progressives.) The historical differences and inequalities between regions may appear to be flattened out and disappear from the consciousness of privileged publics, though they continue to have economic consequences. As Colás states, in an extension of Jameson's thought: "In postmodernism, late capitalism obliterates the nature of the Third World and paralyzes our sense of historicity." [20] An era of indulgence for the privileged would be nothing for Latin American intellectuals to celebrate.

On the other hand, postmodernism was all but inevitable in major Latin American cities, which had become centers of modernist innovation. Buenos Aires, Mexico City, and São Paulo had been the site of important avant-gardes. São Paulo, in hosting the renowned Semana de Arte Moderna (Week of Modern Art) of 1922, left a lasting reminder of modernism's presence in Latin America. For many years, new construction in Latin American's urban centers was generally in the spare modernist manner. Once having embarked on the twentieth-century quest for modernity, these cultural centers, unless they were to become museums of the avant-garde period, had to move into the postmodern age.

Concerned with cultural autonomy, Nelson Osorio has opposed the application of the term *postmodernism* to Latin American culture; he sees it as periodizing culture and literature based on foreign cases. In his view, the attempt to make this largely European and U.S. term fit Latin American realities is a wrong move. Of greater benefit would be an effort to generate new period terms more faithful to the particular historical dynamic being played out in Latin American nations. [21] Since the current term and concept *postmodernism* had been in circulation for some time before they became part of Latin American intellectuals' agenda in the mid-to-late 1980s, there was an often-voiced apprehension that another product had been exported southward after losing its novelty or being deemed undesirable in wealthier countries. Even those studying Latin American postmodernity at times voice this anxiety. Colás, wondering whether the domestic U.S.-European market for postmodernism has been exhausted, asks, "why, then, especially, would I write a book that dumps the concept—like so much First-World toxic waste—onto Latin America?"[22] However, talk of postmodernism does not seem to be vanishing from Europe and the United States. Though the postmodern has been under considerable study since the 1970s, scholarly publications on the theme became more abundant than ever during the 1990s. Popular sources such as newspapers and book jacket copy continue to employ the term. A newer scholar, such as Andreas Huyssen, could still attain international prominence through novel analyses of the tendency. At the same time, an established scholarly observer of postmodernism, Jameson, has expanded his interests to include the transformations the concept requires to apply accurately to Latin America.[23]

In a further complication, many observers have raised the point that features regarded in advantaged countries as signs of postmodernism have been the norm in Latin American nations. If the commingling of stylistic features from different periods was sufficient to demonstrate postmodernism, then many Latin American churches and city centers had already been postmodern for many years. The contact between unlike cultures and the markedly uneven modernization of the region, among a variety of factors, have already produced the anachronistic mixture that distinguishes postmodernism. José Joaquín Brunner, for example, discerns "a sort of regional postmodernism *avant la lettre* that, nonetheless, fully constitutes our modernism."[24] For Brunner, the unique dynamic of Latin America's modernization produced many different "cultural logics" and hence an ability to rework cultural influences with exceptional heterogeneity; he therefore questions whether the term and concept *postmodern* will be of much use in thinking about Latin American societies.[25] (Brunner is also among those who view postmodernity as a decline.) Nicolás Casullo also points to a lack of coherence in the way modernization came to Latin America as evidence that the region has long been experiencing the dislocations associated with postmodernity. He observes: "The fact that the various phases of modernity (and their waves of modernization) have never been able to occur among us except as a modernity in crisis . . . *make the current debate over a postmodern sensibility, a sort of experience of long standing in Latin American history.*[26] This researcher identifies "traces of strong postmodernism" stretching well back into Argentine cultural history.[27]

Jean Franco summarizes this argument: "Not surprisingly, Latin American critics have claimed that in any case Latin America was postmodern *avant la lettre*, since its culture has always been formed from a complex of transactions between other cultures and regional specificities. The hybrid, copy, pastiche that have always been features of Latin American writing are now commonplaces of contemporary culture, which is engaged in a perpetual recycling of a new global repertoire."[28] Indeed, efforts to identify the distinctive features of Latin American cultures have often focused on the prevalence of mixed or *mestizo* forms, much as characterizations of postmodernism emphasize an exceptional heterogeneity that cuts across stylistic and period categories.

The idea of an already-postmodern Latin America seemed suddenly ubiquitous during the late 1980s; the widespread concept was difficult to attribute to any single figure.[29] Yúdice locates its source previous to the debate over postmodernism. He traces it back to the thought and writings of the influential Mexican poet and essayist Octavio Paz, starting with the latter's celebrated book-length essay of 1950, *The Labyrinth of Solitude*.

This attribution may initially seem strange. Paz, who as a poet has pursued an avant-garde line of innovation, has written a great deal about modernity, avant-gardism, and the idea of the modern but has only sporadically addressed the concept of postmodernity.[30] Nonetheless, Yúdice identifies in Paz's essays a line of argument that leads to the conclusion that Latin America was ahead of the central powers in moving beyond modernity: "According to him, the contradictory logic (*tradition of rupture*) of modernity is exhausted . . . at the moment when the central nations of capitalist imperialism lose their center and become just as 'marginal' as the periphery," so that U.S. and European culture belatedly exhibits the commingling of unlike features long familiar to nations on the edges of modernity.[31]

Yúdice, though, rejects Paz's idea that postmodernity represents a move beyond cultural history into a timeless present. Theorizing in the highly abstract mode that typifies his essays, Paz envisions the dawning of a new type of perennial now, open to all styles and modes, transcending historical periods. (A fascination with the attainment of a perpetual present or time outside time has long marked Paz's thought.) With creators released from the modernist pressure to produce striking innovations, features from past periods freely commingle. For Yúdice, it is a mistake to characterize the postmodern present as radically unlike standardly recognized periods and to see postmodernity as having uncoupled itself from modernity. Instead, postmodernity exists in a close relation with modernity and can even be considered a subset or variant of it, as Lyotard has often emphasized.[32]

Yúdice is similar to most participants in the debate over a Latin American postmodernity in that, while he criticizes previous formulations and applications of *postmodern*, he does not urge its abandonment or, as Osorio suggests, seek to develop a different term and concept for Latin America. He encourages the continuation of the debate over postmodernism, but always taking into account the distinctive historical dynamic that marks Latin American societies. Scholars should not simply apply concepts of the postmodern to Latin America. Rather, "such theories need to be deconstructed and reconstructed in relation to Latin American contexts."[33] Yúdice cautions against positing the existence of a purely esthetic and cultural sphere in which art and design develop independently of social factors. At the same time, the globalization of both capital and culture must be recognized as a shaping force: "If by postmodernity we mean local 'esthetic-ideological responses/proposals' in the face of and within capitalist transnationalization, no longer only in the United States and Europe but worldwide, the analysis of Latin American cultures must take this dialogical relation as its point of departure."[34] In asserting that the goods and cultural information now circulate and commingle worldwide, creating a globalized culture, researchers should not lose sight of the inequities that mark interactions between more- and less-powerful nations and regions. Yúdice warns that too strong an association between postmodernism and post–World War II technologies makes the concept poorly suited to the case of Latin America.[35]

The term *postmodern* may not be the ideal one for the current cultural era in Latin America (or anywhere else); it may require careful transformation before it corresponds well to the Latin American context. But in the era of globalization no region, no matter how distinctive its historical situation, can escape either the word *postmodern* or the phenomena widely perceived as postmodern. Latin American architects and visual artists had often been in the vanguard throughout most of the twentieth century; they could not turn away from such a massive new development. Buildings designed in the hard-to-mistake postmodern manner began to appear both in the commercial zones of cities like Caracas and in private residential zones.

The ephemeral culture of postmodernism came quickly to Latin American capitals and began its spread to more remote areas. The first video games of the early 1980s, like Pac Man, were soon available in Mexico City and other major centers. In Latin American cities, compared with U.S. ones, a smaller market exists for sophisticated electronic devices, especially when they are newly marketed and high in price. Yet this obstacle has not stopped the spread of new telephone features, videocassette recorders, compact discs, personal computers, satellite reception of televised programming, and other late-twentieth-century novelties. Users of computers with modems quickly gained access to the Internet. Communications specialists have been struck by the swift and pervasive spread of satellite-broadcast news and programming, not just in Latin America but worldwide. It is John Beverley's observation that not only is "postmodernism . . . bound up precisely with the dynamics of interaction between local cultures and an instantaneous and omnipresent global culture" but the theory that posits the link between postmodernism and global circulation of information and culture is "now itself globally disseminated."[36]

Perhaps the very difficulties of applying the term to Latin American societies have proven stimulating. A lively discussion over postmodernism, including study groups and long-running polemical exchanges, has arisen among Latin American intellectuals and foreign students of Latin American culture; while popular culture studies were long the main focus, literary scholars have also become involved. Large umbrella organizations of Latin American researchers, such as CEDES, CLASCO, and FLACSO, as well as smaller study groups, began to include scholarly activity centered on postmodernism. The journal *David y Goliat* produced a special issue on "Latin American Identity, Premodernity, Modernity, and Postmodernity"; appearing in September 1987, as the concept was taking hold, it aroused considerable excitement.[37] Certain figures became known for their ability to analyze postmodernism in Latin America and to stimulate further discussion on the topic. Examples include the Chilean Nelly Richard, editor of the influential *Revista de Crítica Cultural* (Review of cultural criticism); the Brazilian José Miguel Wisnik; and the Argentine Nicolás Casullo. But beyond such specialists, many intellectuals had little choice but to follow or participate in a debate of such general significance. Many Latin American intellectuals and artists, including such respected figures as the Argentine literary critic Beatriz Sarlo, have adapted the term and concept *postmodern* in their studies of Latin American cultural issues. In her 1994 *Escenas de la vida posmoderna: intelectuales, arte y videocultura en la Argentina*

(Scenes from postmodern life: intellectuals, art, and the culture of television in Argentina), Sarlo transforms the concepts of Baudrillard and others to apply them to Buenos Aires cultural life, with emphasis on the effects of television broadcasting and on intellectuals' diminished ability to function as social critics. Sarlo's book-length essay is dedicated simultaneously to critiquing intellectual life in Argentina and to transforming the concept of the postmodern to apply it to Argentine realities. For example, she takes into account the uneven distribution of wealth in Argentina, where the contrast between poor and rich is more evident than in many European countries. Particularly in her analysis of the effects of television, she recognizes the disproportionate influence U.S. popular culture and media have exercised on countries with less powerful and technically sophisticated cultural industries.

Sarlo's study is directed specifically to an Argentine readership; it expresses the author's judgments on the nation's intellectual life and draws on her extremely detailed insider's knowledge of this phenomenon. Sarlo is especially concerned with what intellectuals do to keep up with the times, either in order to feel satisfied with their own efforts or to continue to earn a living and be taken seriously in a changing milieu. She argues that Argentine intellectuals have become more like those of the United States, having little chance to address a general public and instead remaining hidden and obscurely cultivating their expertise in academic posts. She calls for a return of the public intellectual, who enjoys the attention of a public beyond fellow specialists and students and who can comment on matters broader than his or her field of expertise. The social criticism of *Escenas* is meant to constitute a move away from the intellectual as specialist.

Escenas is simultaneously about Argentine society and about international tendencies. It focuses on a period of time beginning in 1955. The base year chosen has to do with matters specific to Argentine social history, since the first regime of Juan Domingo Perón ended in 1955. At the same time, the span of time the study covers saw changes common worldwide, such as the proliferation of devices for the reproduction of sounds and graphics and the increasing limitation of intellectuals to their disciplinary specializations.

A noted Cuban creative writer and essayist, Antonio Benítez Rojo, has provoked widespread discussion with a highly original interpretation of Caribbean cultural phenomena that draws upon, among many other sources, notions of postmodernism. Of more international interest than

Sarlo's research on Buenos Aires intellectual life, Benítez Rojo's 1989 *La isla que se repite: el Caribe y la perspectiva posmoderna* (*The Repeating Island: The Caribbean and the Postmodern Perspective*) brings in concepts from twentieth-century physics, anthropology, and the cultural criticism of Caribbean thinkers, together with postmodernity, to produce a distinctive interpretation of the Caribbean.[38]

In the period from the early 1980s to the present, many other thinkers have become involved in what John Beverley and José Miguel Oviedo term "the postmodernism debate in Latin America."[39] Not all contributors to the exchange can be included in this chapter. Instead, the goal has been to present the main issues.

During the mid- to late-1980s, the discussion of postmodernism by Latin American intellectuals often took place on quite an abstract level, with relatively sparse examination of examples. More concrete illustrations of how postmodernity affects Latin American societies appear in the work of García Canclini, who studies mass media, popular cultures, and the marketing and exhibition of art and artisanry. While this intellectual has come to be associated with the term and concept *postmodernism*, it should be kept in mind that he is often quite critical of postmodern phenomena. In his assessment, the speeded-up, globalized late twentieth century has not been favorable to creative people. In particular, the influence wielded by capitalist marketing competition cuts into the creators' ability to make choices: "The autonomy of the artistic field, founded on esthetic criteria set by artists and critics, is diminished by the new way that art is determined by a rapidly expanding market, where noncultural forces are the decisive ones."[40]

García Canclini examines the modifications that creators, whether associated with a folkloric tradition or part of the art world, make in the age of urbanization, tourism, art as investment, and increased international movement of people and objects. In comparison with the figures mentioned above, García Canclini makes relatively few overt allusions to postmodernism and has not tended to feature this key term in his titles; more than a theorist of the postmodern, he is an observer and analyst of culture in the postmodern age. Little of his work is devoted to definitions or refinements of the term *postmodern*, although he certainly employs the word; rather, his attention turns to the manifestations of the phenomenon and how groups and individuals cope with it.

García Canclini bases his general statements on case studies, often of popular cultures but at other times of art galleries, museums, outdoor art-work, and advertising for art. Much of his research has centered on sites in Mexico, though his range of reference extends throughout Latin America, the United States, and Europe. García Canclini often associates the post-modern with cultures in contact; for example, he observes that while seek-ing "to study intercultural conflict on the Mexican side of the border, it often occurred to me that, along with New York, Tijuana is one of the major laboratories of postmodernity."[41] While his examples are almost ex-clusively Latin American or U.S. Latino, he draws significantly on Euro-pean postmodern theory, especially the work of Baudrillard and Pierre Bourdieu, as well as theories of culture generally.

García Canclini studies populations and communities that, impelled by necessity, have proven resourceful in dealing simultaneously with very dif-ferent cultural systems. These groups, driven to create inventive syntheses, generate "hybrid cultures," to cite the title of García Canclini's 1991 book.[42] He is probably best known for his studies of possessors of tradi-tional knowledge and skills, such as artisans and folk performers, who have learned to ply greatly modified versions of their trade in a predominantly urban society open to international markets. As García Canclini reminds readers, even though folk traditions such as crafts have not died out, "The fact that 60 to 70 percent of the population is now concentrated in big cities and is connected to national and transnational networks means that the contents, practices, and rites of the past—including those of migrant *cam-pesinos*—are reordered according to a different logic."[43] He examines in-stances in which "what can be observed is that traditional cultures have developed by modifying themselves."[44]

Internationally, he is best known for his 1982 *Las culturas populares en el capitalismo*, translated into English as *Transforming Modernity: Popular Cul-ture in Mexico* (1993), an examination of the production and marketing of articles handmade by Indians in the Tarascan area of the state of Michoa-cán. One of the areas examined, near Lake Pátzcuaro, has seen a rapid growth of tourism and commercial marketing of handicrafts. The items sold originate in native tradition, usually having either a practical or a ritual use. But these handmade articles now travel from their original context and become part of the capitalist marketing system. Now they must be made to appeal to consumers who will display rather than use them. Purchasers of crafts fall into different categories, but tend to be seeking novelty, unusual beauty, and prestige. The result is an ambiguous and hybrid situation in which "Crafts belong and at the same time do not belong to Indians, they both find and at the same time fail to find a place within the household."[45]

García Canclini is known for questioning the common assumption that current-day capitalism and its associated mass media are producing uniformity among the world's cultures. He theorizes about developments in popular culture that run counter to what would normally be expected. To return to the case noted above, as automated production becomes more widespread, one would expect fewer handmade articles. Instead, the production of handcrafted items is accelerated and the articles evolve to increase their marketability. In the context of late capitalism and global media, cultural homogenization is the predicted outcome. García Canclini recognizes that, to some extent, a standardization of tastes and habits is occurring worldwide. Still, this process does not eliminate the appeal of cultural items distinct to particular localities: "But, at the same time, the exigencies continually to regenerate economic demand cannot tolerate the stagnation of production at a level of monotonous reproduction of standardized objects."[46] Local folk manufacture now becomes a source of stimulating novelties useful in maintaining the interest of consumers.

A complex issue is what judgment García Canclini makes on the phenomena he studies. On the positive side, he communicates his admiration for groups and individuals who, without leaving behind their traditional skills and knowledge, are adroit in the intricate contemporary marketplace. Yúdice notes that while many students of traditional communities have described changing customs, García Canclini is unusual in exhibiting "no sense of loss": "Rather than see their cultural adaptation as an accommodation to Euro- and Nordocentric perspectives, he emphasizes the ingenuity of these groups in negotiating multiple demands in several languages, making use of many different kinds of technologies, . . . ably bringing their various knowledges to bear in marketing their products, and so on."[47]

Still, García Canclini is not celebrating the postmodern era for its ability to bring out, through capitalist competition, a resourceful, entrepreneurial vigor in previously traditional people. He notes that the present age, in which capitalist-style marketing pressures have gained such strength, has been a difficult time for artisans and native peoples generally. Though the artisans living in villages near Lake Pátzcuaro might appear, with their expert adaptation, to present a capitalist success story, García Canclini reminds readers that, in the late twentieth century, very few Mexican Indians have enjoyed their relative prosperity. However ingenious and adaptable

Indians may be and however skilled at negotiating between cultures, still "Since the sixties, the chronic problems of the Mexican countryside have worsened," and both rural and urbanized Indians are losing ground.[48]

As he has observed in studying the high-art world, García Canclini finds that under the pressure of market forces, creators and art itself find their autonomy eroded. As he puts it, in a statement about artisans that could apply to all creators in the age of heavily organized marketing: "There will be no truly popular cultural policies as long as producers do not play a leading role, and they will hold such a role only after a radical democratization of civil society."[49]

Transforming Modernity examines the entire system that conveys traditional handmade clothing, earthenware, ceremonial objects, and adornments from their Indian creators to various non-Indian publics. García Canclini shows the transformations produced when Indians, out of economic necessity, enter into unprecedented relations of exchange with the rapidly globalizing culture of late capitalism. His study is also concerned with the expanded range of consumers of handicrafts: tourists, dealers, agents for museums and state-run shops, and collectors striving to give their interiors an exotic, worldly eclecticism. These groups represent such tendencies as globalization and the expanded reach of the mass media. To satisfy the buyers' desire for novelty, the makers commingle features from unlike periods, cultures, styles, and geographical areas: "Industrialization, tourism, and the mass media appear to be . . . effective in making potters from Santa Fe de la Laguna manufacture clay cigarette cases, decorated with reproductions of international labels. . . . They have also influenced designs of trays from Charula . . . which in recent times have increasingly depicted giraffes, an animal that has, thus, suddenly become typical of the central mountains of Mexico."[50]

Literary scholars also began to examine postmodernism as a set of behaviors and attitudes common to recent societies. But since literary critics are always examining or at least pointing out particular texts, whether drawn from literature or popular culture, they cannot stop at a theoretical characterization of postmodernism. Critics cannot escape the task of identifying and studying examples of postmodernism. Their need to refer to textual examples continues even when they become involved in developing concepts of the postmodern. This necessity distinguishes their work from that of social scientists who theorize postmodern culture.

When students of Spanish American literature take up the inquiry into postmodernism, a special terminological problem arises. In Hispanic letters and culture, including architecture and the decorative arts, *modernismo* has a meaning unlike that of the international term *modernism*. (This problem does not arise in the case of Brazilian culture. Brazilian avant-garde writing, art, and design of the 1920s were referred to as *modernismo* and can reasonably be included in the same worldwide movement as the *modernism* of James Joyce and his generation.) In Spanish, *modernismo* refers to a style that originated in Spanish America, traveled to Spain, and flourished from about the beginning of the 1880s into the 1910s. Often highly embellished and artificial, filled with exotic allusions and references to valuable objects, *modernismo* does not correspond very well to *modernism* in the general European sense. The international style known as *modernism* is marked by the reduction to a minimum of exterior ornamentation. Indeed, the *modernismo* of the Spanish-speaking world often resembles late-twentieth-century *postmodernism* in its exuberant desire to embellish.

To give a visual example, *modernista* is the term used in the Spanish-speaking world for the architecture of Antonio Gaudí (1852–1926) and other designers struck with his approach. A number of buildings constructed during the late nineteenth and early twentieth centuries, especially a concentration in one area of Barcelona, are perceived in Spain as exemplifying architectural *modernismo*. Yet it is the *modernismo* of Gaudí that Charles Jencks takes as his starting point of the history of postmodernist architecture. The buildings of Gaudí and his like-minded contemporaries, distinguished by their imaginative and eclectic ornamentation, undeniably resemble the postmodernist architecture that came to the fore in the 1970s.

The lack of terminological synchronization between *modernismo* and *modernism* affects also the terms *posmodernismo* and *postmodernism*. *Posmodernismo* is the transitional style that began to appear in the first decade of the twentieth century and became more evident in the 1910s. *Modernismo*, which had prevailed for some three decades, was losing its appeal. Even its most important practitioner and exponent, the Nicaraguan-born Rubén Darío (1867–1916), had exhausted *modernismo's* resources and was moving beyond it in his late work. The same could be said for the second most prominent *modernista*, the Argentine Leopoldo Lugones (1874–1938). While the established *modernistas* were distancing themselves from the *modernista* esthetic and style, younger writers were often hostile toward it.

The year of Darío's death is a convenient ending date for *modernismo*, but in the mid-1910s no clear countermovement had yet emerged, a situation summed up by the term *posmodernismo*. (By the beginning of the 1920s, Spanish American avant-gardes would constitute the first distinctive movement to follow *modernismo*.) In the 1910s, writers were attempting various strategies to develop a new literary language. Simplicity was widely prized, as a reaction to the ornamentation of *modernismo*. Writers who exemplify *posmodernismo* at times favor regional and rural settings. Since many different experiments were undertaken in the effort to evolve beyond *modernismo*, *posmodernismo* does not constitute a single movement or esthetic, though it is unified by a weariness with *modernismo*'s long-standing dominance. In short, Hispanic *posmodernismo* does not correlate with *postmodernism* in the sense the latter term has taken on internationally.

Various solutions to the problem have been proposed, such as using *posmodernidad*, which has no prior history of usage in Spanish, rather than the already-in-use *posmodernismo*. This slightly modified form of the term is, in fact, sometimes used. Since *vanguardismo* is the Spanish term that most closely corresponds to modernism in the international sense, some scholars employ *posvanguardismo* in lieu of *posmodernismo*. The use of *posvanguardismo* is logical; postmodernism is, indeed, what emerges after the exhaustion of the twentieth-century campaign for striking esthetic innovation, which the avant-garde movement exemplifies. Despite its descriptive accuracy, *posvanguardismo* has never gained wide currency. If it were substituted for *postmodernism*, the terminological difference would to some degree cut Latin American intellectuals off from worldwide intellectual exchange. Whether or not the term *postmodernism* is the most suitable—it does not correspond unproblematically even to the Western European and U.S. contexts in which it was formulated—it is the one that has caught on and dominates the analysis of the present cultural era.

Such terminological problems are not a lasting impediment to the inquiry into postmodernism. Even a careless reader could not proceed far into an essay on *posmodernismo* without discovering whether it concerned the back-to-basics literary movement of the 1910s or the late-twentieth-century social and cultural tendency. A more substantive issue for students of Latin American writing is which texts one may reasonably consider instances of late-twentieth-century literary postmodernism. When those discussing postmodernism are literary critics by background, they often illustrate their arguments by citing cases from popular culture. Literary writing would appear to be one of the cultural forms in which specimens of postmodernism are especially difficult to single out.

Analysts of postmodern writing who have no great familiarity with Latin American literature at times turn to certain widely read novels to exemplify postmodernism in Latin America. Two examples of such scholars and their works are Linda Hutcheon, one of the most frequently cited students of postmodernist narrative, in her 1987 *A Poetics of Postmodernism: History, Theory, Fiction* and 1989 *The Politics of Postmodernism*, and Brian McHale in his 1987 *Postmodernist Fiction*. Hutcheon in particular believes Spanish American literature to be an exceptionally rich source of examples of postmodern writing. Both draw some of their examples from the internationally celebrated novels that Spanish American fiction writers produced during a period from the end of the 1950s to the beginning of the 1970s. While this period was called the *boom* for the unprecedented sales and publicity Spanish American writing enjoyed, the term *boom novel* also evokes experimentation with narrative form and an ambitious drive to produce strikingly inventive masterpieces. The boom authors, such as the Mexican Carlos Fuentes (b. 1928), Gabriel García Márquez of Colombia (b. 1927), and the Argentine Julio Cortázar (1914–1984), have attracted English-language translators and publishers and are among the Spanish American writers best known to an international audience.

The classification of these authors as postmodern, though, is somewhat baffling to critics and readers who have a more long-standing familiarity with Latin American literature before and after the 1960s. Colás, for example, calls Hutcheon's habit of illustrating postmodernism by examining characteristics of boom novels a "misappropriation of Latin American fiction for her transnational canon of postmodern historiographic metafiction."[51] Readers familiar with the history of Latin American literature are more likely to perceive the boom as an era marked by a modernist confidence in the possibility of radical, groundbreaking innovation. The great novels of the era, such as Cortázar's 1963 *Rayuela* (*Hopscotch*, 1967) and García Márquez's 1967 *Cien años de soledad* (*One Hundred Years of Solitude*, 1970), received acclaim for breaking with narrative tradition; the term *new*, as in *new Spanish American novel*, was much in use. Characteristic of the contemporary outlook was Fuentes's 1969 collection of essays, *La nueva novela hispanoamericana* (The new Spanish American novel). Fuentes enthusiastically characterizes Latin American narrative as having undergone a thorough transformation for the better as the second half of the twentieth century began. The drive to create landmarks of novelistic innovations was widespread among "boom" authors; at the time, reviewers and critics often appraised their work based on the criterion of novelty. Much of the experimentation of the "new novel" clearly expressed an avant-garde or modernist intent. It was common for the successful writers of the boom to express their admiration for avant-garde experimentalists or for modernist novelists like Faulkner. For example, many new novels stood out for their highly discontinuous treatment of time and space and the instability of the narrators' and characters' identities.

While the link between the boom and postmodernism is difficult to sustain, some critics view as largely postmodernist the less authoritative, weighty, ambitious, and demanding novels that Spanish American writers began to produce in the late 1960s, as the boom started to decline in interest. While it has occurred to various readers to use the term *postmodern* for the more easily read, frequently light-hearted and parodic fiction of the postboom, Raymond Leslie Williams is the critic who has most thoroughly researched this link. In many articles and in his 1995 book, *The Postmodern Novel in Latin America*, he has pursued the relations between the fading of the boom and the rise of postmodern fiction. In Williams's analysis, the narrative of the boom is predominantly, though by no means exclusively, modernist: "For García Márquez and Latin American writing, *One Hundred Years of Solitude* represented a culmination, in 1967, of a modernist project."[52]

At the same time, Williams insightfully identifies, well before the boom, the inception of what would later flower as the Latin American postmodern novel. He points to probably the most internationally respected of Spanish American authors, Jorge Luis Borges (Argentina, 1899–1986): "Borges . . . planted the seeds for a Latin American postmodern fiction with his stories of the 1940s."[53] As he traces the progression, postmodernist features are evident here and there in fiction written before the postmodernism era in Latin American writing. Williams also finds occasional traces of postmodernism within the boom, especially in Cortázar's 1963 *Rayuela* (*Hopscotch*), noted above and often cited as a quintessential boom novel.[54] The actual postmodern era comes, though, as the boom is ending: "In the late 1960s and early 1970s, the postmodern novel began to appear in Latin America, almost always inspired by either Borges or Cortázar."[55] Williams observes that the writers who had gained prominence as boom-era modernists often moved toward postmodern modes as the boom became exhausted. A successful example is the 1975 novel *Terra nostra* (*Terra Nostra*) by Fuentes; "Although *Terra Nostra* has some modernist totalizing impulses, it shares closer proximity to the postmodern."[56] More important, in Williams's analysis, is the work of a new generation of novelists who made their names with postmodern fiction. The greater part of *The Postmodern Novel in Latin America* is devoted to a country-by-country survey of these more recently emerged authors. While many of the scholars surveyed here are critical of postmodernism, Williams expresses his admiration for postmodernity—or postmodernities, as he prefers to say—in fiction by Latin American authors. His account of the postmodern Latin American novel is a knowledgeable and sympathetic one.

Williams correlates the shift in Spanish American fiction from boom to postboom to the transition, in culture at large, from modern to postmodern. In linking postboom fiction to postmodernism, Williams examines with particular care the way narratives present information as being true within the fictional world. Boom novels, motivated by the modernist drive for technical experimentation, are often narrated in a noncontinuous sequence and contain many sudden changes of locale. Though these innovations slow down readers' discovery of the events of the plot, with persistence the reading audience can usually reconstruct most of the narrative data; modernist novels, for all their nonlinearity, move toward a greater order. In Williams's analysis, postmodern postboom novels do not offer a clear picture of what holds true in a novel. For example, he notes that postmodern novels may contain many speaking voices but none to supply guidance: "they present no privileged narrator upon whom the reader can rely, nor is there an authoritative discourse or figure to whom the reader can turn for something like an objective, final truth regarding its fiction."[57] Postmodern writing is marked by instability, uncertainty, and indeterminacy. The modernist quest for some overarching order or structuring logic is largely abandoned. Narratives are not merely fragmented or arranged in unexpected sequence. Instead, even a careful and patient reader will be at times unable to determine what was supposed to have happened in a given narrative.

Williams's characterization of postmodern Latin American fiction refers in part to the way in which narratives are constructed. However, it goes beyond issues of narrative technique. Williams is also speaking of a general shift in the status attributed to truths, resulting in a relativistic vision of truths as indeterminate or less than absolute: "Selected Latin American postmodern novels question the truth industry of modernism. What is at stake for the Latin American postmoderns who have arisen since the late

1960s . . . is not truth."[58] The association between Latin American post-modern fiction and the relativism of truths is not unique to Williams's research. Colás makes similar findings in his examination of Manuel Puig's narrative. In Colás's analysis, an outstandingly postmodern feature is the latent suggestion that "utopian (pure and uncontradicted) truth is an illusion," and that even scientifically demonstrated truths are superseded by other, similarly supported, truths.[59]

Not all critics perceive a strong association between postboom and post-modern. Donald L. Shaw, who has developed a critical characterization of the postboom, says of this tendency: "it seems clear that there are great difficulties in the way of regarding it (except for the New Historical Novel) as a postmodern movement in any familiar sense of the term. . . . We must keep in mind that Postmodernism is a far wider-ranging concept than that of the Post-Boom, and that it arose and developed in relation to the culture of advanced industrial or post-industrial societies, whereas Post-Boom is a much humbler and narrower term restricted to fiction on one continent."[60] Shaw recognizes that certain postboom texts, such as some of those that parody popular subgenres of the novel, may present aspects of the post-modern. Yet overall, he sees postboom literature as largely separated from international postmodernism by such factors as Spanish American fiction writers' more vivid concern with social issues.

There is another reason to be cautious in identifying postboom fiction with postmodernism. Critics have had little success in their efforts to single out particular literary works as postmodern. In books and articles on literary postmodernism, there is little agreement about which texts illustrate the tendency. Uncertainty over which features mark a text as postmodern is great for Latin American writing, since the term and concept are still undergoing adaptation to correspond to the region's conditions.

It seems unlikely that individual literary works can ever be analyzed, in isolation, for their postmodern traits. Literary intellectuals involved in the discussion of postmodernism do well to examine a broad range of cultural phenomena, including popular works and contemporary beliefs about what literature can accomplish. This more ample panorama helps provide a context in which the word *postmodernism* has greater meaning than it does when applied to works one by one.

Keeping these cautionary remarks in mind, it is still possible to examine a limited number of instances in which postboom writing manifests some of the characteristics associated with postmodernism. At the same time, one should take into account the extreme difficulty of isolating any literary text and analyzing the postmodern strain that runs through it. Postmodernism is present in many cultural manifestations simultaneously, often in unintended forms. It is not concentrated specifically in texts deliberately composed by professional writers. There has always been a poor consensus among critics concerning which literary texts may most accurately be characterized as postmodern.

Postboom writing first appeared before the boom was over, in the latter half of the 1960s; the postboom period continued unabated into the 1990s. Though postboom fiction originally arose while important boom novels were still being published, it was not difficult to distinguish from the former, with its serious and determined innovation. The first large-scale movement toward a newly light-hearted mode probably came with the *onda* (literally *wave*, meaning *hip writing*) in Mexico. The *onda* was a youth movement. The authors were younger than the boom writers, who were born in the 1920s, or, in Cortázar's case, the 1910s, and attained their celebrity in the 1960s. In contrast, the *ondero* José Agustín (full name José Agustín Ramírez Gómez), born in 1944, had published the novel *La tumba* (The grave) by 1964. But, more importantly, the narrators and characters of *onda* writing were speaking from the youth culture of the 1960s. The speech represented in the novel was that of disaffected young people and included a good deal of the hip slang of the 1960s.

The comments provoked by the *onda* writers show, as well as a reaction to the youth counterculture in Mexico, a similarity to the response to postmodern art. The leading writers of the *onda*, Agustín and Gustavo Sainz, were often dismissed as inconsequential, and their works seen as offering too easy and accessible a form of enjoyment. Much commentary centered on the relations between *onda* novels and popular culture, especially 1960s rock music, hip slang, and the psychedelic subculture. There were predictions that such novels as Sainz's 1965 *Gazapo* (which bore the same title in English translation), while providing momentary excitement, would become unintelligible in a few years because of their close correlation to ephemeral popular phenomena. These novels were often perceived as less substantial than their predecessors. In more measurable terms, they were generally briefer than the great novels of the boom years, which often required a considerable number of pages to unfold their ambitiously complex narrative design. On the other hand, the writers of the *onda* in many ways continued the experiments in narrative construction for which the boom had been noted.

The *onda* writers, both in their fiction and in their public images, moved away from the high-modernist seriousness of purpose that had characterized their literary elders. These writers stressed their debt to contemporary rock music and other nonelite forms. Agustín, especially, was known for his ties to celebrities of the entertainment world. Parody, irreverent mimicry, and a flippant stance marked the early work and personae of these writers.

The brief-lived *onda* was one of the first signs of a tendency that would be confirmed in the novels of Manuel Puig. The Argentine-born author, achieving an international celebrity, is probably the most widely recognized practitioner of postboom fiction. As had the *onda* writers, Puig drew heavily upon commercial, popular culture for allusions and references as well as novelistic subject matter. Puig's two most-studied novels are *La traición de Rita Hayworth* (*Betrayed by Rita Hayworth;* first published in 1968, though it won a wide public later) and his largest international success, *El beso de la mujer araña* (*Kiss of the Spider Woman,* 1976). Both of these texts devote considerable space to the narration of scenes or entire plots from popular films, some of which were actually made and others that are Puig's invention. In both works, the protagonists' absorption in watching movies and recreating them in memory is a major thematic issue.

Puig's writing is also among the most likely to be cited in comments on postmodern literature from Latin America. Colás asserts emphatically: "*El beso de la mujer araña* represents, in my view, a turning point in recent Latin American narrative from a Latin American modernity, critical but still within the logic of European modernity, to a Latin American postmodernity that operates from a point beyond the exhaustion of those paradigms." [61] This same critic identifies in *Kiss of the Spider Woman* a rejection of puristic and absolutist outlooks, such as those of devoted believers in a cause: "By contrast, the postmodern viewpoint, for which Puig's text begins to clear a space, does not require such purity but rather views it as myth." [62]

Of the characteristics that earn Puig's writing the designation of postmodern, probably the most salient is the thorough fusion of elements of high and popular culture. When Puig first won widespread notice, his distinctive mode of fiction was often referred to as the *novela pop*, but this designation is inexact. While he had done screenwriting before he became a celebrity, Puig was generally known for his work in a form regarded as art—the "serious" novel. With the intricacy of their narrative form, his novels provided material for the type of close textual analysis in which literary critics are trained.

At times Puig mimicked popular subgenres. For example, the 1969 novel

Boquitas pintadas (*Heartbreak Tango*) imitates the form of a *folletín*, a serialized novel designed to exercise a sentimental appeal to a largely female reading public. His novels also included many citations from popular culture, such as the excerpts from tango lyrics that serve as epigraphs throughout *Heartbreak Tango*. Obviously, his novels stand in an intimate relation to popular culture; the relation varies from derisive parody to affectionately nostalgic recreation. Still, his fiction cannot be placed completely in the terrain of popular culture, in great part because of its complexity. It has a dual identity, bringing together features of popular and elite culture. In addition, Puig's novels, like many postmodern works, are relatively brief and can appear insubstantial next to the great boom narratives. The novels include material that makes them seem more ephemeral than boom novels, which in many cases strove for an air of timeless significance. Allusions to popular culture are only one variety of the seemingly inconsequential material that Puig works into his fiction. Conversations between characters often include surprisingly banal observations. Puig, who had a talent for the mimicry of low styles, often provided narrative information via fictitious documents composed in heavily conventionalized official jargon. Beyond the heterogeneity that inevitably results when various styles are parodied, the imitation of "officialese" shows a lessened solemnity toward the literary enterprise. Puig is willing to display levity and to appeal to his readers' sense of the ridiculous; he also risks using material that may soon go out of date. These practices set his work at a distance from the seriousness of high modernism.

Since Puig's work began to attract the label of *postmodern*, this label has been applied at one time or another to many texts, most of them narrative fiction. Rather than attempt to name every author and work that has been identified as postmodernist, it might be more useful to review another approach to tracing Latin American manifestations of the postmodern. A different perspective on the issue may be obtained by going outside the type of writing that would normally be examined by literary critics. The point is to seek signs of the postmodern attitude in a broader range of cultural activities and productions. Yúdice, for example, proposes that scholars in quest of a Latin American postmodern work examine the poetry written by nonprofessionals in workshops sponsored by the Sandinista government in Nicaragua. He also brings into the discussion the social-activist reinterpretations of Biblical narratives common among radicalized Christian groups and the new social movements of the late twentieth century, whose members make common cause for reasons unlike the standard ones of class or national solidarity. As these and other of Yúdice's examples clearly indicate, he is concerned with bringing to the fore the democratizing tendencies in current-day culture and with questioning the special status critics assign to elite art forms.[63]

It is a valuable practice for researchers of literature to consider new developments beyond what is standardly considered their purview. Yet, realistically, few literary critics will feel capable of analyzing in detail poetry from revolutionary workshops, revisionist Biblical exegeses, or such new social movements as those of ecological activists or resistance groups united by a common ethnic identity. While critics may make note of them, these phenomena do not offer the type of text that students of literature need to utilize their analytical skills as critics. Yúdice offers a more useful point of departure for critics: to consider testimonial literature (to be discussed in the next chapter) when they examine postmodernist culture.[64] Critics have many reasons to scrutinize and analyze testimonial literature; an association has often been made between postmodernism and testimonial writing.[65] This form of writing, which has provoked many students of Latin American literature to examine some of their concepts of literature and authorship, is the next topic of this survey.

3   Testimonial Narrative: Whose Text?

The discussion of *documentary* and *testimonial narrative* has occupied a good deal of attention in recent years. Critics' eagerness to think about this class of writings surely arises in great part from the abundance of documentary works published during the 1960s, 1970s, and 1980s, including some striking international successes. At the same time, texts in this category raise some difficult questions that require critics to think about, in Jean Franco's words, "ethical questions that are normally set off to the side in literary studies."[1] Noteworthy innovations in documentary literature have occurred worldwide. Truman Capote's 1966 *In Cold Blood* is a memorable example. Capote produced what he called a *nonfiction novel*, a narrative version of a multiple murder and its consequences based on his interviews, over a period of years, with the killers. While documentary narrative is not exclusive to any region, Latin American writing has been unusually vigorous in its production of texts in this vein.

By 1970, so many new works of this type were appearing every year that the Cuban state publishing house, Casa de las Américas, established a category for *testimonio* in its annual awards competition. John Beverley and Marc Zimmerman posit that with the creation of this prize, "Latin American *testimonio* coalesces as a clearly defined genre."[2] Even so, examination of the titles that have earned awards in this category shows a low degree of uniformity. Many of the prize-winning works are first-person participants' narratives of resistance movements, such as the memoirs of *guerrilleros*, the type of text that concerns Beverley and Zimmerman in their research. But others are descriptive accounts of primarily ethnographic interest, such as interviews with subjects representing little-known segments of Caribbean culture. They have the traditional ethnographic purpose of preserving a record of culture that may soon vanish. Certain testimonial works deviate from the eyewitness-account pattern by offering summaries and interpretations by scholarly observers. Some are composed by a literate participant in history, while others involve the collaboration between such a participant and a more skilled writer. The selections for the *testimonio* award suggest a more general nonfiction category of testimonial narrative than would the works Beverley and Zimmerman examine in their "Testimonial Narrative." The examples they analyze are all recent first-person accounts by persons involved in anti-government resistance activities; nearly all are from Central America.[3]

Documentary writing has been one of the areas in which Latin American writers have produced notable innovations. It has been a topic much discussed on the Latin American intellectual scene. The discussion has resulted in numerous efforts to define documentary or testimonial narrative. To generalize about the meanings these terms have taken on, *documentary literature* appears vaster and more difficult to specify, including many works with a strong claim to factuality. *Testimonial* writing would seem to be a subset of documentary literature, generally indicating the first-person accounts of participants in or witnesses to significant events or little-known subcultures. Yet, as the debate continues over the decades, neither term has been defined with much precision.

The working assumption here is that it is impossible to identify the exact beginnings of documentary fiction or to set its boundaries. Writers, especially those following a realist program, have always made use of current news or historical events as points of departure for fiction. Realist writers eager to represent the world with the least possible degree of mediation have quite naturally been inclined to supplement their invention with factual material. In many cases, authors have sought out and conversed with eyewitnesses to exceptional historical or personal events before composing their fictional versions of the same or similar occurrences. Writers of realist and naturalist fiction have in many cases recorded samples of real-world conversations and other interactions, particularly those of lower-class speakers, to lay the groundwork for their own narratives. The Goncourt brothers, with their extensive fieldwork and notebooks, present a well-known instance of this practice. Testimonial literature is somewhat easier to characterize because it offers readers access to the words of witnesses and participants. Yet, as the following discussion will show, this category is also complicated; the words of the testimonial speakers are theirs to varying extents.

This chapter does not attempt to devise a definition either for documentary or testimonial literature. Still, these categories present a valid problem for students of literature and have given rise to some highly sophisticated analyses. Critics have utilized their studies of the issue in order to test certain difficult-to-specify boundaries. These include the distinction between literary and nonliterary writing and that between fiction and nonfiction narrative.

David William Foster's "Latin American Documentary Narrative," published in the widely distributed literary journal *PMLA*, drew critics' attention to the struggle to establish conceptually a distinctive category for the writing specified in the essay's title.[4] Foster, quite reasonably, does not attempt to construct a definition for documentary narrative. Rather, he delimits a category within which he situates the five texts he analyzes. His article begins with a frank recognition that Latin American literature has always included an unusually high incidence of historical documents and various types of factually based writings, so that documentary literature cannot be called new or assigned a recent starting date. Foster keeps the category broad so as to analyze jointly diverse texts. They include the results of investigative journalism presented in narrative form, a diary composed retrospectively, and edited versions of first-person participant and witness accounts.

The problem these critics are working on—delimiting a category for documentary or testimonial narrative—is a perennial one. For example, while Foster's essay presents scrupulous arguments to support his working characterization of documentary narrative, it has certainly done nothing to lay the discussion of this point to rest. The succeeding decade brought more debate than ever over the boundaries of documentary and testimonial narrative. Reading, for example, the 1986 collection edited by René Jara and Hernán Vidal, *Testimonio y literatura*, it is easy to feel that there are almost as many implicit or enunciated definitions of *testimonio* as there are essays in the book.[5] However intelligent the definition of the terms and concepts, there will always be too many borderline or ambiguous cases of such writing for the definition to maintain distinct outlines.

The point here is to examine one particular tendency within testimonial literature that has recently received a good deal of attention. This is the effort to bring to the reading public the self-accounts (often tape-recorded) of individuals who would not normally have the opportunity to publish autobiographies or statements about their special communities and cultures. In the most typical case, the speakers are representatives of a group outside the general, literate culture—usually Indians, African-Hispanics, or members of the underclass. While they would ordinarily never become published authors, these speakers have a claim on the reading public's attention. They are valued as the possessors of information and experience that would otherwise remain unknown to a standard, middle-class audience.

This chapter's discussion of documentary or testimonial literature focuses above all on one issue: the status that the finished text assigns to the less-literate people involved in its making. My concern is not with discovering behind-the-scenes information about how these narratives came into being, for example, whether a tape recorder was used and how extensively the writer reorganized the material obtained in interviews. (The genesis and gestation of the most successful testimonial narratives have often been the focus of intense curiosity, speculation, and polemic.) Rather, the approach here is to rely on published sources, both testimonial narrative and critical writing about it. Special attention goes to the presentation of the less-lettered and worldly of the collaborators. No attempt has been made to cover all the important works that have been called *testimonial narrative*. Instead, a few examples have been selected to illustrate different aspects of the issues involved.

Beverley and Zimmerman's "Testimonial Narrative" gives a brief prehistory of the phenomenon: their examples run back to the beginnings of Latin American writing, when discoverers and colonizers set down their experiences.[6] Obviously, if such a vast body of texts is included as documentary literature, then the category becomes too cumbersome to discuss. Still, Beverley and Zimmerman have a point: the works generally studied as Latin American literature include an unusually high proportion of nonfiction narratives.

Juan Pérez Jolote, biografía de un tzotzil (*Juan the Chamula: An Ethnological Re-Creation of the Life of a Mexican Indian*) by Ricardo Pozas (Mexico, 1917–1994) may be considered a more immediate, mid-twentieth-century forerunner to testimonial narrative as it is currently discussed. Following extensive conversations with a Tzotzil Mayan informant, Pozas composed a first-person account of one life that encapsulated the problems of Mexico's native population. Literary readers have regarded *Juan the Chamula* as an extreme case of the anthropological current in *indigenista* (Indian-themed) narrative. Writers following this tendency utilized their indigenous characters as opportunities to impart information about native traditions and problems facing current-day Indians. In fact, Pozas was a cultural anthropologist who originally published his fictionalized study in the professional journal *Acta Anthropologica* (1948). Still, the work had a character and plot; it proved its ability to reach a general readership when reissued in 1952 by the Fondo de Cultura Económica house. *Juan the Chamula* is not so different from contemporary Mexican novels designed to educate readers about the native population. To cite the best-known examples, the 1936 *El indio* (English version also entitled *El Indio*) by Gregorio López y Fuentes (1897–1966), and *El resplandor* (1937; English title *Sunburst*) by Mauricio Magdaleno (1906–1984) also carry a didactic load of data and opinions about indigenous customs and modern social problems. As Joseph Sommers has pointed out, later writers would reject this information-heavy approach as treating Indians too externally, turning them into composite figures. The next generation of Indian-theme writers, in reaction, focused on native peoples' experience, attitudes, and vision.[7]

While poised between anthropology and literature, *Juan the Chamula* leaves little ambiguity about the roles of Pozas and his native informant. Pozas is the author, and the Indian is the supplier of data for a case study. Juan is not meant to stand out as an autonomous subject; he serves to exemplify the traits of a population and the factors affecting it. In his introduction, Pozas says of his informant: "Our example is typical, since he characterizes the behavior of many men of his group (except for the participation in the armed phase of the Mexican Revolution, which was an accident of his life). It is not an exceptional biography; on the contrary, it is perfectly normal within its environment."[8]

Pozas's remarks and tone recall an era—the thirties and forties—when many students of society were striving to establish themselves as scientists maintaining an objective relation with the cases they examined. The remarks cited above certainly contrast with statements made later in the century, in which the researcher stresses his or her empathy and the informants' human particularity. For Pozas, the information is what counts, not the informant.

Some anthropologists and linguists carrying out research in Latin America will always depend on native informants. Consider, for example, that instruction in a native American language, unlike the teaching of European languages, has generally required the participation of a native speaker. In the making of a dictionary or grammar of a native language, many informants offer bits of information. Even if it were desired, not every contributor of information could be recognized. However, there is a great difference between obtaining lexical and grammatical information from an informant and obtaining the story of a person's life. What disturbs readers in Pozas's work is that the researcher has extracted such a significant, intimate contribution from his subject and has shown such little regard for his status as a person.

It is fair to say that widespread discussion of documentary narrative in Latin America was ignited by the appearance of the works of Oscar Lewis (1914–1970), the U.S. anthropologist whose best-known works centered on the collection of first-person accounts of life in poverty. Though not himself a Latin American researcher, Lewis obtained from Mexican, Mexican-American, Puerto Rican, and Cuban subjects the tape-recorded reminiscences that formed the raw material of his widely recognized books. He constructed his most celebrated work, *The Children of Sánchez: The Autobiography of a Mexican Family* (1961), from the statements, elicited by interview questions, of a family of Mexico City slumdwellers. He spent a great deal of time in Spanish American countries, trained a number of research assistants on site, and indisputably made an impact on Latin American documentary writers, even if their response was in some cases to react against him.

Lewis's principal contribution to anthropology may be his postulation of an international culture of poverty, which transcends national and ethnic differences. But for readers with a literary background, his techniques for presenting his material were his most electrifying innovation. They cast a new light on a problem in realist fiction. Lewis, in his introduction to *The Children of Sánchez*, confidently presents "the use of a new technique whereby each member of the family tells his own story in his own words."[9] Besides exhibiting a sanguine belief in his work's ability to represent poor people, Lewis shows an awareness that his technique would reopen old questions in literature. He suggests that his methods of revealing the lives of the poor supersede not only those of anthropologists and sociologists but also those of novelists: "Nor have the novelists given us an adequate portrayal of the inner lives of the poor in the contemporary world. . . . The tape recorder, used in taking down the life stories in this book, has made possible the beginning of a new kind of literature of social realism. With the aid of the tape recorder, unskilled, uneducated, and even illiterate persons can talk about themselves and relate their observations and experiences in an uninhibited, spontaneous, and natural manner."[10]

Lewis's repeated reference to the tape recorder as an indicator of his care to transmit the exact words of his subjects begins a tradition of focusing on this device. The professional writers responsible for documentary narratives frequently refer in their prefaces to tape recording. Readers of these works often express curiosity as to whether the sessions were edited from tape recordings or recreated from memory. In a common perception, the taping of sessions signals a higher degree of verbatim fidelity to the source's testimony. There seems to be a belief that, no matter how the resulting transcripts have been edited and reorganized, the words themselves can be counted on to be a true representation of the subjects who lived the experiences narrated. Discourse recreated from memory seems to betray a greater mediation on the part of the more literate author.

For literary readers, Lewis had pursued a new angle in the old problem of representing the talk of uneducated people. A realist writer most typically invents unsophisticated and poorly educated characters and then devises a form of speech—dialogue or autobiographical monologue—for them, striving for a lifelike effect. In contrast, Lewis obtained the monologues he presented from real-world peasants and the urban poor. While in this sense even a subliterate informant could be said to "tell his own story in his own words," Lewis enjoyed a good deal of the novelist's freedom in organizing his tape-recorded material into the narratives published under his name.

Over the years, Lewis has on many occasions been accused of manipulating the words of those he interviewed and of making their testimony appear less mediated than it is. For example, Jean Franco cites several points on which she believes that Lewis has understated or camouflaged his control over the narrative. In her analysis, Lewis benefited unfairly from the common tendency to perceive information from oral sources as natural, direct, and true to the speaker's experience. Franco also claims that Lewis failed to acknowledge that some of his material was written out by a member of the Sánchez family.[11]

Although he was looking for traits common to members of the "culture of poverty," Lewis individualized and spotlighted his tape-recorded subjects to an extent unusual in a social scientist's representation of informants. Like a novelist, he expected his readers to keep track of a full cast of characters by name. Lewis's prefatory remarks stand in contrast to Pozas's. While the latter refers to his informant as an "example," Lewis draws the reader's attention to the differences in outlook that distinguish his tape-recorded speakers. He uses pseudonyms to protect his subjects, who had admitted to forbidden behaviors. At the same time, he recognizes them in a way Pozas had not. For example, *The Children of Sánchez* is dedicated to the Sánchez family.[12] Its rural counterpart, the 1964 *Pedro Martínez: A Mexican Peasant and His Family*, credits the Martínezes, alongside professional colleagues, in the acknowledgments. Consider the contrast between Pozas's allusions to his informant and Lewis's "To the Martínez family, whose true identity must remain anonymous, I am grateful for their cooperation and friendship over these many years."[13]

Lewis's books beyond any doubt belonged to him; his ability to edit the transcripts and to introduce the material with his own generalizations made that clear. Still, he moved away from the standard notion of the informant chiefly because, while his texts were his, the bulk of the words in them were those of his subjects. Secondarily, he focused an unusual degree of attention on his research subjects themselves, apart from the information their accounts contained.

Carolina Maria de Jesus (Brazil, 1914–1977) in 1958 excited widespread, but unfortunately sensationalized, discussion of the problem of obtaining first-person accounts of lives spent either in poverty or in ethnically marked enclaves. De Jesus, an African-Brazilian dwelling in a São Paulo slum, gained celebrity as the author of *Quarto de Despejo* (published in English as *Child of the Dark*). In this instance, Audálio Dantas, at that time a young reporter for the *Diário da Noite* (Evening news), encountered her and published *Child of the Dark* as de Jesus's own writing; he presented his role as that of de Jesus's discoverer and agent. Controversy broke out around this surprise best-seller. Some skeptics questioned whether de Jesus could have composed her story without substantial assistance, while others were convinced her writing was her own, but inadequate in style and structure.

The complicated story of de Jesus's career is a side issue to the main problem presented in this chapter. Unlike the other cases, it does not involve one collaborator who offers material orally and another who develops it into a written narrative. However, the phenomenon of Carolina Maria de Jesus, which created a great stir at the time, makes one point relevant to this discussion. Even if a representative of a disadvantaged and marginalized population is literate enough to compose a written account, he or she is still dependent upon a partner from the mainstream culture to bring the writing into print and obtain publicity. Robert Levine, in his retrospective commentary on de Jesus's career, notes how little benefit she derived from the spectacular success of *Child of the Dark*. Despite outselling even the nation's most read novelist, Jorge Amado, for some time, she received disproportionately little in royalties, public respect, or in the ability to impress her message upon Brazilians. In addition, Levine finds that de Jesus's discoverer-agent sought to limit her to realistic, first-person accounts of life in poverty, discouraging her efforts to publish imaginative writing.[14]

Since then, certain Latin American writers, such as Elena Poniatowska, a French-born Mexican journalist and creative writer (b. 1933), and the Cuban anthropologist and poet Miguel Barnet (b. 1940), have become known for the composition of documentary narratives based on interviews and other first-hand accounts.

Poniatowska first won notice as an engaging, disarming interviewer who, even on brief acquaintance, could elicit unguarded remarks from her subjects. Her most-lasting fame came from works developed out of lengthy familiarity with her interview subjects. The most-celebrated instance was her profound collaboration with the woman whose voice and self-account she recreates in her 1969 *Hasta no verte, Jesús mío* (*Until We Meet Again*). This text is not an edited transcription of interviews but rather a first-person life story that Poniatowska wrote. In composing *Until We Meet Again*, Poniatowska mimicked the language, narrative style, and experiences of one specific lower-class woman. The author was still an adolescent when, out of curiosity, she sought out this woman, who had lived an exceptionally rugged and varied life. She conversed with the woman, who was often begrudging with information, over a period of many years before undertaking the composition of her life story. These circumstances were not mentioned in the text of *Until We Meet Again*, but the author clarified them in many interviews.

The first-person speaking subject of *Until We Meet Again* stands out with unusual clarity, not just for the story she has to tell, but for her marked personality: crusty, judgmental, distrustful, frank, and skilled at oral narration. Although Poniatowska never claimed to be relaying her source's actual words, readers seemed convinced that the voice in the novel was, in fact, that of a real-life, lower-class Mexican woman. While assigning her longtime conversation partner a pseudonym, Poniatowska makes her stand out as a unique individual with many identifying traits and not as a composite figure representative of a given population under study. After the success of the book, Poniatowska's real-world source became the object of great curiosity on the part of the reading public. Journalists persistently asked Poniatowska questions about "Jesusa Palancares"; the woman's real name soon became public. The relations between Poniatowska and "Jesusa"—for example, whether the former had used a tape recorder during their sessions and how profound their friendship had been—also became the focus of widespread interest.

Second in importance among Poniatowska's works is the 1971 *La noche de Tlatelolco* (*Massacre in Mexico*). This book on the 1968 killing of protesters in Mexico City's Plaza de las Tres Culturas includes testimony from many different sources: organizers of the student movement, participants in and bystanders at the ill-fated protest, and people who simply had some comment to make; a few of Poniatowska's own observations appear as well. She also incorporated written texts such as a statement of protesters' demands. *Massacre* was innovative for its editing, which organized diverse fragments of text into something approaching a narrative. However, it was not part of Poniatowska's experiment in working in great depth with a particular individual who would then emerge as the autobiographical narrator of the text.

The 1979 *Gaby Brimmer* is exceptional among Poniatowska's long-term work with sources and throws some light on her collaborations with less literate collaborators. Here Poniatowska not only identifies her principal subject by name, but Brimmer is listed as the senior author. Brimmer is different from Poniatowska's typical sources; she is a well-educated, literate person and an aspiring writer. Her ability to communicate her story was inhibited by cerebral palsy and by being an unknown author. The implication is, to some extent, that Poniatowska's services were engaged to assist Brimmer in reaching the reading public.

Miguel Barnet began as a disciple of the Cuban anthropologist Fernando Ortiz, whose influence went well beyond his discipline to affect the way a broad range of intellectuals perceived Caribbean culture. It should be remembered that Ortiz won his following not only for his anthropological thought but also for his inventive manner of expressing his ideas, particularly appealing to a literary public. Barnet was also eager to utilize the resources of literary narrative to present ethnographic and historical information. His most memorable work stemmed from his conversations with an African-Hispanic man, 104 years old by his own account, whom he located in a nursing home. This is Esteban Montejo, the forthcoming, observant, witty raconteur whose speech and life story Barnet recreated in the 1966 *Biografía de un cimarrón*. (The English translation is retitled *Autobiography of a Runaway Slave*, and Barnet is credited as its editor rather than its author. I will refer to the work as *Biografía*, reflecting the franker title Barnet gave it.) Born about 1860, Montejo had witnessed virtually all the major turning points in Cuban history since that date. The book casts him in the spotlight to a degree unusual for an informant; for example, a full-page photograph of the ex-slave precedes the introduction and appears on the cover of some copies.

Almost since *Biografía* appeared, observers have pointed out, on some occasions in a scholarly way and on others with polemical fervor, how heavily Barnet engaged his own inventive and, indeed, literary skills in the composition of the ex-slave's narrative. Critics have often skeptically treated *testimonio*'s apparent claim to offer an exceptionally pure view of history, unencumbered by either the interfering generalizations of social science or the complications that literary form introduces. For instance, Roberto González Echevarría examines *Biografía* jointly with a contemporary Cuban novel. He is concerned with documentary narrative as an effort to compose absorbing narratives but at the same time "to bypass literature." [15] In the resulting analysis, González Echevarría shows *Biografía* as inescapably rooted in literary traditions. He calls it an important work but does not attribute its significance to any exceptional ability to reveal the lived experience of history: "The book purports to be factual, the result of a series of interviews with an informant, strung as a first-person narrative for the sake of continuity and convenience. Yet there is a peculiar literary propriety to Esteban Montejo's figure and to *Biografía* in general." [16] For González Echevarría, the notion that Esteban Montejo can be "the living word of history" does not represent a realizable possibility, but rather a dream that Barnet expresses with authoritative force. [17]

Elzbieta Sklodowska, a determinedly skeptical analyst of testimonial narrative, has warned against perceiving *Biografía* as an unobstructed window thrown open onto history: "Obviously, it would be naive to assume a relation of direct homology between history and the text." [18] Her analyses of this and other testimonial texts serve to sharpen readers' awareness of the intervening steps between the experience of history and the testimonial narrative that retells it. Several factors mediate between history and the testimonial text: "The witness's speech cannot be a reflection of his or her experience, but rather its refraction, owing to the vicissitudes of memory, intention, ideology. The intentionality and the ideology of the author-editor is superposed on the original text, creating more ambiguities, silences and lacunae in the process of selecting, putting together, and arranging the raw material according to the norms of literary form." [19]

Sklodowska's complaint is primarily against an unthinking reading of *Biografía*. However, she also suggests that Barnet's text can be inherently misleading. The first-person account, well-known for its ability to sound convincing, together with the literary mimicry of direct speech, can lull unwary readers into forgetting how much authorial intervention entered into the composition of the narrative. Other critics find Barnet guilty of outright misrepresentation, of being too much the inventor of a witty, observant character and not enough the editor-transcriber of testimony. It should be noted that Barnet's title—*biography* rather than *autobiography*—carries the frank implication that Montejo's life is being narrated by someone other than Montejo himself. Barnet has not encouraged readers to expect literally an eyewitness account of history. For example, his "Introduction" to *Biografía* explains that he completely rearranged the material to bring it into chronological order. As well as acknowledging his own creative participation in the writing of the book, Barnet recognizes Montejo as exceptionally expressive, with "an outgoing volubility uncommon in people of his age. He spoke with ease and in many cases he himself was the one to choose the topic."[20] Barnet singles out Montejo's ability to place his personal stamp on narrations, conveying "How he has seen things. He gives us an image of life in the mountains, of war, that is his own image."[21]

Even though Barnet would seem to some extent to have disarmed criticism by admitting that both he and Montejo were drawing upon literary resources, controversy has continued. In a pattern typical of the discussion of documentary writing, many scholars have become excited over issues that go behind the published text. They raise questions about the making of the document and the initial decisions that preceded its undertaking. There has been a great deal of heated commentary, for example, over the fact that, while Barnet speaks in the "Introduction" of preserving some of his sessions with Montejo on audio tapes, he has never produced a copy of these tapes.[22] Readers have at times wondered why Barnet chose that particular ex-slave; his introduction rather tantalizingly mentions a 100-year-old woman, also born in slavery, with whom he at one point considered working.[23]

The objection to Barnet's creative mediation represents an unusual variant of one of the most typical complaints against anthropologists. Ethnographers (and, for that matter, archaeologists and museum curators) have aroused indignation by appropriating for their own uses what by right belongs to less powerful populations. Their fault, beyond the theft or expropriation of others' heritages, is in not recognizing poorer and less literate groups as possessors of their own past. Barnet was generous in the recognition he extended to the ex-slave. His alleged misdeed was not expropriation of another's memories and words but excessive attribution, ghostwriting in order to satisfy the contemporary desire to hear the words of marginalized groups. Sklodowska, who has extensively analyzed collaborations between literate authors and testimonial sources, uses the term "ventriloquism" to characterize the peculiar form of misattribution, or excessive attribution, of which Barnet has been accused.[24]

Whether or not it should be regarded with a degree of suspicion, *Biografía* succeeded in turning attention not only to the African-derived current in Cuban cultural history but to issues involved in developing narratives with information culled from informants. The incessant questioning of the perennially controversial *Biografía* has thrown the text into question but at the same time has added to its value.

Biografía also represents a step in the direction of referring the reader's attention toward the informant, not just toward the information of which he or she is a supplier. Esteban Montejo, as his voice is recreated in *Biografía*, is another distinctive speaker with a quickly recognizable personality. He stands out for his sly wit and eye for women, his skill at noting and describing folkways, his concept of himself as an observer of society, and his light-hearted tone even when recounting hardships.

Barnet theorized about, as well as wrote, documentary narrative. Three years after *Biografía* appeared, he published a much-cited programmatic statement, "La novela testimonio: Socio-literatura" (The testimonial novel: socio-literature).[25] With the term and concept *novela testimonio* he defends the right of those composing such works to employ some of the expository freedom of the novelist. At the same time, he insists that the person responsible for writing testimonial narratives—for whom he invents the term *gestor*—should not pursue literary ends; such texts should serve a practical function in society. Barnet has often returned to the issues of "La novela testimonio" in interviews. Of his own works, he has said: "They are studies of real cases, but recreated, or what might be termed equally, written by me. It is testimony from whose contents I take the juice, the essence, to turn them into fiction and reality."[26] Barnet's efforts to define what he has done in *Biografía*, and what might be done in other such works, have touched off as lengthy a discussion as has *Biografía* itself.[27]

Texts by Barnet and Poniatowska have been translated, but both are known principally to readers concerned with Latin American writing, whether Latin American literary publics or foreign specialists in this literature. *Until We Meet Again,* which had created tremendous excitement in Mexico, made relatively little impact on the international literary scene; perhaps it requires too much previous knowledge of Mexican history and relies on the nuances of the Mexican Spanish in which Jesusa couches her comments on events.

The 1976 *"Si me permiten hablar," testimonio de Domitila, una mujer de las minas de Bolivia* (*Let Me Speak! The Testimony of Domitila, a Woman of the Bolivian Mines*) exercises a more international appeal. Domitila Barrios de Chungara (b. 1937), widely known by her first name, is a miner's wife from Bolivia who became active in labor organization. Though her father was an Indian, she notes that she cannot describe his ethnicity more exactly. She shows little sense of herself as belonging to an ethnically defined community; instead, she identifies herself using the terms *peasant* and *working class,* and her community is composed of the local workers and their families.

Moema Viezzer organized the book from the first-person statements of this labor activist. While Viezzer interviewed Domitila for the book, she also used material from a variety of more public occasions during which the noted activist was tape recorded. In an unusual note, Viezzer states that after creating a composite narrative from these sources, she reviewed the resulting text with Domitila. Viezzer explains: "What I present here is not Domitila's monologue with herself. It is the product of numerous interviews I had with her in Mexico and Bolivia, of her speeches at the Tribunal, as well as discussions, conversations, and dialogues she had with groups of workers, students, and university employees, people living in workers' neighborhoods, Latin American exiles living in Mexico, and representatives of the press, radio, and television. All of this taped material, as well as some written correspondence, was organized and then revised with Domitila, and resulted in the present volume of oral history."[28]

Let Me Speak! makes above-average demands on the concentration of readers, especially foreign readers. The story it recounts takes place over a lengthy period; to grasp it, one must correlate developments in Bolivian political and labor history with struggles in Domitila's community. Indeed, the book is so densely packed with information that the English edition provides readers with a supplementary timeline of the principal events. Though its middle section is the narrative of Domitila's life, this story of labor activism is less intimate than any of the narratives discussed above. Its principal appeal is to a liberal or left-tending public interested in the formation of an activist's outlook and in women's growing role in political organization.

Let Me Speak! never aroused the suspicion that Barnet and Montejo's *Biografía* provoked; it was generally accepted as a fair representation of Domitila's statements. One important difference is that Barnet's readers had no opportunity to verify that the real-life ex-slave spoke with the sly wit and sharp recall displayed in *Biografía*. Domitila, in contrast, was a public figure who often spoke to groups and gave interviews, especially after *Let Me Speak!* increased her celebrity.

The work that definitively focused international attention on the phenomenon was *Me llamo Rigoberta Menchú* (*I, Rigoberta Menchú: An Indian Woman in Guatemala*). This is Menchú's life story, developed into a written narrative on the basis of tape-recorded sessions. In January 1982, Rigoberta Menchú (b. 1958), a radicalized Quiché-Mayan Indian, was visiting Europe as a spokesperson for the armed resistance in Guatemala. She was interviewed over the course of a week by Elizabeth Burgos Debray, who then undertook the actual composition of *I, Rigoberta Menchú*. Burgos was a Venezuelan-born Paris resident who had studied anthropology but, when she met Menchú, was making her living as a journalist and editor. As Burgos notes in her preface, she is not a Guatemalan specialist and Menchú was in no sense her research subject.

Menchú was attractive to Latin American and foreign readers as a witness to repression, a resistance spokesperson, and a village Indian in the process of becoming a radical and an intellectual. Even though the writing was not Menchú's, *I, Rigoberta Menchú* seemed to approach fulfilling, for a nonspecialized and international readership, the hope announced by the celebrated thinker José Carlos Mariátegui. Mariátegui had anticipated a step beyond the *literatura indigenista*, Indian-themed writing of the late 1920s, whose authors often had some Indian ancestry but were certainly not members of native peoples: "It is still a literature of mestizos. That's why it's called *indigenista* and not *indígena* [Indian]. *Indígena* literature, if it should come, will come in its time. When Indians themselves are in a position to produce it." [29]

(One should keep in mind that there is a lengthy history of books or manuscripts produced, in various ways, by native communities or individual Indians in Latin America since the Spanish and Portuguese conquest. Many of these have as their purpose to preserve in writing narratives, verse, or other traditional knowledge that a community has been maintaining through the less dependable means of oral transmission. Others offer the opinions, protests, experiences, and literary work of individual Indians, though very few of these latter have reached a wide audience.)[30]

Menchú's life story is accessible to general readers. It requires extremely little previous knowledge of Central American history or politics; Menchú makes little reference to specific details of Guatemalan politics. Unlike the veteran labor organizer Domitila, Menchú is a young person, twenty-three when she told her story, and her experiences have occurred principally on the family and community level. Menchú frequently discusses feelings, her own and those of her community, and her narrative makes an affective appeal.

Besides having a story that is easy to grasp, *I, Rigoberta Menchú* features a narrator able to draw in readers through dramatic accounts of episodes she has witnessed and lived through. Beverley has given some thought to Menchú's skill at riveting the reader's attention, especially with scenes of torture and death. He is particularly concerned not to treat Menchú as simply the source of information. If she is perceived as relaying nothing but data or unimpeachable testimony, the implication is that she is not sophisticated enough for invention and artistry. In Beverley's judgment, Menchú should receive credit for the imaginative and evocative qualities of the narrative that bears her name. This is so even if a recognition of Menchú's art as a narrator entails a diminution of *I, Rigoberta Menchú*'s value as a literally true statement of facts. Beverley has suggested that *I, Rigoberta Menchú* has some of the qualities that, in Latin American fiction, are characterized as magical realism.[31] In a similar vein, Doris Sommer suggests that it is unfavorable to Menchú and her narrative to perceive them as artless and transparent, offering nothing but "sincerity" and "an inviolable truth."[32] Sommer's commentary encourages greater acknowledgment of the rhetorical strategies to which Menchú has recourse.

The text that Burgos composed from the taped interviews enjoyed international success when launched in 1983. It was the recipient of the Casa de las Américas *testimonio* prize. In translation, it attracted foreign readerships concerned with human rights and with women's studies as well as those interested in Latin America. Menchú's narration of the deaths by slow torture of her mother and brother, filled with disturbing details, electrified many readers and helped make Menchú an emblematic figure of the international campaign for human rights. Adding to the fascination Menchú aroused, she had grown up in a Quiché community that had preserved a good deal of its traditional folkways and knowledge. While the main line of her narrative is her radicalization, the earlier portions of Menchú's narrative supply abundant ethnographic detail on village life and the beliefs of the community. At the same time, Menchú describes herself as the possessor of important ancestral secrets that she cannot divulge.

In addition to attracting general readers, Menchú's book raised issues of great interest to scholars of Latin American literature. Critics found in it many of the features they had been examining in their research into more established types of narrative. Some observers, including Beverley and George Yúdice, have argued that testimonial narratives could be seen as the manifestation of a specifically Latin American form of postmodernism; Beverley offers *I, Rigoberta Menchú* as his principal example.[33] Postmodernism is frequently viewed as offering relief after a lengthy stretch of arid avant-garde sophistication; Rigoberta Menchú, of peasant origin, may seem an odd choice for this category. However, there are several reasons to make the association.

Beverley identifies in testimonial writing a feature that Lyotard attributes to the postmodern era: diminished confidence in "master narratives," all-encompassing explanations such as those propounded by orthodox Marxists or sanguine believers in scientific progress. In Beverley's analysis, by its very nature testimonial writing cannot presume to offer large-scale explanations of and solutions to social problems.[34] He is correct in that such figures as the grassroots Indian organizer Rigoberta Menchú focus attention upon cases specific to a historical time and place.

Beverley notes that not only have other scholars linked testimonial texts with postmodernism, but "it is not surprising . . . that Menchú explicitly denounces 'modern things' in her *testimonio*."[35] Beverley also observes that the anthropologist David Stoll, in raising questions about the accuracy of Rigoberta Menchú's most vivid scenes, is involving himself in a polemic with "postmodern anthropology."[36]

Yúdice has urged researchers of Latin American writing to extend their search for signs of the postmodern beyond the works commonly studied as literature. He argues that the inquiry into postmodernism should not overlook "the struggles for interpretive power on the part of peasants, women, and ethnic, racial and religious groups." The texts that result from these struggles reveal "rearticulatory practices [that] are both old and new: old because they draw from their traditions; new because they no longer operate solely within the framework of class or nation."[37] Yúdice's observation that testimonial writing makes a postmodern fusion of the old and the new applies well, not only to *I, Rigoberta Menchú*, but to Menchú's entire situation. She represents an ethnicity with long-held customs and lore and generally makes public appearances in traditional dress. At the same time, in her efforts to unite Mayan communities by appealing to their common identity and plight as Indian peasants, Menchú emblemizes the new social movements of the late 1980s. Bringing long-maintained lore into the speeded-up information society, Menchú began life as a member of a traditional native community and became a radicalized intellectual. Following the success of her book, she emerged as an international figure of human rights, her image and message spreading via global media.

The relations between testimonial writing and postmodernism are a lively issue that has elicited comments from a number of critics. However, this examination of *testimonio* centers on the question of whose texts these hybrid narratives are. The appearance of Domitila's and Menchú's narratives immediately raised difficult questions about how to characterize the authorship of such texts. Beyond any doubt, Domitila Barrios de Chungara and Rigoberta Menchú were the names that became known through the success of these two texts; Burgos and Viezzer remain relatively obscure. Though the original Spanish assigns to Burgos sole-author status, the 1984 English translation of *I, Rigoberta Menchú* lists Menchú as the principal author, with Burgos as editor. (It seems extremely likely that the change was prompted, not by analysis of the issues involved, but by the name recognition Menchú had garnered since the original publication.) Clearly, there is a generalized desire to view these narratives as literally the words of poor authors of indigenous ancestry.

Readers who give thought to the matter are almost certain to realize that the relationship between the more literate editors of these works and the autobiographical speakers is more complex than the texts readily indicate. For example, Burgos in her preface characterizes Menchú's narrative as very lightly edited, saying that she asked as few questions as possible, often prompted her subject to speak on her own without interrogation, and made few changes in Menchú's language.[38] Her preliminary observations minimize Menchú's creativity as a storyteller as well as Burgos's own mediation, which is reduced to that of a scribe: "Rigoberta has chosen the weapon of the word as a means of struggle and it is this word that I have tried to ratify in writing."[39] However, the idea that the narrative offers Menchú's nearly unmediated testimony does not hold up very well once one begins to read *I, Rigoberta Menchú*. The published book is organized in the pattern of an autobiography and makes use of fairly sophisticated literary conventions, especially the placement of epigraphs at the outset of chapters. Under the scrutiny of literary critics, or any other readers attentive to details of the text, the narrative reveals itself to be the work of more than a single voice.[40]

The attribution of the authorship of *I, Rigoberta Menchú* is a puzzling issue. While in some cases a project is the intellectual property of the individual who conceived and designed it, Burgos's preface states that her collaboration with Menchú was initiated and negotiated by a third party. Unlike Pozas, Lewis, Barnet, and Poniatowska, who sought out their informants and won their confidence, Burgos did not find Menchú; the two only met after other parties had arranged their collaboration.

If neither author developed the original project, Burgos clearly presents herself as the individual in charge of the actual making of *I, Rigoberta Menchú*. While Menchú tells the story of her life, Burgos in her preface tells the story of the book. Menchú in her narrative does not say anything to indicate that she is engaged in a book project. Perhaps it was felt that, if Menchú's narrative contained references to the making of the manuscript, it would contaminate the work with self-consciousness and diminish its effect of being natural, direct testimony. Menchú's silence about the editorial project can also be read as suggesting that while Menchú is the possessor of her experiences and her community's legacy of knowledge, the book—as book—belongs to Burgos.

Fredric Jameson, in his considerations of the issues involved in attributing authorship, suggests that testimonial narratives are a postmodern, Third-World form of "counter-autobiography," an alternative to the individualistic account of the personal development of an exceptional subject, such as an intellectual at odds with the community. In Jameson's vision, one should expect postmodern counter-autobiographies to manifest "the return of anonymity." The anonymity that he discerns in *testimonio* is not that of a native informant, who supplies data to an expert, resulting, in Jameson's words, in "a faceless sociological average or sample or a lowest common denominator."[41] Rather, he sees a more positive form of anonymity, that of a collective voice or voices. Testimonial narratives, though anonymous in this sense, exhibit "not the loss of a name, but, paradoxically, the multiplication of proper names. *I, Rigoberta Menchú*, by Elizabeth Burgos or *Let Me Speak! Testimony of Domitila* by Moema Viezzer; these adjunct names are not merely names of editors or transcribers, and surely we as yet have no appropriate category to name their specific work, which can be seen as analogous to the creativity of a translator." [42] The parallel with a translator's reinvention of a text is an excellent one; it recognizes the extent of the more learned author's involvement in the making of the text, yet does not suggest that this participation is illegitimate tampering with the original testimony.

Jameson further explores the peculiar coauthorship of *testimonios* using concepts developed by the noted literary theorist Mikhail Bakhtin. Bakhtin especially valued, and often analyzed, narratives in which different voices coexist and, through their interaction, give the text qualities of a dialogue or an interchange among many speaking participants. Jameson finds the dialogical concept useful in appreciating the hard-to-specify collaboration between more and less literate authors. Ideally, testimonial narratives produced by such disparate coauthors could offer "the use of the discourse of an other in a situation that liberates us from the 'authority' of the old centered-subject, private-property type and establishes a new collective space between known subjects and individual human beings." [43] Jameson cites in support of his case Rigoberta Menchú's much-noted assertion, in the opening passages of *I, Rigoberta Menchú*, that the experiences she narrates are not unique to her. Rather, she presents her first-person story as being one lived out by many people, and herself as a collective spokesperson representing an entire community. [44]

Sklodowska, too, suggests that Bakhtin's thought about the plurality of voices in narratives can be helpful in the effort to perceive and characterize testimonial narratives fairly and accurately. In her judgment, such a way of understanding the dual-authored *testimonio* allows for consideration of the many factors that mediate between the history the protagonists have lived and the text that narrates them. As such it is a great improvement over approaching these texts with the ingenuous expectation, or the impossible demand, that they render direct witness to history. [45]

Jameson is right in saying that current-day critics have no satisfactory way of describing the authorship of works like *I, Rigoberta Menchú* and *Let Me Speak!* Bearing out his observation are the shifts in assignment of author credit by publishers of these texts. As noted, Barnet was credited as author of *Biografía* in its original Cuban edition; nonetheless, some libraries classified the book as if its author were Montejo. Montejo then appeared listed as author and Barnet as editor of the English edition, whose title now began with the word *Autobiography*. A 1968 reissue by Ediciones Ariel of Barcelona lists *Biografía* as by Montejo and "as told to" Barnet. These changes suggest that testimonial narratives confuse standard notions of authorship. The fact that *I, Rigoberta Menchú* could be published in Spanish under Burgos's name and in English under Menchú's should give one pause. It suggests that the attribution of sole authorship to either of the two is arbitrary; whichever one is singled out by name as author, the other's voice is still present in the work. The contributions of the two have become indistinguishable and inseparable, no matter how much curious readers manage to discover about the methods they employed in their collaboration. Yúdice, recognizing the collaborative process by which testimonial narratives come into being, cites them as dual-authored works regardless of the authorship assigned by the publishing house.[46]

The study of collaborative testimonial narratives is almost necessarily different from the examination of work that is undisguisedly literary in nature and attributed only to the person responsible for the actual writing. Inevitably, issues external to the published text make their way into the discussion. In some cases, the discussion appears to stray far afield, into the realm of rumor and speculation. Such is the case when commentators conjecture about what transpired out of the public eye during the interview and editing process, suggesting that the more educated collaborator secretly falsified or adulterated some of the supposedly first-hand, oral testimony.

However, even limiting debate to evidence available to all interested researchers, testimonial narrative presents a number of legitimate issues that go beyond the text. Some observers see testimonial narratives as test cases that provoke writers and scholars of literature to explain better the unique contribution that literature offers. The idea of a challenge to literature is certainly present in Lewis's previously cited suggestion that his techniques in *The Children of Sánchez* are superseding the realist writer's efforts to represent the experience of living in poverty. González Echevarría obviously does not share Lewis's confidence that edited interviews represent real life. Yet he expresses the same sense that documentary variants of narrative challenge types of narrative whose reliance on invention is undisguised: "*Biografía de un cimarrón* and Cuban literature of the Revolution play an important role in Latin America . . . by forcing literature to stake out its domain anew."[47] In a similar spirit, Sklodowska says that Barnet's concept and practice of testimonial narrative "enriches our notion of literature and demonstrates the inexhaustible possibilities of a referential novel."[48]

Other significant issues are those that Franco, in the citation at the beginning of this chapter, accurately characterizes as "ethical."[49] Any reflective reader must be struck by the degree to which someone like Rigoberta Menchú, in her campaign to communicate her version of events, is dependent on a collaborator more literate and worldly than herself.

The introductions written by the more literate partner in such texts have been accorded much closer scrutiny than is usually devoted to the prefaces of authors or editors. The ostensible purpose of these introductions is to inform readers of the process by which the book came into being, as well as to give an idea of its thematic focus. But readers also examine them in an effort to assess how open and fair the writer has been. The volume's writer should do justice both to the less literate collaborator, who is dependent on the former's composition skills and worldly connections, and to the reader, who will be defrauded if the writer has misrepresented the narrative's provenance. This type of justice is difficult to achieve and to ascertain. Undoubtedly, the current-day tendency is to strive to give full credit to disadvantaged and native peoples when their memories and traditions are displayed. On the other hand, a literate author who states too simply that the text belongs to a less literate collaborator invites disbelief. Readers who spend much time engaged in reading and writing tend to be very aware of how much the discussion of a given subject changes as it moves from conversational to written form. This awareness needs to be present during the conceptual struggle to characterize and understand testimonial narrative. The best analyses are the ones that take into account the transformations information undergoes as it becomes progressively more organized. An individual's memory of historical or personal events is not very coherent before it begins to be told. It requires a good deal of shaping to be presented in the form of a story. During the making of a testimonial narrative, this work of organization is performed in great part by the speaker in the course of generating the original material; here is where the literary invention mentioned by Beverley and Sommer comes into play. As the material from interviews takes shape as a written document, another set of transformations occur. These are clearly the work of the more literate partner. Testimonial narratives contain substantial factual material but also an element of invention that deserves acknowledgment. This includes both the creativity of the collaborator who provides the oral story and that of the writer who reorganizes it to make a written narrative.

4 Literary Intellectuals and Mass Media

As previous chapters have indicated, scholarly discussion of mass culture has generated a large number of studies from a variety of often overlapping perspectives. They have been carried out by researchers in such varied fields as communications, art history, music, sociology, and anthropology. The purpose of the present chapter is to focus more specifically on how intellectuals from Latin American countries have sought to interact creatively with—as well as to examine from the outside—mass media in the twentieth century. These creative individuals have sought to go beyond literature as such. Their goal has been to develop new genres of writing that depend upon the new forms brought by twentieth-century technology. Research from other fields will be mentioned only insofar as it has significantly affected the outlook of those who study literature. These influences on literary thinkers include the work of members of the Frankfurt School (to be discussed), media theorists, and scholars and activists seeking grassroots participation in the making of popular culture.

In recent years the Argentine-Mexican anthropologist Néstor García Canclini has challenged the concepts of popular culture most widely in evidence in Latin America. García Canclini's research examines the effects of commercialization and accelerated global movement of capital, individuals, and objects on cultural phenomena that were formerly folkloric and local. In doing so, he has called into question well-entrenched definitions of popular culture, or, as he prefers, popular cultures. García Canclini has found two conceptions of popular culture to hold sway in Latin America and has criticized both. The one favored by nonspecialists, "formulated in Europe by romantic populism and in Latin America by conservative nationalism and *indigenismo*," tends to idealize folk cultures as the spontaneous expression of the people.[1] The other, "concerned with scientific precision," is more common among those with some anthropological background; in García Canclini's analysis, it has "ignored the political meaning of symbolic production among the people."[2]

Because dependency theory and the outlook of García Canclini have been examined (in Chapters One and Two respectively), they will be only briefly mentioned here. Literary intellectuals have at times carried out academic research in mass communications. The emphasis here is not on their formal scholarship but on their creative experiments and their more free-form essays. So many well-known literary people have had some involvement with the creation of mass culture that full coverage has been impossible. As in earlier chapters, the goal is to bring to the fore some important issues concerning the topic. The writer who is singled out for closest examination is the Argentine Julio Cortázar (1914–1984), known for his novels, essays, and multimedia experiments.

Before turning to writers who have sought to renovate popular culture from within, taking an active role in its shaping, a brief look at the study and criticism of folkloric and mass culture will be useful. It is most likely inevitable that literary critics will occasionally function as analysts of popular culture. Even before the great expansion of commercial mass culture during the twentieth century, some scholars with a literary background examined poetry, lyrics, drama, and narratives of folk origin. Researchers trained in the analysis of literature, especially when based in areas where folksong or folktales were readily accessible, have often turned to the collection and study of this popular production. These scholars were generally admirers and cognoscenti, rather than critics, of folkloric forms. They sought to preserve them despite the decline of the isolated communities where folksong is most apt to survive. Among scholars of Iberian literatures, the lyrics of folkloric ballads have for many decades been established as a worthy object of research. Studies long tended to be descriptive or to trace sources and influences; critical analysis was underdeveloped.

In Latin American countries, as elsewhere, folklorists have come from literature, anthropology, linguistics, and sociology. A case well-known in twentieth-century Spanish American literature is the interdisciplinary career of José María Arguedas (Peru, 1911–1969). Arguedas, who earned an international reputation as a writer of fiction, pursued a research and teaching career as a folklorist. Though his university appointments identify him as an anthropologist, throughout his career he published essays on literature as well as collections and studies of folk lyrics and narrative. As a scholar, Arguedas was more an anthropologist than a student of literature, but his work increased literary critics' awareness of the folkloric traces in elite literature.

While literary studies have long made room for folklorists, a more recent and controversial development is literary critics' analyses of twentieth-century commercial culture, such as film, advertising, television, and reading matter aimed at a very popular audience. Here the term *mass culture* will be used for this type of production. Unlike folkloric culture, it is designed and produced, not at the local level, but in a more centralized manner and with more specifically commercial ends. Also in contrast to folk culture, in which innovations spread slowly, mass culture relies on the rapid spread of novelties that will quickly capture the interest of a widely dispersed public. Mass culture depends upon communications technologies and the expertise needed to use them. This discussion will make little use of the term *popular culture*, whose meaning varies among scholars of differing orientation and between English-language and Latin American researchers.[3]

It would be difficult to set a starting date for mass culture. As soon as typesetting became widespread and relatively cheap, printed copies could be generated and marketed. Lyric sheets, broadsides, caricatures, and other similar publications have long been directed to an expanding public. Still, it is clearly in the twentieth century that mass media have been most influential. The growth of mass culture, as it is defined in this chapter, has been a direct result of the development of more numerous and rapid communications technologies.

The spread of radio and film during the early decades of the twentieth century prompted responses from intellectuals, including both writers and critics of literature. The response of intellectuals was nothing like the reverence accorded folk culture by its dedicated researchers. Worldwide, a number of respected thinkers expressed alarm over the emergence of a mass culture and the new power accorded to mass taste. In the Spanish-speaking world, as well as throughout Europe and the United States, the thought and statements of José Ortega y Gasset (1883–1955) exercised great influence. Ortega is identified as a Spanish philosopher, social critic, and arbiter of tastes. It should be remembered, though, that he spent considerable time in Buenos Aires and developed strong ties to intellectuals in various Spanish American countries, especially during his lengthy exile (1936–1948) from Spain.

Ortega did not provide specific commentary on the new mass media and manifested little interest in novel communications technologies as such, apart from their possible influence on elite art. Yet his most influential writings coincide with the period when these media were gaining ground; he is clearly writing in reaction to the changes they bring. It is noteworthy that, while Ortega is virtually silent concerning the technical novelties that characterize the new media, he makes some detailed observations about the innovative techniques developed by writers of avant-garde fiction. As he characterizes the techniques, they suggest the influence of twentieth-century media; yet, they are literary techniques. This divergence suggests that Ortega did not judge that the new media, such as films aimed at a general public and radio broadcasts, deserved careful scrutiny and thought.

This thinker's focus is less upon media themselves than upon mass taste and mass publics and the effects of their triumph, a "massification," in Ortega's word, of culture and society. Massification can occur not only through new media but also through works, such as romantic novels and dramas, that are traditional in form and genre. Literary texts constitute mass culture when they are read by a less-educated public whose primary goal is emotional identification with the protagonists. Ortega placed great importance on the perceptions of the reader or viewer, who had the power to bring out a work's artistic features or to reduce it to mindless entertainment. A literary text could function as art, when analyzed by critical readers concerned with its form, yet lose its esthetic status when consumed by an audience eager only for sentimental gratification. Conversely, Ortega's criteria do not rule out the possibility of a worthy work of art being executed in a form previously used for popular entertainment. Ortega epitomized those high modernists who pitted experimental art against all cultural manifestations appreciated by a broad public.

Ortega's 1925 *La deshumanización del arte* (*The Dehumanization of Art*, 1925) and 1929 *La rebelión de las masas* (*The Revolt of the Masses*, 1932) both lent significant support to an elitist outlook on cultural and intellectual life. Ortega fostered a belief that if crowd-pleasing entertainments and political populism spread through society, barbarism and disorder would result. This defense of high art and exclusive audiences strengthened a current of elitist thought already present among certain Latin American intellectuals, as witness the remarkable influence of the 1900 *Ariel* (identically titled in English) by the Uruguayan essayist José Enrique Rodó. Rodó had made a lasting impression by enjoining young Latin Americans to focus their minds upon higher intellectual and esthetic concerns. The general public and its enthusiasms were, according to the "Arielist" program, distractions to the elevated mind.

The elitism that spread with the success of Ortega's philosophy justified the aloof disregard in which many intellectuals and artists held mass culture. Still, some innovative figures in the arts and humanities found the new media and cultural forms stimulating, or at least felt that to exercise full citizenship in the new century they should respond in some way to such a widespread new phenomenon. This was the case for intellectuals who rejected both the classical, timeless ideal of art and puristic modernism. Instead, they saw themselves as participants in the twentieth century, marked by accelerated change and impermanence. Writers who were determined to keep pace with the times paid close attention to the new technologies and the art and entertainment forms associated with them. Avant-garde writers, whose agenda required them to generate novelties, were particularly eager to draw influence from, or to participate in the making of, new mass-media forms.

The Chilean poet Vicente Huidobro (1893–1948) exemplifies those literary figures who admired the new media because of their newness. Huidobro was a dedicated avant-gardist known for his extreme love of novelty and desire to keep pace with the new century. He was fascinated with recently developed technologies, and his poetry contains many allusions to new forms of communication, as well as rapid transportation and the armaments designed for the First World War. One of his most-noted poems, "Tour Eiffel" (first version 1917), celebrates and to some degree mimics wireless-telegraph broadcasting from the tower.

With his characteristic drive to take part in the first manifestations of any new phenomenon, Huidobro attempted to make a place for himself in the early film industry. He worked for some time on a silent film to be entitled *Cagliostro*. The script won an award but was never filmed; apparently, Huidobro had not anticipated the imminent shift to sound film.[4] Successful as a writer, he seemed unable to make the transition to the movie industry. However, undeterred by his failure to make a film, he translated the concepts he had envisioned for cinema back into written narratives. Huidobro created a mixed genre he called the *novela-film*. The version of *Cagliostro* (English title *Mirror of a Mage*) that he published in 1934 is a prose narrative using techniques of silent film.[5] Huidobro reacted to the popular culture springing up around him and, as a creator, sought to influence its development. Yet he never won notice as a commentator or analyst of the new forms.

Such ardent experimentalists as Huidobro were not the only ones who came up with ways to respond intellectually to the new media. The Mexico City-based Contemporáneos group (1920s–1940s), as their name indicates, pursued an up-to-the-minute esthetic and endeavored to keep abreast of all new cultural tendencies, including those that others might consider ephemeral. These writers cultivated the ability to comment critically upon other recently emerged cultural forms. One of the Contemporáneos, the poet and dramatist Xavier Villaurrutia (1903–1950), distinguished himself as a movie critic. At that time, very few individuals knew how to comment intelligently on cinema, and Villaurrutia virtually invented a new genre, the film commentary. More than a movie reviewer in the current-day sense, Villaurrutia composed elegant, meditative commentaries that gave readers a sense of the film under discussion but also stood on their own as creative essays.[6]

Villaurrutia stood out for his ability to move between elite and mass culture. While one of the most respected poets of the 1930s and 1940s, he also composed lyrics for popular songs. These lyrics were considerably more romantic than the sophisticated verse and experimental prose with which he made his reputation. Though Villaurrutia signed his film commentaries with his real name, as a lyricist he preferred to remain anonymous.[7] Villaurrutia's decision reminds one that literary figures run less risk of losing prestige by commenting on extremely popular forms than by participating in their making. In addition, particular forms are more likely to be viewed as furthering the massification of culture. Twentieth-century intellectuals are generally most disdainful of genres tinged with sentimentality, such as popular song lyrics and romantic novels directed toward a female audience.

Writers of Villaurrutia's generation were at times said to use cinematic techniques in narrative, as Huidobro had. It is difficult to determine the extent to which film subtly altered the vision and writing habits of writers during the 1920s, 1930s, and 1940s. Critical discussion of this issue has been plentiful, including a lengthy survey devoted exclusively to parallels between film and narrative practices in Mexican fiction.[8] On the whole, such research belongs more to the study of narrative construction than to the examination of intellectuals in a media-saturated society.

The innovations of Huidobro and Villaurrutia are difficult to appreciate in retrospect because, in succeeding decades, numerous well-known elite writers from Latin American countries have been engaged as screenwriters (Gabriel García Márquez of Colombia, the Mexicans Juan Rulfo and Carlos Fuentes, Mario Vargas Llosa of Peru, the Argentine Manuel Puig [discussed in Chapter One, on cultural autonomy], and the Cuban Guillermo Cabrera Infante, among many others) and film reviewers (the most noted case being Cabrera Infante). Though not enjoying the status accorded the writing and analysis of literature, screenwriting and film commentary have established themselves as among the most prestigious ways in which intellectuals from a literary background can involve themselves with mass culture.

When Villaurrutia began to write his commentaries on film, very little theory had been developed concerning cinema and the new communications media generally. If there was any set of concepts on which to draw, it was the debate over elite vs. popular culture and values that Latin American intellectuals had been pursuing since the mid–nineteenth century. However, the concept of "civilization versus barbarism" was not altogether suited to the new mass media. The dichotomy had been developed to pit Enlightenment and European-style urbanity against a more rustic, tradition-based, home-grown populism. The new mass culture did not fit well into either category; it was aimed at a popular audience but was often imported, as elite culture typically had been, and was not itself rural, even if its settings sometimes were. One of the notable features of Villaurrutia's film commentaries is his recognition that at least some movies possessed enough complexity and sophistication to bear analysis. His confidence that film merited scrutiny was a statement at a time when many intellectuals still categorized movies as part of the massification of culture deplored by Ortega.

If the 1910s and 1920s were marked by a paucity of theory specifically about mass culture, by the 1930s and 1940s thought on the topic had grown more systematic. This change was in part the work of theorists associated with the Frankfurt School (originally an actual Institute of Social Research founded in 1923 in Frankfurt; later, a general current in neo-Marxism that became known also as critical theory). Especially after members of the Frankfurt group were forced to emigrate to the United States in the mid-1930s, they examined the effects of new reproduction, broadcasting, and marketing systems. The Frankfurt scholars, in their writings about the mass media, show both curiosity about this quickly spreading phenomenon and Ortega-like pessimism about its effects. They, and those influenced by them, include the propagation of mass culture among the harmful changes being wrought in society by advanced capitalism.

Walter Benjamin (1892–1940) and Theodor W. Adorno (1903–1969) are probably the Frankfurt thinkers who exercised the greatest influence on critics, scholars, and creative people in literature and the fine arts. Benjamin, an art and literary critic, won admiration not only for his ideas but for his aphoristic, suggestive manner of exposition. "Art in the Age of Mechanical Reproduction" typifies Benjamin's work in its effort to demonstrate the intimate link between new techniques of reproducing and distributing images and changes in the overall culture. This frequently quoted essay is also characteristic of Frankfurt thought in its apprehensive view of mass production and marketing of cultural items, including those previously understood to belong to high art. Benjamin sees new techniques for reproducing images spreading art as never before, yet posing a danger to it.

Adorno was a sociologist and, by avocation, a musicologist. He was like Ortega in championing avant-garde experimentation, in opposing modern art forms to mass culture, and in examining the attitudes and perceptions of the cultural public. But Adorno stands out for his specific focus on the large and technically sophisticated production, marketing, and distribution systems that had arisen around mass culture. The term *culture industries*, in wide use today, originated in the discussions and writings of Adorno and his colleagues.

The displacement of folkloric culture by mass culture was a source of concern for Adorno, who, as well as promoting twentieth-century modern music, looked with favor upon locally produced folk music. In Adorno's analysis, the effects of mass production and marketing disrupted the often fruitful interaction between folk music and art music. In his *Introduction to the Sociology of Music*, Adorno asserts that, until partway into the romantic era, composers not only drew on folk forms such as lullabies and ballads but added to the repertory of popular music. Popular and concert music were close enough that composers could create music simple enough for a broad audience, yet artful enough for an elite public. Evidence of the exchange between folk and art music is the large number of melodies that, generated by a renowned composer, have gone into general circulation.

Adorno views the twentieth century, especially from the 1920s onward, as a time when elite and general publics were driven apart. At the same time, nonspecialists such as local musicians began to lose confidence in their creative capacities and to look to the entertainment industry for models. He attributes these changes to the rise of enterprises, such as record companies, which thrive by whetting a passive, acritical public's appetite for novelties. Popular compositions become hits by being catchy and unusual rather than through their musical qualities. They are designed to capture the public's fancy only briefly, then pale in interest as more recent hits are marketed. Consumers of this ephemeral mass culture constitute, not so much listening, viewing, or reading publics, as a buying public that must be kept passively awaiting new releases. This outlook offers scant hope that members of the public can creatively adapt, to suit their own situation, the products that come to them through the media. Adorno exhibits little respect for the mass audience, which appears helpless to resist the manipulation of marketing experts.

The Frankfurt School's apprehension of mass media is not limited to concern over the fate of art or the maintenance of taste. Mass communications and entertainments were seen as potentially reducing the autonomy of members of society. The social critics of this group were especially preoccupied with conformism and an unthinking acceptance of authority. In their writings, the term *art*, when not used ironically or suspiciously, implies a form of communication with an inherent element of social criticism. Mass culture appeared, to these social critics, to inhibit citizens' ability to imagine any society unlike the existing one. With a few outstanding exceptions, its products tended to idealize existing arrangements rather than to draw attention to needed changes. Commercial entertainment was viewed as "making no demands on its audience to think for itself."[9]

The ideas of the Frankfurt School eventually became widespread. By the mid-1960s, the work of two Frankfurt colleagues, the social philosopher Herbert Marcuse (1898–1979)—then greatly in vogue—and Adorno, was easy to obtain in Spanish translation. References to Marcuse, Adorno, and Benjamin began to appear in the work of literary intellectuals from Latin American countries. In a well-known playful homage, Julio Cortázar named his cat Teodoro W. Adorno. (It was formerly standard Spanish-language practice to Hispanicize the given names of noted foreigners.) Cortázar referred to, and included one of his photographs of, this cat in two mixed-genre works that are largely an effort toward a rapprochement between literature and mass culture. These are the 1967 *La vuelta al día en ochenta mundos* (Around the day in eighty worlds) and *Ultimo round* (Final round), originally published in 1969.[10]

It should be noted that the spread of Frankfurt-style thought and research did not necessarily imply an unquestioning acceptance of all the assertions made by members of this group. Of particular importance to the present discussion is one point on which thinkers later in the century, both from Latin American countries and from other regions, often diverged from the Frankfurt line. This deviation consists in seeing positive qualities, and even a potential for liberation, in certain mass-produced cultural items. Cortázar, for example, was an aficionado of jazz, including not only live performances but recorded jazz numbers. Adorno had singled out jazz recordings as a debased, commercial musical genre. The fact that Cortázar would develop adaptations of mass forms demonstrates that he held some hope for these expressive media.

Adorno was an attractive figure not only for his ideas and judgments on mass culture but for his efforts to establish it as a worthy object of study and reflection. The Frankfurt-School outlook, which legitimized scholars and creators spending time and thought on the new mass-produced cultural forms, was an alternative to the vision epitomized by Ortega. According to the latter, educated people should concern themselves with esthetic considerations and not allow their minds to be cluttered with commercial diversions.

The Frankfurt-School suspicion of mass culture and its producers and marketers would later fit well with the distrustful outlook characteristic of dependency analysis, discussed in Chapter One. The Frankfurt association of mass culture with the evils of late capitalism dovetailed with the notion that the capitalist ruling class would seek to establish an undeclared empire by dominating the media. Indeed, such characteristic Frankfurt terms as *culture industries* recur in studies by dependency theorists. The thought of the Frankfurt School and dependency theory both represent, of course, revisionist variants of Marxist theory. In both cases, the public for mass culture was viewed, to some degree, as passive consumers manipulated by those skilled in manufacturing and packaging a product. The producers of mass culture, in this view, encourage the acritical acceptance of the status quo by supplying a rosy picture of existing society.

Many other figures could be named for their willingness to pay close attention to mass-culture forms. Among the most influential in Brazil (where he lectured and taught) and Spanish America is the highly respected Italian literary theorist and novelist Umberto Eco (b. 1932). Often cited by Latin American scholars is Eco's *Apocalípticos e integrados* [The apocalyptic and the integrated ones] (Spanish edition, 1968; Brazilian edition 1970). The title refers to two possible stances toward mass culture: a belief that the media spell doom for civilization, and an acritical acceptance of mass culture.[11] The work contains detailed analyses of both the narrative content and the repertory of graphic signs used in comics. Readers were impressed, both favorably and negatively, that such a prominent and complex literary theorist was now analyzing comics. Eco had earned his place largely through his contributions to semiology, a methodology useful in studying systems of signs that communicate meaning. He was now demonstrating the general applicability of this approach by scrutinizing the graphics and text of a very popular form. Eco helped extend mass-culture studies to a literary public by treating the products of this culture as texts to be analyzed.

In a sense, Eco paid comics a compliment: he recognized in them a complexity that justified the scrutiny he devoted to individual frames and sequences. As his much-cited title suggests, he did not see mass culture as bearing doom. Still, his stance toward this mass narrative is not that of a fan. Though not as pessimistic as the Frankfurt social critics, Eco maintains an ironic and critical distance toward mass culture, and a vivid awareness that it is, most often, a baldly money-making venture.

Cortázar occupies an unusual and somewhat contradictory position within these lines of argument. He comes from a generally leftist perspective but does not exhibit the oppositional, distanced stance toward mass culture typical of the left. Cortázar at times resembles the Frankfurt social critics in associating commercial mass culture with the ills endemic to late capitalism. Yet, in his experimental writing he often strives toward an intimate rapprochement with riveting jazz performances, hit records, irresistibly memorable slogans, popular adventures, posters, and the advertising of new gadgetry. As a writer immersed in and changing with the times, he seeks to create close links between his creative work and the expressions of the twentieth century. His undisguised fascination with mass culture, and his desire to create new variants within it, stand in a complex and sometimes contradictory relation to his political outlook. Cortázar's unusual closeness to mass culture is one of the features of his career that brought him persistent criticism from the left.

Cortázar had long had some acquaintance with Marxism; in his circles, support for the Cuban revolution was widespread. Until the late 1960s, though, he showed little concern for the ideas behind radical movements. *Ultimo round* showcases Cortázar's enthusiasm for the protest movements and neo-Marxisms of the era. The anarchistic current running through the New Left, and the love of the absurd exhibited by young protesters, appear to have struck Cortázar in a way orthodox Marxist thought had not. A French resident, he had been an approving witness to the revolutionary efforts of May 1968. These and other late-1960s protests were influenced by Marcuse's ideas, especially the philosopher's urgings not to delay radical action while waiting for historical forces to produce a revolution. Cortázar, clearly struck with Marcuse's anticonformism and belief in immediate action, cites the philosopher both directly and through the statements of youthful protesters struck with the philosopher's approach.[12]

Yet Cortázar went against Adorno's and Marcuse's critique by his warm fondness, not only for certain variants of commercial mass culture, but even for the processes of mechanical reproduction that had made it possible. *La vuelta al día en ochenta mundos* and *Ultimo round* are distinguished by Cortázar's efforts to be a participant in, not just an observer of, the mass-produced art of the twentieth century. At the same time, he seeks to maintain his autonomy as an innovative writer, unlike the paid hands who produce much mass culture according to rigid guidelines.

When these two works first appeared, the feature that drew most attention was their format. Both works are a mixture of graphics and text, set in various faces and fonts and with the type sometimes facing different directions. Their segments are not arranged in any readily identifiable order. In the original 1969 edition of *Ultimo round*, the pages are split in two by a horizontal cut. The "upper floor" and "lower floor" resulting from this division carry different material. The unusual arrangement reflected not only the continuing influence of the surrealists, with their predilection for the collage, but also the 1960s fascination with the simultaneous use of unlike media.

It should be remembered that it was during the mid- to late-1960s, during the writing of *La vuelta al día* and *Ultimo round*, that such terms as *multimedia* came into use. The spread of transistorized electronics increased the number of devices in use and sharpened awareness of being bombarded with messages and images from the media. While some observers deplored the resulting overload of trivial information, others seized upon the chance to theorize about the resulting social changes. A celebrated case of the latter was the Canadian "media guru" [Herbert] Marshall McLuhan (1911–1980), who during the 1960s exerted influence via his many interviews and his 1967 book *The Medium Is the Message: An Inventory of Effects*. McLuhan urged the public to be aware of the effects of mass media. He postulated that the structure or "grammar" of electronic media was closely analogous to the organization of the central nervous system, allowing these forms a rapid impact upon perception and cognition. He predicted the demise of standard books and tried alternatives that, in their mix of text and image, resemble Cortázar's two mixed-format works.

While some multimedia experiments were limited to art-world circles, others reached the mass public. (The use of *multimedia* for teaching and reference tools is of later date.) Light shows, developed as a complement to rock concerts, spread to many types of events. Cortázar recognizes the more avant-garde vein of multimedia and experimentation with new technologies in "What happens, Minerva?" (*La vuelta al día*), a celebration of happenings.[13] Here Cortázar admiringly cites such artists as the Korean-born Nam June Paik (b. 1932), who during the 1960s gained renown for his adept manipulation of video images and his use of numerous television sets in assemblages.

This essay provides a few clues to the motivation behind the unusual format of *La vuelta al día*. The epigraph from Dick Higgins speaks of "the necessity to explore the art that lay between the arts," a suitable citation in a book that is an effort to create a genre of writing between or beyond the known ones.[14] Cortázar also expresses the anxiety that he is too old to appreciate some aspects of the 1960s avant-garde; this reflection suggests that *La vuelta al día* is an effort not to be left behind by the new techniques flourishing in the latter part of the century.

The content of both books is heterogeneous. Some sections take the form of fiction or poetry. Other portions are informal reflections, parodies, and the nonsense writing that was one of Cortázar's specialties. The graphics range from reproductions of avant-garde art to cartoons, Cortázar's photographs, and illustrations taken from novels and advertising. While the volumes give a playful and whimsical effect, Cortázar included in them such serious position statements as the essay entitled "On the situation of the Latin American intellectual."[15]

A number of the pieces include reflections on mass culture and the means of its reproduction. Cortázar is an observer of the globalization that, all during the 1960s, was being produced by rapid and inexpensive long-distance communications. Reading a letter from the celebrated Mexican poet and essayist Octavio Paz, who is in Nepal, Cortázar reflects: "*Mass media:* to follow the events of May in France he bought a short-wave transistor radio, with the voice of the Radio Luxembourg newscasters mixing in with the Buddhist litanies at sunset."[16]

Though Cortázar shows a desire to think about new developments, he affectionately favors the period from the late–nineteenth century to the Second World War. This is the era in which it was still possible for an ingenious technician, knowing mechanics but little theory, to win success as an inventor. In Cortázar's nostalgic vision, it appears as an innocent time when even crude reproductions of cultural forms were still a thrilling novelty. In one segment of *Ultimo round*, Cortázar expresses a preference for early phonographs over later sound reproduction systems, largely because of the awe the earlier technology produced in the public. "I was raised in a household that had seen the birth of the record," writes Cortázar, recollecting "gatherings around the phonograph with its green loudspeaker, his master's voice, the needle scratching in the warped groove, the heavy Bakelite slabs recorded on only one side."[17] Listeners of the early systems enjoyed a sharp awareness that sound was being reconstructed long after its initial production. A public accustomed to technological advances is numb to their significance: "It is painful to go into music stores and see the customers handling those fabulous pieces of frozen time, space, and life, so often buying voices of the dead, violins of the dead, pianos of the dead, leaving with an exquisite death in their hands to listen to later between two puffs on a cigarette and a chance remark."[18] The audience Cortázar portrays for early recordings little resembles the stagnant consumers posited by Adorno. Rather, Cortázar remembers excitable listeners who sought to interact with the music and the technology that conveys it; he recalls, as a child, attempting to extract hidden sounds from the reverse side of single-sided records.[19]

A similar tribute to the advent of mass-produced sound recordings appears in *La vuelta al día*. Cortázar expresses his pleasure over the acquisition of early recordings by the tango star Carlos Gardel, along with a victrola to play them. Cortázar's judgment is that "Gardel must be listened to on the victrola, with every imaginable distortion and skipping."[20] This noise, which a still-new technology cannot yet control, draws attention to the medium. For Cortázar, it also marks the sound as having been reproduced for a mass public, far from its original source. The scratching and crackling are a reminder that Gardel's recordings were heard by a large, poor listening audience: "the people, who could not listen to him in person."[21] *La vuelta al día* embodies this outlook in an homage to Jules Verne; Cortázar evokes the excitement once stirred by imagining wondrous technical advances that would later seem routine.

Many readers were struck by the close relation between Cortázar's two multimedia works of the 1960s and mass culture. Some observers felt he had joined the forces of massification. David Viñas exemplifies this perception when he contrasts Cortázar's often light-hearted works in experimental format with the dense, complex novel of 1963, *Rayuela (Hopscotch)*, on which the author's fame depends. He states: "In the course of Cortázar's career, the pace of production to which he held himself used to be that of the skilled craftsman; he has ended up being sucked into the pace imposed by an industrial market, of whose workings he has no inkling."[22] Viñas here classifies Cortázar's *Ultimo round* as fully part of mass culture. Certainly the volume exhibits an involvement with culture produced for mass consumption. One might note, though, that the unusual format of the original edition of *Ultimo round* made its production difficult and expensive; in this sense it is a book for the elite.[23] The most serious of Viñas's assertions is that the experimental volume lacks the critical dimension that art should maintain.

Cortázar was undoubtedly pulling away both from the mandarin disdain of "massification" and, to a significant degree, from the Frankfurt School's despair over this culture. One should hesitate to label his approach, since he was a creative writer who drew on his own experiences and reflections more than on theoretical sources. Yet it is fair to say that his mixed-media experiments strongly parallel the alternatives to Frankfurt-School pessimism that were beginning to emerge. Though these approaches varied, their distinctive feature was a recognition of the active role of non-elite publics. In some cases, the emphasis was on consumers' creativity in reinterpreting and even customizing mass-produced cultural items. The term *cultural studies* became a convenient handle in English-language countries for evoking this upward reevaluation of the general public. Reacting against the earlier portrait of an easily manipulated public, cultural-studies scholars viewed this audience as resilient, adaptive, and imaginative in dealing with the media's onslaught.[24]

In Spanish American countries and Brazil, the term and concept *transculturation*, discussed in Chapter One, served a similar purpose. Developed by the Cuban anthropologist Fernando Ortiz (1881–1969), *transculturation* referred to the process whereby an enterprising community creatively transforms elements of a new culture to which it has been exposed.[25] The work of the anthropologist Néstor García Canclini and those associated with his approach also encouraged a belief in the resourceful adaptability of a less educated public. (One should note, though, that García Canclini warned against the wishful belief that the resistance of audiences was strong enough to counter the effects of mass media and marketing.)[26] The two terms are not parallel: *cultural studies* is an activity carried out by researchers, while *transculturation* occurs as part of the cultural existence of a well-functioning community.

In the years following *Ultimo round*, Cortázar continued to be drawn both to the new radicalisms and to the possibility of bringing writing into the age of mass media. His 1974 novel *El libro de Manuel* (*A Manual for Manuel*), set among activists, made relatively limited use of innovative format. Newspaper articles were reproduced within the text in a different type from that of the principal narration.

In 1975, Cortázar made a full-scale effort to generate a new type of mass culture. His *Fantomas contra los vampiros multinacionales* (*una utopía realizable*) (Fantomas versus the multinational vampires [a realizable utopia]) integrated text, segments narrated via comic strip, and other graphics. The Mexico City-based Excélsior, primarily a newspaper publisher, produced an edition whose cover and strip narration replicated the style of an adventure comic, albeit a somewhat sumptuously produced one.[27] Some longtime Cortázar readers expressed an astonished sense that, as Wolfgang Luchting put it, "yes, Cortázar has written a comic strip." [28]

Fantomas has an immediate goal: to showcase the findings of the Second International Russell Tribunal held in Brussels, with special emphasis on ITT's involvement in the September 1973 military coup in Chile. The results of investigations into this and other wrongdoing by transnational corporations appear as a report following the *Fantomas* adventure.

The volume also seeks to correct certain features of mass entertainment. Cortázar resists the celebration of lone heroes, which imbues comic books with a conservative ideology. The 1960s–1970s critics of the mass media had been faulting action adventures for promoting values associated with capitalism, such as individualism.[29] The critic Ariel Dorfman, along with the communications scholar Armand Mattelart, discussed in Chapter One, were the most-noted analysts of the ideology embedded in comic books. Many other contemporary researchers found in mass-culture narrative the same emphasis on competition and the attainment of personal distinction and wealth.[30]

Formal innovation is also present in *Fantomas*. The narration diversifies comic-book storytelling with an elaborate framing story. Cortázar's persistent concern with graphics and layout is evident in his reworking of the conventions used by comic-book illustrators.

The principal section is an adventure story, "La inteligencia en llamas" (Intelligence in flames). In it, a worldwide conspiracy begins to destroy books and threaten authors. Writers are the principal protagonists of the story. With a Marxist emphasis on labor and working people, *Fantomas* situates writers among society's workers. The story begins with the statement that the narrator, a writer, has been working hard all week and has more work to do when he returns home. As co-workers, authors band together against a common threat to the book. Cortázar goes against the common image of the writer as a unique creator, set apart from society and devoting less time to labor than to a mysterious and solitary quest for inspiration. (Nonetheless, one difficulty in portraying writers as united working people is that the authors shown all have attained individual distinction and celebrity.) In addition to the united literary community, the crisis attracts the asocial mastermind Fantomas.

Fantomas, of French origin, became familiar to both an elite and a mass audience via his adventure tales. He is an urbane but sociopathic man of mystery wearing evening clothes, a cape, and a mask, "the king of the night."[31] As the protagonist of a current-day Mexican comic book, he is still "the elegant menace." His identity obscured by an enveloping mask, he deftly exercises his criminal talents. Cortázar transforms him into a well-meaning superhero who volunteers to serve on the side of right but proves unsuited. Fantomas offers his services to the endangered writers. His resources include his concealed identity, powers of flight, and his headquarters equipped with state-of-the-art electronic devices and staffed by the beautiful women of his harem. Fantomas's flaw is his inability to become part of a community effort. A typical action hero, he is designed to perform virtuoso feats that demonstrate his superiority to ordinary human beings. When the narrator wonders whether Fantomas will fight alone, he answers, "Solitude is my strength, Julio."[32] As the narrator expresses overt doubts about the efficacy of his plan, Fantomas gives a fiery defense of individualism and flies off to right wrongs single-handedly. The writers harbor little hope, and as time passes they see no results from his exertions. They recognize that a broadly based coalition, rather than individualistic heroics, is required to counter the misdeeds of international entities, whether the mysterious antibook conspiracy or transnational corporations.

It is difficult to know whether Cortázar's *Fantomas* succeeded in reaching a general public. Luchting reports that "the book has not . . . sold well."[33] He suggests that Cortázar made a mistake by using avant-garde formal innovation in a work designed for a popular audience. The public for Cortázar's *Fantomas* was necessarily different from that for standard comic books because of its author's celebrity. As well as a modified comic book, *Fantomas* was a narrative text by a noted writer. For example, copies of the alternative *Fantomas* were acquired and preserved by research libraries and literary critics as part of their Cortázar holdings.

Another factor that set the experimental comic apart is expense; the 1975 edition of Cortázar's *Fantomas* was lavishly produced compared to the comics one might ordinarily buy from newsstands. As in the cases of *La vuelta al día* and *Ultimo round*, the reissue of *Fantomas* was a cheaper production; the austere 1989 version lacked even cover art. Though Cortázar never wrote another *Fantomas* adventure, the writer Rubén Sánchez and the illustrators of the Estudio Martínez continued to develop his concept of a politically progressive *Fantomas*. This sequel was conventionally produced and was almost indistinguishable from the usual *Fantomas* comic until one began reading it.[34] These circumstances suggest that the more complicated production required by unusual formats inhibits efforts to innovate within mass-culture genres.

A precedent for Cortázar's experiment deserves mention: the educational comic books of the popular Mexican illustrator Rius (Eduardo del Río). Rius, who came into prominence in the 1960s, falls somewhat outside the scope of this chapter; he is not a literary writer or critic but a cartoonist and educator. Rius made his name with the comic-book series *Los Supermachos;* when he lost control of this series, he founded *Los Agachados* (The hunched-over, i.e., beaten-down ones). He was first recognized for political satire and denunciation of corruption, but his work spread into many thematic areas. Rius's graphic style has also grown more diverse; he supplemented cartoon characters with caricatures of public figures, photographs, nineteenth-century illustrations, and reproductions of documents such as newspaper clippings and manifestoes.

Rius is not fundamentally a creative writer or tale-teller. Though he sometimes sets his presentations within a brief framing story, his comics are self-teaching guides, muckraking exposés, and warnings about the dangers of the present age. In certain didactic comics, such as his *Marx para principiantes* (*Marx for Beginners*), Rius showcases important figures in progressive and Marxist thought, emphasizing their concepts over their biographies.[35] He also explores such events as revolutionary movements and scandals that reveal the exploitative collusion between business and capitalist governments. Though Rius's humor is slangy and often frivolous, he does not refrain from applying it to figures and texts he respects. Making himself a third author, after Marx and Engels, of the *Communist Manifesto*, he adds visual humor and verbal clowning absent in the original version.[36]

Rius has many themes other than the political; he is a consumer advocate who advises his readers to distrust certain products. Holding strong opinions about health, Rius has waged a crusade against meat and contaminated edibles; a denigrator of the cult of expertise, he encourages readers to rely less on physicians and manufactured pharmaceuticals and more on preventive self-care and natural healing. A strong rationalistic current runs through Rius's work; he derides superstition and belief in the supernatural, along with the mystique generated by advertising and publicity campaigns. Some of his comics, such as *The Chicanos*, are designed to sharpen Mexican readers' vision of phenomena that the mass media have presented in a sensationalist fashion.[37]

Though Rius is fundamentally concerned with presenting a critique of society, his transformation of comic-book format has been an attractive topic to academics. Researchers of culture and media, including a number of literary scholars, have examined Rius's thorough reworking of a seemingly rigid narrative genre.[38] Others, concerned with instructional media or with spreading progressive thought and exposés, hope to duplicate, through translations of Rius or works modeled on his, the illustrator's success in enlivening what are in great measure self-paced instructional guides.[39] Rius developed his comics to provide alternatives to the information available from the standard mass media, textbooks, and official publications and spokespeople. Seeing his work catch on, these very entities, such as government agencies, began to imitate it, using comics in information campaigns about hygiene, birth control, and other issues.

Dorfman and Mattelart also promoted the idea that the mass media could be used to spread more desirable messages. So did their various collaborators, students, and other contemporaries who took a similar approach. Dorfman, who made his name as a literary critic, taught students in literature programs to be critical analysts of mass media. Those associated with their approach, unlike Cortázar, often focus primary attention upon ideological content. Cortázar placed great importance on the graphic communication of information and reformed both structure and theme. Critiques like *How to Read Donald Duck*, discussed in Chapter One on dependency, were content analyses without reference to issues of form. The virtual absence of commentary on the graphic signs used by comic-book illustrators is often noted as a weakness of Dorfman's research, even by those who admire his content analyses.[40]

During the administration (1970–1973) of Salvador Allende, the Chilean government increased its involvement in the mass media. Government-owned media provided an opportunity to experiment with changing the ideological messages implicit in popular entertainment. In 1971, the government acquired the bankrupt Zig Zag publishing concern, which had a large comic-book division. Drawing on the expertise of media critics, the state-run publisher initiated an experiment in the reform of this type of narrative. One of those working on this project was Manuel Jofré, who had studied with Dorfman and Mattelart. Jofré's detailed report on the experiment appears in his and Dorfman's 1974 *Superman y sus amigos del alma* (Superman and his bosom buddies).[41] Jofré, who is clearly a literary critic as well as a student of ideological persuasion, generally follows the lead of Dorfman and Mattelart. However, the terminology and concepts he employs reveal that he is more concerned than these two mentors with making a semiological analysis of culture and with studying the formal aspects of the comic-book text.

The Chilean experiment resembles Cortázar's in some respects but diverges in others. Jofré and his collaborators shared the concern over the single-handed derring-do of superheroes. In comic books produced under new guidelines, story lines concentrated on problems facing communities and on common action. As did the reworking of *Fantomas*, the new adventures showcased work and shared concerns among co-workers.

Jofré and his colleagues were not just seeking to reform comics themselves. Part of their program was to involve the workers in the comic industry—many of whom were accustomed to simply following instructions—and even actual readers in the process of change. This was congruent with a widespread concern for attaining "horizontal communication," to cite the title of a contemporary book urging wider participation in media affairs.[42]

From the 1960s into the 1990s, many projects were launched to loosen the grip of media professionals and allow a non-elite public more of a say in its own cultural lives. A lengthy study could describe efforts toward a people's culture, which really involved many different cultural levels. Some of the activities were not much different from previous attempts by various agencies to keep folk arts alive. Other undertakings attempted to bring members of the working class into forms of culture generally associated with the elite; an example is the people's poetry workshops sponsored by the Sandinista government (1979–1990) in Nicaragua. In other cases, such as the one described by Jofré, the objective was to give workers in and consumers of a mass-culture form unprecedented input into the creative process. While Cortázar admired the ideal of grassroots participation in culture, as a cosmopolitan literary celebrity he had little opportunity to be part of it.[43]

Another important difference between Cortázar and the Chilean team is the issue of verisimilitude; closely associated with the demand for greater realism in comics is a focus on values and ideological content over matters of form and graphic elements. Cortázar, with his scant interest in realism, situates *Fantomas* in the comic-book tradition of fantasy; for example, only Mexican magazines are to be found in Brussels, and the narrator inexplicably materializes in Barcelona. The Chilean team strove for a lifelike resemblance between the adventures and readers' lives. Jofré uses the term *cotidianización* ("everydayization") for the effort to reduce the fantastic and the exceptional.[44] One comic book, *OVNI* (UFO), was discarded at the outset; as the title suggests, encounters between human beings and extraterrestrials were its mainstay, leaving little opportunity to explore social relations.[45] Other series were abandoned after failures to make them reflect issues in society.

Jofré recognizes that the initial drive for realism may have decreased the comics' attraction. Consultation with readers revealed that, even when approving of the reforms, they desired entertainment; more humor, more extended storytelling, and better color reproduction were among the requests. A number of readers asked for more fantasy and imagination; Jofré judges these readers to be unsympathetic to the progressive measures.[46] If one follows his line of thought, a taste for the fantastic element in popular narrative correlates with indifference to or evasion of social problems.

Though Jofré maintains his defense of narrative realism, in a retrospective appraisal of the project he unexpectedly departs from the strict content analysis typical of Dorfman, Mattelart, et al. In this afterword, Jofré speaks as a scholar of the arts and as a communications analyst, and takes a more semiological approach to the art of comics. Turning his attention to the rigidly conventional system of graphic signs employed by comic-book illustrators, Jofré wonders whether their monotonous visual shorthand might not also come in for rethinking, saying, "The overall structure of the comic book has not been changed."[47] Jofré earlier suggested that illustrators are undervalued in comparison with the story writers, who consider themselves an elite of creators.[48] He has observed that "The technical training of cartoonists and colorists is poor and minimal," and suggests that stronger support for these neglected artists would result in a more imaginative use of color.[49]

Cortázar's *Fantomas* and the Chilean experiments of the early 1970s are just two examples of an outlook that flourished, above all, in the late 1960s through the mid-1970s. Writers and educators often turned serious attention to the most disdained of mass-culture forms, such as comic books and televised melodramas ("soap operas"). They viewed these genres as capable of inculcating in viewers such values as excessive competitiveness, stereotyped views of male and female behavior, and a belief that everyone deserved his or her place in society.

This was a period when a number of intellectuals made efforts to influence the content of television programming. These were not the perennial campaigns to suppress sexual and violent scenes and profanity. Rather, a more analytical critique of programming came largely from writers, university faculty, and other educators. Criticism from these sectors led to the curtailment or reworking of certain types of programming under the Allende government in Chile noted above and, in Peru, the leftist military government (1968–1975) headed by Juan Velasco. During 1970–1975, the Peruvian regime undertook the nationalization of a number of media enterprises. It then undertook programs for the "socialization of the means of communication" that were similar in many ways to the Chilean experiment. These are two unusual cases in which the state was heavily involved in the reform of communications and recruited the participation of intellectuals, including such well-known writers as Dorfman in Chile and the Peruvian novelist and essayist Julio Ortega.

Even when the government did not seek out consultants for media reform, there were many cases in which writers, researchers, and educators urged state agencies to control particular cultural manifestations. A much-discussed case was the opposition to *Sesame Street* when it was aired in Latin American countries under the titles *Plaza Sésamo* and *Praça Sésamo*. The Children's Television Workshop hoped to avoid perception of its show as a foreign intrusion. Local production in Mexico and Brazil and extensive consultation with Mexican and Brazilian educators were intended to adapt the show to its new audiences. Nonetheless, the show provoked a storm of criticism from writers, researchers, and educators. It was not allowed to air in Peru, and persistent complaints eventually shut down the Mexican and Brazilian productions.

The polemic over *Sesame Street* centered on the perception that, despite local production and cultural allusions, the underlying values and concepts were those of U.S. capitalism. Critics saw the show promoting an individualistic striving for personal advancement over others, an excessive dependence on authorities to guide and regulate everyday life, and a lack of community among the denizens of Sesame Street. By stressing the positive values of neatness, cheerful obedience, and productivity, the show seemed designed to produce hard-working individuals who would not be likely to band together and question society's fairness.

For the present discussion, the particular criticisms of *Sesame Street* are less significant than the involvement of numerous researchers, educators, and well-recognized intellectuals in the controversy. The fact that established figures were willing to lend their time and names to a dispute over a children's television show is evidence of the importance increasingly accorded to mass media and their contents.

Looking at intellectuals' varying attempts to interact with mass media and the culture they bring, a few overall tendencies stand out. Over the course of the twentieth century, it has become more and more accepted for writers and literary critics to work as reviewers and analysts of popular forms. The idea that educated individuals should keep their minds clear of the clutter of mass entertainments and information has been steadily losing ground. Obviously, the analysis of comics, television programming, video games, and other ephemeral cultural manifestations is not as prestigious an activity as the study of literary texts. Still, well-regarded intellectuals have become less inhibited about commenting on these phenomena. Literary intellectuals find it relatively easy to discuss mass culture because their commentary is transmitted via media—essays and lectures—in which they are already skilled.

More problematic for literary intellectuals are their efforts to actually participate in the making of mass culture. In some cases, such as Huidobro's efforts to work in silent film, literary figures have not had the practical expertise or insider knowledge to become full-fledged participants. New variants of mass culture devised by innovative outsiders are likely to be considerably less profitable than conventional products turned out by the routinized employees of a given culture industry.

5 Latin American Women's Writing and Gender Issues in Criticism

Issues of gender have no doubt always appeared in commentary on literary works. It would be possible to compose a lengthy survey of assertions about masculinity and femininity and women's and men's status in critical writing from Plato to the early twentieth century—that is, before a special category such as *feminist criticism* or *women's studies in literature* had come into existence. Some of these writings argued in favor of women's right to self-expression and in this sense can be called feminist.

Though antecedents are abundant, it is only in the latter half of the twentieth century that the concept of *feminist criticism* has emerged clearly. This chapter principally concerns itself with the ways in which critics of Latin American literature have, from the 1970s onward, manifested a renewed interest in women writers and in women's role and status as evidenced in literature.

The last portion of the chapter deals with a more recent development in research into gender in Latin American literature: gay and lesbian studies. By reviewing research on this topic in the same chapter with feminist criticism, I am in no way implying that feminist literary studies are necessarily linked to lesbian and gay issues. Rather, feminist theory and research sparked an interest in issues of gender that spread beyond feminism. One extension of the reexamination of gender is research into writing by gay men and lesbians and into homoerotic themes in literature. While it could be argued that these studies deserve a separate chapter, the published research on gay and lesbian issues in Latin American writing is not yet extensive enough to sustain a chapter-length review.

The development of feminist criticism and women's studies internationally is an extensive and complex story. Sweeping coverage of literary feminism will not be a goal of this chapter. Rather, it will concentrate more specifically on the issues that have claimed greatest attention as late-twentieth-century feminism began to affect the study of Spanish American and Brazilian writing. In addition, this chapter seeks to provide readers with a general idea of which Latin American women writers deserve to be more widely read and studied. The assumption in writing this chapter has been that readers will be interested, in great part, in finding out who Latin American women writers are. The following discussion is intended to offer leads to readers eager both to learn more about the authors and their writing and to recognize major questions in this area of research.

This book has been written with an English-reading audience especially in mind. For this reason, many of the works cited are those for which good English translations are available. Readers who encounter Latin American literatures only through translations often have a struggle gaining a historical perspective on that body of writing; recent writers tend to loom disproportionately large. To counter this distortion, this chapter emphasizes the lengthy historical development of women's writing and feminist thought in Latin American cultures.

First, a brief look at post–World War II international feminist criticism is in order. Although it is principally known as a work of social criticism, Simone de Beauvoir's 1949 *Le deuxième sexe* (*The Second Sex*) includes a section entitled "The Myth of Woman in Five Authors." Beauvoir's book exercised great influence. Although worldwide feminism often appeared somewhat dormant during the 1950s, Beauvoir's book is generally recognized as the first stirring of the women's movement that gained strength in the late 1960s. (The more immediate starting point is the 1963 *The Feminine Mystique* by Betty Friedan, the founder of the National Organization of Women. Unlike the other works discussed here, it makes virtually no reference to literature.) The chapter Beauvoir dedicated to detailed literary analyses may be considered the precursor of much subsequent feminist criticism. Beauvoir brings to readers' attention the distortions male writers introduce into their representations of women characters.

Beauvoir's critique was groundbreakingly original. As late as 1970, there were still few studies of gender issues in literature. Kate Millett's *Sexual Politics* (1970)—a feminist analysis of fiction—and Germaine Greer's *The Female Eunuch* (1970)—examining female images in commercial art and writing and the popular imagination—won considerable publicity as controversial novelties. Subsequent years have brought such a proliferation of feminist analyses of literature and popular culture that it is difficult to imagine any single work producing a stir similar to the reaction elicited by these early works. Worth noting is Beauvoir's, Millett's, and Greer's concentration on images of women projected by male writers or cultures in which a male perspective predominates. The effort to denounce stereotypes and inaccurate images was more important in early feminist criticism than later versions and on the whole was more characteristic of English-language than Spanish- and Portuguese-speaking literary cultures.

During the 1970s, scholars and nonspecialist readers of Latin American literature began to pay increased attention to women writers and to gender issues in literature. In the process, feminist concepts were adapted to be useful in literary studies and to apply to different types of societies. As will be noted in the following survey, terminology and ways of framing issues varied both from one society to another and within a single society. The feminism that arose in the late twentieth century was at first based in Western Europe and the United States. Its framers were largely middle-class white women who wanted the same rights and opportunities enjoyed by the males in their circles. As it moved beyond the fairly homogeneous context in which it originated, it was forced to diversify and transform itself. A sizable number of women in Spanish American and Brazilian societies became involved with current-day feminism, giving rise to much discussion of the aspects of the women's movement that would need modification to fit local realities. Gabriela Mora has ably summarized, through an invented composite dialogue, the types of comments Spanish American feminists make concerning this issue. Many of these are common-sense observations about linguistic and cultural differences. For example, Mora captures a greater fear among feminists in Spanish American countries of being perceived as lesbians. She notes the belief that feminists in U.S. universities, even those from Latin American countries, exhibit greater detachment from the region's social problems. Notable, too, are such traits of U.S. intellectual style as the ability to examine one factor in isolation; U.S. feminism often separates gender issues from other social problems. Other of the opinions Mora samples are more debatable. Her imaginary debaters air the perhaps romantic idea that pre-Columbian civilizations could reveal forgotten ways to give women a valued place in society.[1]

Yet feminism is not entirely a foreign import to Spanish America and Brazil. There has also been a homegrown feminism, often arising more from women's own experiences and observations than from their readings. Long before the current (1960s forward) feminist movement, there were feminists and proto-feminists in Latin America. Sor Juana Inés de la Cruz (real name, Juana de Asbaje y Ramírez de Santillana, Mexico, 1648? – 1695), to be discussed later, expressed views that would in retrospect be recognized as feminist. Sor Juana's critique of women's status cannot be attributed to any outside influence; it was the fruit of experience and observation.

In actual practice, feminist analysis of Latin American writing draws on both international feminism and lines of thought developed within the region. In her much-cited 1992 study, *Talking Back: Toward a Latin American Feminist Criticism*, Debra A. Castillo considers the ways in which foreign-generated concepts of feminism become synthesized with the creative writing and theoretical work that have arisen closer to home. If critics bring these elements together without devoting critical thought to the task, the result is confusion: "in the perceived absence of indigenous theory, the Latin Americanist tends to conscript other theories to fill the gap, ironically, uncritically, and sometimes inappropriately utilizing the resources of a first-worldist approach in the service of the critique of capitalism, creating strange hybrids of dubious applicability and—in the context of the nations of Latin America—with unacceptable political ramifications."[2]

Despite the danger of an unthinking application of international theory, Castillo argues that feminist critics of Latin American writing would be impeding their own research if they were to reject the contributions made by contemporary theory. She recalls Alice Jardine's observation and warning that "those who had chosen to reject or ignore the major theorists . . . most often produced no theory at all."[3] While Castillo cautions against drawing upon existing theory without carefully assessing its applicability to Latin American literature, she encourages an effort "to build an applicable feminist strategy based on an infrastructure of evolved and evolving Latin American theory, while taking from first-world feminist theory that which seems pertinent and complementary."[4] Both in her own work and in the recommendations she makes to other scholars, Castillo gives relatively little importance to the origin of the ideas and phrases she borrows, and lays considerable significance upon their applicability to the critical problems she is examining. She draws attention to the fact that she quotes thinkers, such as Friedrich Nietzsche, generally regarded as unfavorable to women's causes, as well as others who might be dismissed as reactionaries. Their words suggest insights that lead toward the type of analysis she cares to make. The critical evaluation and use of citations count more than the current reputation, sex or gender, or national origin of those quoted.

Castillo notes that, in casting a wide net for sources from which to form a feminist criticism, scholars would do well to avail themselves of the ideas that appear in the work of Latin American women writers. When writers make direct statements, speaking in their own voices, Castillo finds them more frankly feminist than researchers.[5] In their creative writing, using the less direct rhetoric that distinguishes imaginative literature, Latin American women writers have long made implicit assertions that by today's standards would be deemed feminist.[6]

(It should be remembered that the actual term *feminist*, while it has a long history in progressive circles, did not come into widespread circulation until approximately the 1910s. Organized campaigns for the emancipation of women, or for equal education and opportunity for both sexes, date from the late eighteenth century. Nonetheless, individual women had long been pointing out their disadvantaged situation. In addition, since the middle ages, treatises had been written either pointing out women's moral flaws or defending them against previous criticism; these last are at times in retrospect referred to as feminist.)

The first wave of feminism was an outgrowth of the Enlightenment, with its ideals of personal autonomy and equality. During the French Revolution, women's organizations formed to demand the same rights then being claimed by men. The American Revolution, which followed similar ideals, also gave rise to scattered women's-rights movements. English-language readers are most familiar with early feminist thought through the nonconformist circles that included the poet Percy Bysshe Shelley and the novelist Mary Wollstonecraft Shelley. The latter's mother, Mary Wollstonecraft (1759–1797), had in 1792 published *A Vindication of the Rights of Woman*, the first important modern feminist treatise.[7] It is worth remembering that Wollstonecraft's advocacy of equal education and opportunities for women was considered extremism in its day.

By the nineteenth century, feminism had spread beyond radical enclaves to a broader spectrum of progressives. Educated people worldwide were becoming aware of the tendency, though the women's-rights movement did not spread at an even rate. In the Spanish-speaking world, as in other Catholic regions, feminism often met with clerical disapproval as a threat to the institution of the family. Less industrialized societies were not as receptive to feminism as those that registered the full impact of the Industrial Revolution; the movement of women into the paid workforce strengthened their demands for equality.

Despite inhibiting factors, the goal of female emancipation was attractive to a number of progressive women in Latin American countries. As was the case in the United States, women involved in antislavery campaigns were often struck by resemblances between slaves' lack of rights and their own. The abolitionist movement gave women practice as social critics and reformers, which they then applied to improving women's status. The link between abolition and women's emancipation is clear in the writing of the Cuban poet, novelist, and playwright Gertrudis Gómez de Avellaneda (1814–1873). Avellaneda's celebrated first novel, the 1841 *Sab* (also named for its protagonist in English), is feminist fiction even by late-twentieth-century standards. It repeatedly draws parallels between the status of slaves and that of wives and uses the same rhetoric to advocate the outlawing of slavery and improvements in women's situation.

Because few nineteenth-century women were public figures as was Avellaneda, and because of her desire for independence, many aspects of her life especially illustrate the situation of women in her time and place. (It should be noted that much of her career took place in Spain.) She struck many contemporaries as an example of the emancipated woman. At a time when women devoted much thought to maintaining a reputation for chastity or fidelity, Avellaneda's tumultuous amorous life was public knowledge. She was likened, and indeed compared herself, to the then-scandalous French novelist George Sand (1804–1876; real name Armandine Aurore Lucile, Baronne Dudevant).

Avellaneda's very success brought into clear relief some of the obstacles facing women intellectuals. In 1853, an opening occurred in the Royal Academy of Letters. Avellaneda was proposed, but the vote went against her. The basis was not an issue of merit but resistance to admitting a woman. This decision disturbed many contemporary intellectuals, and an extensive polemic ensued. Although she had won acclaim as a poet and novelist, Avellaneda drew harsh criticism when her plays began to be staged, though their content was not inflammatory. The occupation of playwright was held to be unsuitable for a woman.

While Avellaneda is the most outstanding example of a nineteenth-century Spanish American literary feminist, many other women writers were drawn, with various degrees of enthusiasm, to the contemporary ideal of the emancipated woman. In reading nineteenth-century Spanish American novels by women, one occasionally encounters allusions to the need to improve women's place in society. Yet these nineteenth-century assertions of women's entitlement may strike twentieth-century readers as timid or ambivalent toward the advancement of women.

Clearly, even women intellectuals dissatisfied with their role in nineteenth-century Spanish American societies frequently shrank back from the European concept of the New Woman, emancipated from her home and able to enter the public sphere. Feminist ideas were transformed and adapted for Spanish American audiences by combining them with more traditional concepts of womanhood. Advocates of women's rights often linked the improvement of women's education and social status to an idealized image of motherhood. One of their fundamental arguments was that, given women's lofty mission in raising future world leaders, female education was an imperative.

An outstanding example of this distinctively nineteenth-century, Spanish American feminism is *Aves sin nido* (*Birds without a Nest*), the 1889 novel by Clorinda Matto de Turner (Peru, 1852–1909). The narrator stresses that women make their contribution as wives and, above all, mothers. The novel's one explicit reference to emancipated women, who seek new roles outside the home, is a condemnation. No doubt many twentieth-century readers have been astonished to encounter this passage in what is otherwise a highly progressive novel. It is fair to wonder whether it was not included to forestall adverse reactions by readers who associated women's independence with the decline of the family.

At the same time, the heroines of *Birds without a Nest* frequently leave their homes unaccompanied and involve themselves in public matters. They take an active hand in dealing with social and political problems, with or without the help of the male protagonists. *Birds without a Nest* unambiguously promotes a complete education for girls. (At that time, girls' schooling was not mandated and was often limited to subjects considered ladylike; geography, science, and mathematics, beyond a rudimentary level, were taught principally to boys.) The principal heroine and her husband enjoy an exceptionally egalitarian marriage based in large part on intellectual companionship. Their relationship exemplifies the marital ideal expounded by feminists, as for example in Wollstonecraft's previously noted *A Vindication of the Rights of Woman*. Women's lack of education and opportunities is, however, only one of several social ills and individual moral failings that the novel denounces. The exploitation of native Andean peoples, clerical celibacy, schooling by rote memorization, poorly chosen and un-scrupulous small-town officials, and abusive, drunken husbands are among its many targets.

Efforts to make feminist ideas palatable to a contemporary Spanish American public were common among intellectuals like Matto and her friend the novelist-journalist Mercedes Cabello de Carbonera (Peru, 1845–1909). The latter, an essayist and novelist, linked her defense of women's education to the philosophy of positivism, then enjoying a widespread vogue. Both Matto and Cabello de Carbonera exemplify the advanced woman of nineteenth-century Spanish America. Their feminism is not an issue complete unto itself but is part of a general struggle to reform society. In their writing, fairly bold statements against the current status of women co-occur with what, by the antiromantic standards of the twentieth century, are sentimental and stereotyped portrayals of female characters. Despite the care these women took to make their feminism and advocacy of other reforms acceptable to their readers, both became targets of hostility.

Twentieth-century curiosity about women intellectuals has brought back to light the life and writings of Flora Tristán (France-Peru, 1803–1844), who among other things was the grandmother of the painter Paul Gauguin. Her imagination fired by Wollstonecraft's *A Vindication of the Rights of Woman*, Tristán wrote essays advocating the emancipation of women and utopian socialism. She also composed a document of great interest today, since it narrates the experiences of a single woman traveling in early-nineteenth-century Peru: *Mémoires et pérégrinations d'une paria* (*Peregrinations of a Pariah*, *1833–1834*).[8] New editions and translations of Tristán's essays and memoirs began to appear in the late twentieth century, the direct result of literary feminism.[9]

In addition to the support lent to feminism by celebrated nineteenth-century authors, a number of little-known women in Spanish America and Brazil published fiction that, to varying extents, delivered a critique of existing gender arrangements. The possibilities for research into barely known nineteenth-century Argentine women writers were impressively demonstrated in Francine Masiello's 1992 *Between Civilization and Barbarism: Women, Nation, and Literary Culture in Modern Argentina*. Obscure figures as well as celebrated women in the creative arts are examined in Jean Franco's widely cited, interdisciplinary study of 1989, *Plotting Women: Gender and Representation in Mexico*.

Other women, who were more journalists or pamphleteers than literary writers, worked in grassroots women's movements. In some cases, feminists promoted women's rights by founding their own newspapers. These nineteenth-century feminist publications, though they are somewhat beyond the range of literary analysis, today constitute valuable source material for feminist scholars.

With the twentieth century underway, the poet Alfonsina Storni (Argentina, 1892–1938) propagated feminist ideas through her journalism and, in some cases, through her poetry itself. In such widely read Argentine periodicals as the magazine *Nosotros* and the newspaper *La Nación*, Storni advocated the improvement of women's status. Victoria Ocampo (Argentina, 1890–1979), the powerful editor and publisher, was a feminist and an admirer of Virginia Woolf. Rosario Castellanos (1925–1974), an author who worked in several genres, was the first well-known Mexican intellectual to associate herself with feminism. Castellanos brought to her readers the new feminism that gained strength in the 1960s. She aligned herself with the women's movement at a time—the late 1960s and early 1970s—when few readers were familiarized with feminist thought. Though the principles of equality Castellanos advocated would today be considered a moderate feminism, during her lifetime she provoked hostility with her ideas. It should be noted that, even before she began to show the influence of international feminism, Castellanos had been critical of society's treatment of women; her critical outlook was the result of what she had lived and seen.

In addition, certain writers became associated with women's issues without being completely marked as feminists. An example is the novelist and journalist Marta Lynch (Argentina, 1925–1985), whose reporting often centered on such topics as women's perspectives on society, reproductive rights, and women in the workplace. The examples cited above stand out because they involve women from generations in which feminism was rare and its adherents extremely controversial. For women writers of subsequent generations, avowed interest in feminism was less exceptional, and they could count on a public that shared the same concerns. Already by the late 1970s and early 1980s, the writing of Rosario Ferré (Puerto Rico, b. 1942) shows a more comfortable familiarity with contemporary feminism than Castellanos, who was venturing into new terrain. By 1982, Ferré refers easily to Beauvoir and Woolf in "La cocina de la escritura" ("The Writer's Kitchen"), an account of her beginnings as a writer. She does not need to explain who they are or why they are significant. Her essay is directed to an audience that did not yet exist for Castellanos, composed of feminist critics familiar with Beauvoir and Woolf and eager to hear how women approach the task of writing.[10]

The word *feminist* itself is among the most variable terms in this entire area of discussion. In liberal U.S. usage, especially at academic conferences and among editors who deal with a public interested in women's issues and experience, *feminist* at times loses its connotation of social activism. In this context, where feminism enjoys acceptance, the term may mean nothing more polemical than "concerned with women's status." Using this broad definition, one might remark that all professional women are to some degree feminists because they all desire the same opportunities as male co-workers. A novel that focuses attention upon women's experience or women's difficulties in society may, simply on these grounds, be called *feminist fiction*, especially by publishers eager to reach the women's-studies market. Writers who cannot be said to promote feminist thought or programs nonetheless become used to hearing themselves described as feminists. Critics who often write about women writers and questions of gender are sometimes described as feminist scholars, without reference to whether feminist thought is clearly present in their work.

Although *feminist* is often used in this broad way when feminism is assumed to enjoy a certain acceptance, resurgences of antifeminism keep the term charged. When discussion of women's issues takes place in the public arena, where opposition is likely to be strong, the term *feminist* is not used as lightly and is sometimes avoided.

Readers who have grown accustomed to the relatively attenuated use of *feminist* characteristic of U.S. liberal enclaves are often surprised to discover that in Spanish America and Brazil the term *feminista* is, on the whole, more strongly loaded. In this latter context, to call a woman a *feminista* suggests that she is an activist, possibly a member of an organized movement, and that she expounds a feminist program. Women working and writing in Spanish American societies and Brazil often resist being referred to as feminists. The denial of a feminist identity does not imply a rejection of the ideal of gender equality or a lack of concern over the issues facing women. More likely, it reflects an understandable desire not to acquire an image as a doctrinaire or tendentious writer.

Another complication comes through the association of feminism with a Western ideal of a progressive, internationalized society. Here is another variant of the pattern discussed in the chapter on autonomy and dependency. Dominant societies tend, consciously or unthinkingly, to exert pressure on weaker ones to resemble them. U.S. observers are apt to applaud such indices of Western-style progress as more women in the workforce and women's increased ability to go out alone in public. There has been a widespread belief among social planners that women's participation in work and public affairs will boost the world economy and improve international relations. In this outlook, women's adherence to traditional ways, whether regional, ethnic, or religious, hinders progress. Hoping to produce a world united in its modern development, such agencies as the World Bank and the United Nations have helped fund women's organizational activities in poorer countries.

The association between feminism and the drive toward a homogeneously modernized world has produced some negative reactions. Perhaps the most dramatic example of a backlash against the pressure for women to modernize is the adoption of Islamic dress by a number of Arab and Iranian women who had previously worn Western women's clothing. Though no such vivid symbol of resistance can be found among Latin American women, nonetheless there has been some criticism of concepts of feminism framed in the United States and Europe. One can hardly quarrel with the statement that ideas arising in one social context require adaptation to apply elsewhere. Still, it is an unfortunate turn when the very idea of women's autonomy is seen as a foreign imposition.

Gwen Kirkpatrick observes that, regardless of the society in which they arise, feminist organizations, when on the defensive, often substitute the term *women* or *woman*. They seek to avoid the association of *feminist* with "elitism, North American imperialism, lesbianism, and antagonism toward men."[11] Literary critics whose focus is women authors and questions of gender have often devoted discussion to the relative merits of such terms as *feminist criticism, women's-studies approaches*, and *gender studies in literature*.

Kirkpatrick is correct in noting that such name changes are often motivated by a desire to avoid provoking hostile responses, rather than because of conceptual shifts. Many observers have noticed that the same research presented as *feminist* at an academic conference may go under some blander name, such as formulations using *women* or *gender*, at a conservative university. However, the avoidance of the term *feminist criticism* is not always an effort to shy away from controversy. To cite a noted example, one of the most polemical students of women's writing, the French theorist Hélène Cixous, objects to the use of the term *feminist*, associated with reformism, to describe her work. Cixous prefers the word *woman;* in her lectures and writing, she has drawn attention to woman's body and to a radically divergent new writing associated with woman.

The reservations of Cixous and other French theorists such as Julia Kristeva about *feminist* were usually stated in polemical terms, which sometimes struck outside observers as counterintuitive. Some French critics called themselves *antifeminists,* not because they urged women to return to traditional roles, but because they found existing feminism too moderate and liberal. These terminological distinctions helped fuel a lively debate on the French intellectual scene. However, theorists' objections to the term did little to inhibit the use of *feminist* outside those involved in the debate. In fact, the very critics and theorists who found the term inadequate were often identified as contributors to feminist theory rather than with such less recognizable designations as *French women theorists.* Whatever the objections to *feminist,* it was still the most useful handle for scholars whose research centered on gender issues in literature.[12]

Extensive debate has never produced a single best designation for studies that focus on gender issues in literature and writing by women. Nonetheless, the lack of an agreed-upon overall rubric has not inhibited the growth of research and teaching in the field. The present discussion will not attempt to determine the best possible designation for this area of studies, since in this case the terminological discussion seems primarily of concern to specialists. Rather than debate lexical choices, the point here is to survey women's writing and the research issues it raises. Since the most indisputable achievement of literary feminism has been to increase the reading and study of women writers, Spanish American and Brazilian female authors will be as much the focus as problems in criticism.

In thinking about the difference between European and U.S. and Latin American feminisms, it is useful to keep in mind a general, and perhaps obvious, difference between intellectuals from the regions. Those from the more prosperous areas are less likely to view their societies as urgently in need of drastic change. While the unequal distribution of wealth and opportunity between social classes is certainly a feature of U.S. society, it is not widely recognized as constituting a crisis. Relatively few U.S. intellectuals have a thorough grounding in Marxist theory, and European thinkers have widely varying degrees of acquaintance with Marxism, while Latin American university education has tended to provide a strong Marxist background. This difference affects the discussion of feminism generally and of gender issues in literature. U.S. and European scholars at times appear to their Latin American colleagues to be oddly indifferent to class inequities while focusing on detailed nuances of the unequal relations between the sexes. This difference at times has led to a perception that feminisms of U.S. and European style are somewhat self-indulgent practices cultivated among relatively privileged scholars.

Not too surprisingly, this criticism of feminism has also arisen internally within the United States, Spanish American societies, and Brazil. Representatives of underprivileged racial and ethnic groups and classes and scholars with a Marxist outlook are often the ones to voice this dissatisfaction with feminism. For example, within English-language feminist criticism, Lillian S. Robinson has sought to take into account factors of class and race along with those of gender.[13]

A much-noted manifestation of this critical attitude occurred at the 1975 Encuentro de Mujeres (Women's Meeting) in Mexico City, with United Nations sponsorship. Among those attending was Domitila Barrios de Chungara, the representative of the Bolivian miners' movement and the daughter of an Indian father. Domitila expressed a sense of alienation from the predominantly middle-class participants. Saying, "Do you have anything like my situation? Do I have anything like your situation? . . . We are not the same, even as women," Domitila suggested that the struggles of economically exploited, ethnically marked groups possessed for her an involving urgency and that her solidarity was with other similarly oppressed workers. In contrast, the concerns of well-off women appeared remote.[14] Though dramatic and strongly felt, the debate over the relative importance of gender, class, and ethnic issues was more important to feminism as a social movement than to feminist criticism. For example, Domitila's often-cited assertion of her alienation occurred at a conference on women's status in society rather than one devoted to literary discussion.

The habit of singling out gender issues from others is less problematic in literary analyses than in social criticism or policy studies. In thinking about the problems of an entire society, a comprehensive outlook is desirable. In the practice of literary criticism, it is common for one aspect of a text or group of texts to be isolated for the purposes of a certain type of analysis. A focus upon questions of gender, with other social considerations kept in the background, was not very unlike the usual procedures of literary critics, who must delimit their scope to make an analysis. While feminist literary theory has been extensively developed, in the methodology of their analyses feminist critics show more similarities than differences with existing literary studies. As Sara Castro-Klarén plainly states, feminism "is not a methodology for literary criticism. In fact, that is what it lacks,"[15] so feminist critics use existing methodologies. Obviously, if considerations of class and race or ethnicity were absent from all of feminist criticism, it would be a great flaw. Yet, given the tight focus demanded by specialized studies, no one can reasonably expect every analysis to include all these factors; feminist studies by their very nature focus special attention upon issues of gender.

While the degree to which feminists should specialize in gender issues is a matter of opinion, there are more practical dilemmas confronting feminist scholars of Latin American writing. There is the task of adapting the terminology of feminist criticism to Spanish- and Portuguese-language discussion. A persistent source of trouble is the distinction between *sex* and *gender*, which is difficult to communicate clearly in Spanish and Portuguese. To speak of *differences between the sexes* implies that these dissimilarities have a biological basis, while reference to *gender differences* carries the notion that cultural forces are operating. The exchange of views over whether to use *sex* or *gender* reflects sharply divided opinion over which behaviors and outlooks are biologically determined and which are formed by culture. Spanish- and Portuguese-language discussion of this issue is further complicated by the circumstance that *género*, the word for *gender*, has long been established as the word for *genre* in literature. Hernán Vidal records a number of alternative formulations that feminist critics have proposed as less ambiguous translations of *gender*.[16] He notes that the discussion has remained inconclusive and classifies it among the "dead ends" of feminist debate.[17]

Mora suggests that *género*, whose ambiguity makes it an obvious source of confusion, is only one of many problematic terms.[18] She includes a list of words and phrases in use among English-language feminists that have no immediate equivalent in Spanish.[19] Mora's treatment of this problem does not imply that the feminism developed in English-speaking countries is poorly suited to Spanish American societies. Rather, scholars should exercise care in the translation of all terms and concepts.

A term and concept debated extensively during the late 1970s and early 1980s was that of a distinctive *écriture féminine*, *women's* or *female writing*, or *escritura femenina*. The reason for using the French phrase first is that the polemic over the term and idea broke out in France and was strongest there. One confusing factor is that *feminine* in English is not a perfect translation of the French *féminine* or the Spanish *femenino/a* and Portuguese *feminino/a*. While these Romance-language terms mean simply *having to do with women*, the English-language term often brings to mind traits stereotypically associated with women. (For example, it would be acceptable to say *estudios femeninos* or *Letras Femeninas;* the latter is the name of an important journal of criticism on Spanish-language women writers. Yet *feminine studies* or *feminine letters* would not sound right.) An indication of the sharply divided opinion over the term is that it carried two divergent meanings. For some scholars, a woman writer was virtually the only one who could generate female writing. The exception might be a man who had lost all identification with the male role and experience.

Cixous propounded one variant of this notion. In her vision, a writer may produce *écriture féminine* by inscribing, with rule-breaking boldness, the experience of the female body upon the literary page. Ideally, this process results in an avant-garde writing with the power to disrupt the masculine symbolic order. The new writing offers an alternative to literature contaminated by the patriarchal vision. While Cixous often refers to women, and especially to women's bodies, her focus is not on the experiences that real-world women have lived through or texts that they have written.

Of the texts that women have actually written to date, few would qualify as *écriture féminine* under these criteria. So Cixous, unlike the majority of feminist critics, is only occasionally interested in discovering and learning about women writers and examining the texts they have produced. A very notable exception is the extended attention she paid to the Brazilian novelist Clarice Lispector (1920–1977). But more typically, in the avant-garde spirit, Cixous shows scant concern with the literary past and looks to present and future possibilities. Cixous's essays are more a call for a radically deviant writing than a description of it. This concept of female writing is favored principally by those struck by the approach of Cixous and the like-minded analyst Luce Irigaray. Many aspects of their activity have been controversial but none more so than their insistent references to women's biological differences from men.

Other scholars, outside French literary theory and its debates, found a distinctive women's expression in broader ranges of writing. Markedly female literature included, in some cases, all creative writing by women. *The Female Imagination* (1975) by Patricia Meyer Spacks represented the tendency to find shared traits in all work by women authors.[20] This work was translated into Spanish and provoked considerable discussion.[21] It raised, in the era of feminism, a question that had a long history of debate: whether women thought and wrote differently than men.

More typical of the French discussion of *écriture féminine* is a focus on the characteristics of writing that, in its radical deviance, has the ability to counter patriarchal thought. In this view, the biological sex of the author loses some or all of its importance. Instead, *écriture féminine* is identified by the way the speaking subject or self is constituted and by the language of the literary text. Whatever the writer's biological sex and life experiences may have been, the writing must attain a subversive fluidity, avoiding the rigidly defined patterns associated with patriarchal social organization.

During the late-1970s debate in France, the literary theorist Julia Kristeva was the most-noted advocate of a notion of *écriture féminine* based almost exclusively on the characteristics of the literary text. While her ideas on this topic were taken up in women's studies, they did not really originate in this field. Her central concerns are those of French literary theory of the 1970s, the heyday of poststructuralist thought. The emphasis on the subject, language, and writing's ability to undermine or destabilize established assumptions is characteristic of contemporary French theory and criticism generally. As Kristeva's concept of *écriture féminine* was taken up by feminist critics in other countries, it necessarily underwent changes. These adaptations occurred, not so much because foreign critics failed to grasp French poststructuralism, as because their emphases and needs were invariably different.

Students of Latin American women's writing were not always concerned with the problem of the subject in literary language. However, they were eager to construct some theoretical basis for their studies of women's writing and drew elements from this French discussion to help them in this task. Of the concepts generated by French feminism, perhaps the most valuable was the idea that writing could be efficacious in undoing the mindset of the patriarchal system.

Students of Latin American literature also drew to varying degrees upon Anglo-American feminist criticism, which was on the whole less abstract than the writing of French women theorists. English-language feminist critics have had many ways of conceptualizing and characterizing their research. One strong commonality, though, is a drive to research the history of women writers, their work, and their links with literary tradition to date. The connection studied could be either the difficult relations of female authors to the entire literary tradition, in which male writers and values were of most concern, or links between emerging and already established women writers ("mothers and daughters"). The inquiry into women writers in historical context spread through such influential works as Elaine Showalter's 1977 *A Literature of Their Own* and Sandra Gilbert and Susan Gubar's 1979 *The Madwoman in the Attic.*[22]

Nonetheless, the feminist theory and criticism that arrived from France and the English-speaking world required continuous adaptation to make sense when applied to Latin American literature. Castro-Klarén notes several points at which French- and English-language feminist thought must change to fit Latin American literary tradition. She points out that feminist critics tend to make certain assumptions when working with literatures that are securely established worldwide. Critics representing these long-established literatures presuppose the existence of a seldom-questioned tradition of entrenched, in most cases male-authored works against which they contrast less accepted texts by women. In the case of Latin American literature, virtually no author can be said to enjoy the mainstream enshrinement accorded Shakespeare or Goethe. For Castro-Klarén, the characterization "of Woman as Other, is almost ironic in relation to Latin American literature and literary studies, where . . . we have learned to posit an entire discourse, even the discourse of the national dominant classes, as the discourse of the Other."[23]

The concept of a writing that was *feminine* in the sense of, roughly, *antipatriarchal, antiauthoritarian,* or *subversive* was attractive to many thinkers as an alternative to the search for features exclusive to writing by women. The focus on the difference of texts by biologically female authors struck many observers as a version of the idea that women were programmed by their bodies to think and act unlike men, a notion that had often proven disadvantageous to women. Those worried about a reversion to Freud's "biology is destiny" hailed the concept of an anarchistically liberating writing attainable by writers of either sex. This ideal drew the support of such noted women as Beauvoir and the novelist Marguerite Duras.

The debate over a hypothesized female or feminine writing, notable for its intensity in 1970s France, has since lost some of its impetus, owing perhaps to the extreme difficulty of establishing clear evidence of the existence of such a special form of writing. The discussion spread in some measure to Latin American letters, though nowhere was the polemic as sharp as it had been on the French scene. There were a few cases of women literary intellectuals convinced of the existence of a distinctive women's writing. The writer of fiction Luisa Valenzuela (Argentina, b. 1938) and the art critic and novelist Marta Traba (Argentina-Colombia, 1930–1983), postulated the features of an *escritura femenina*. Even before feminist criticism became widespread, Valenzuela had been devoting attention to the topic of women's special relations with language. As a writer concerned with unequal relations of power, she often centered her fiction on ways in which women were dominated by men more skilled in the use of coercive language. An alternative theme was women's ability to escape domination by a more aggressive use of language.

Traba's "Hipótesis de una escritura diferente" (Hypothesis concerning a different writing) was several times reprinted. It tentatively postulated the signs that a given text was the work of a woman. Traba had developed a set of five distinguishing attributes of women's writing in her teaching in the late 1970s. She believes that "stories and novels written by women . . . do not seem to focus on the conception and planning of a text organized from outside the literal/material."[24] Women are less likely to rely on symbols and metaphors and more apt to focus readers' attention on concrete specifics. Traba suggests that "this may occur in part because of women's disadvantage in acquiring training in thinking through synthesis and abstractions."[25] She also suggests that women's writing is closer to oral discourse than is that of men.[26] Her hypothesis came to the attention of larger audiences at the Congreso Interamericano de Escritoras, held in Mexico City in 1981, and other meetings. She had formed her hypothesis based on a sample of creative writing by nine Spanish American and Brazilian women. Though the texts examined were all Latin American, Traba believed that scrutiny of women's literature from other societies would yield similar results.[27]

The assertions of Valenzuela and Traba about the traits that mark women's writing represent one extreme of the spectrum. While many critics and writers discussed the possible existence of an *escritura femenina*, few felt that they possessed enough evidence to posit or hypothesize its identifying features. More characteristic is the cautionary essay of the Peruvian critic Sara Castro-Klarén.[28] Castro-Klarén observes that "This thesis of 'the female imagination,' that entails the tremendous risk of turning into a version of 'biological determinism,' in other fields, would be recognized as a prime example of the anti-feminism and the sexism we saw in Freud."[29] She also decries a methodological weakness in studies that examine writing by women to identify its hallmarks: "If we assume that women's texts, texts written and signed with women's names, indeed contain or become a category for the analysis and constitution of the female subject, it could be said that we are constructing a tautology instead of an analytical tool."[30] She notes that even when characterizations of women's writing are offered as hypotheses, they tend to convince readers that women possess some special mentality.[31]

Despite disagreements over terms and concepts, one element has been common to nearly all forms of literary feminism. This uniting factor is the drive to bring the writings of women authors to the attention of both academics and the general reading public. Examination of the required reading lists used in schools and universities, and of dictionaries and encyclopedias of authors, revealed a clear underrepresentation of women. If widely read literary texts by women were relatively few, substantive analyses of these texts were even rarer. Educators grew concerned that women were growing up with only a meager exposure to previous women's written self-expression. The task of bringing more women's works to the reading public was more urgent than the effort to clarify terms and develop theoretical frameworks for feminist criticism.

Many readers who had considered themselves fairly well versed in Spanish American literature began to notice the limited number of women writers with whom they were acquainted. For example, although Spanish American fiction had earned international attention during the 1960s "boom," this sudden increase in sales and publicity seemed scarcely to have benefited women writers. The "boom" novelists, such as Gabriel García Márquez of Colombia and Mario Vargas Llosa of Peru, had all been men.

While the "boom" was at its height, few observers noticed the imbalance. It was the increased awareness of women's issues that made this curious oversight stand out clearly in retrospect. As the "boom" ended and critics began taking a new interest in women's writing (approximately 1970), it became evident that not a single living Spanish American woman commanded an international readership of any size or had a major, widespread reputation, although a number had built up followings and critical esteem within their own countries. Women were actually less prominent and influential in Spanish American literature than they had been earlier in the century. The scene in 1970 was in contrast to Spanish American letters of the 1910s to the 1940s, when a number of women poets (noted below) were attracting both popular and critical attention. When the 1982 novel

La casa de los espíritus (*The House of the Spirits*) by Isabel Allende (Chile, b. 1942) became an international success, many foreign readers ahistorically perceived its author as the first important Spanish American woman writer.

The situation of female writers in early-1970s Brazil at first glance appeared somewhat more favorable. Two Brazilian women novelists, Clarice Lispector (1920–1977) and Nélida Piñon (b. 1937), were already enjoying international reputations when literary feminism made its impact in the 1970s. Lispector's work had been the object of studies by major Brazilian critics and had been appearing in translation since the early 1960s. Without reaching any sizable foreign readership, the poet Cecília Meireles (1901–1964) had won great respect among readers of Portuguese. The novelist Rachel de Queiroz (b. 1910) had also had a distinguished career. In addition, some current-day authors, such as the fiction writers Lygia Fagundes Telles (b. 1923) and Dinah Silveira de Queiroz (1911–1982), had fairly extensive readerships. However, women writers from earlier periods were little known. Publishers' and required-reading lists, good indices of the authors considered noteworthy, seldom included works by women born before 1900.

One of the principal accomplishments of women's studies and literary feminism has been to increase awareness of the work of women authors and to improve scholarship on these writers and their texts. As scholars began to inventory women's writing and the criticism dedicated to it, some anomalies became evident. A number of women writers were recognized figures in Spanish American or Brazilian culture, and their most popular works were read both in school and for pleasure. Although they could not be called undiscovered, since in many cases they were household names, these authors often did not seem to be taken as seriously as comparable male writers. They had attracted relatively little substantive criticism, and it was often difficult to find complete bibliographic information concerning their work.

Writers in this category include Sor Juana Inés de la Cruz, noted above for her early defense of women's rights; Gertrudis Gómez de Avellaneda, the Cuban poet and novelist mentioned earlier for her attraction to nineteenth-century feminism; Clorinda Matto de Turner, the Peruvian novelist mentioned for her synthesis of feminism and traditionalism; Teresa de la Parra (Venezuela, 1889–1936); Gabriela Mistral (Chile, 1889–1957; Nobel Prize, 1945), a tremendously influential poet in her time; the novelist and short-story writer María Luisa Bombal (Chile, 1910–1980); and Rosario Castellanos, noted above for her bold endorsement of the 1960s–1970s women's movement.

Critics and editors concerned with women writers also brought new attention to talented but lesser-known women than the celebrated authors mentioned above. An example is Elena Garro (Mexico, b. 1920). Her 1963 novel *Los recuerdos del porvenir* (*Recollections of Things to Come*) had been well received and shared many of the features prized in "boom" novels. Yet Garro and *Recollections* had never benefited from inclusion in the "boom."

In other cases, critics rediscovered women who had earlier enjoyed critical recognition but who represented literary tendencies now out of fashion with scholars (though not necessarily with ordinary readers). This was the situation of regional realists like Marta Brunet (Chile, 1897–1967) and of the *posmodernista* women poets who had flourished during the period 1910–1940, such as Delmira Agustini (Uruguay, 1886–1914); Alfonsina Storni, already mentioned for her feminist writings; and Juana de Ibarbourou (Uruguay, 1892–1979).

As these latter writers came in for rediscovery, late-twentieth-century critics were often amazed at the comments that contemporaries had made about the women poets, or *poetesses* as they were then known. During the first half of the twentieth century, critics often referred to women writers in what today would be considered excessively personalistic terms, often singling them out for their beauty and feminine charm; a fairly common assumption was that women wrote directly from their personal experiences and feelings. To cite a much-noted case, contemporary commentators often referred to Agustini as if she were a young girl, even when she was well into her twenties.[32] Women poets of this generation were certainly not forgotten; for example, Juana de Ibarbourou was regarded as a national cultural heroine. What appeared lacking, though, was up-to-date critical analyses of these authors' actual writing.

While these more or less recognized figures were receiving closer scholarly attention, other, little-known writers came to the awareness of critics. Some had been disadvantaged not only by being women but by coming from regions where literary life and publishing attracted little international attention. Such are the cases of the poets Eunice Odio (Costa Rica, 1922–1974), Claudia Lars (real name Carmen Brannon; El Salvador, 1899–1974), and Carmen Lyra (Costa Rica, 1888–1949), who gained readers owing to renewed interest in women authors. Others had been known only to relatively limited publics despite their outstanding originality, such as Nellie Campobello (b. 1900), the Mexican writer of short fiction; and the Argentine poet Olga Orozco (b. 1920).

The search for women writers often coincided with fresh interest in intellectuals as activists. The Peruvian Magda Portal (1903–1989) became the topic of research both for her poetry and her extensive political activism, which came to include the women's movement. Patrícia Galvão (Brazil, 1910–1962, known as Pagú), an avant-gardist and activist who had been remembered in great part for her personal life and her imprisonment, was now reencountered as a novelist eager to deliver a social critique. The Puerto Rican poet Julia de Burgos (1914–1953), who had been involved with Puerto Rico's independence movement and many other struggles, began to attract a new wave of readers.

While the women mentioned above came in for rediscovery in the late twentieth century, there was also an increased interest in women writers whose literary careers were still unfolding. The works of Adélia Prado (Brazil, b. 1936), Albalucía Angel (Colombia, b. 1940), Cristina Peri Rossi (Uruguay-Spain, b. 1941), the previously noted Luisa Valenzuela, Sônia Coutinho (Brazil, b. 1944), and Ana Lydia Vega (Puerto Rico, b. 1946) were attractive to the large number of critics who sought to explore women's writing.

The campaign to explore writing by women coincided with the drive for the inclusion of work by representatives of minority groups. Domitila Barrios de Chungara and Rigoberta Menchú, whose work was discussed in Chapter Three on testimonial literature, awakened readers' interest both as women and as people of indigenous ancestry: Menchú was a Quiché Maya, while Domitila, though not a member of a native community, was aware that her father had been an Indian. Marilene Felinto (Brazil, b. 1957) first drew attention as a writer capable of representing, from firsthand experience, the situation of the urban, literate Brazilian woman of African descent. Her novel *As mulheres de Tijucopapo* (*The Women of Tijucopapo*) is feminist fiction, especially in the episodes involving an Amazon uprising. At the same time, it is an account of the life of an alienated young black woman.

Another noteworthy development was the appearance of fiction by women who, as academic critics, were familiar with contemporary literary theory and criticism, including feminism. The Brazilian literary theorist Helena Parente Cunha (b. 1929) had long been producing short, experimental creative texts as well as her academic research. In 1983, her first novel, *Mulher no espelho* (*Woman between Mirrors*) became both an award winner and a best seller. This novel is the involving narrative of a seemingly docile wife and mother who, in midlife, is forced to struggle toward autonomy. At the same time that it draws readers into an absorbing human story, it makes sophisticated use of contemporary theory in its novelistic construction. Sylvia Molloy (Argentina-United States, b. 1938), one of the most noted critics of Spanish American literature, in 1981 published the novel *En breve cárcel* (retitled in English *Certificate of Absence*). Strongly emphasizing its heroine's relation with her body, of which she has an exacerbated awareness, the novel attracted feminist critics. The novel's protagonist is a lesbian, a feature of interest at a moment when gay studies in literature were just emerging.

The next section of this chapter concentrates on the changes in approach and methodology that necessarily occurred as critics began to carry out studies of rediscovered or new women writers.

Critics began to make the effort to discover and explore more fully women's writing from previous centuries. To recover this heritage, critics had to adjust to analyzing texts unlike the usual canonical ones, while readers had to learn to appreciate some out-of-fashion styles. Though it made new demands on critics and readers, the effort to reclaim women's literary past was successful. Until the 1980s, few readers knew much, if anything, about such authors as the autobiographical nun La Madre Castillo (real name Francisca Josefa Castillo y Guevara; Colombia, 1671–1742), the prolific novelist Juana Manuela Gorriti (Argentina, 1818–1892), and Mercedes Cabello de Carbonera, noted above for her efforts to strengthen education for girls and women. Now research on their lives and works has begun to expand.

In addition to investigating these somewhat forgotten authors, researchers have gone beyond the usual literary genres to discover what women wrote in earlier periods. From the Colonial period onward, there had been at least some literate women eager to express themselves in writing. Yet women were apt to be viewed with suspicion if they assumed the public role of author. As a result, they turned to forms, like diaries and journals, more private than published treatises and literary works. During the nineteenth century, a limited number of women stood out as literary authors. Others worked in journalism, including some early feminist publications. Writing published in long-discontinued magazines and journals is often difficult to obtain, but provides a sample of what contemporary progressive women thought and wrote.

An outstanding example of investigations into extraliterary women's writing is the new inquiry into the intellectual life of Colonial-era nuns. Specialists in the Spanish Colonial era have long been aware of the many autobiographical statements by nuns preserved in archives, especially those of Mexico City; in addition, there are a number of accounts of nuns' lives composed by male clergy. Now these archival documents have become of vivid interest for researchers of women's writing. Electa Arenal and Stacey Schlau, in collaboration, have won considerable attention for this research topic. Their widely noted 1989 *Untold Sisters: Hispanic Nuns in Their Own Works* provides both the results of their investigations and a sampling of the nuns' writings.[33]

Arenal and Schlau found in Colonial convents an uneasy situation. In a sense, the nuns were meant to stand out as inspiring models of piety and emblemize the spiritual loftiness of the Spanish colonial enterprise. At the same time, they were expected not to call attention to themselves and their individual expressive talents. Schlau explains the types of writing that resulted from this tension, citing one of the better-known cases: "As a professed nun was required to follow the rules of her order and the tenets of the Spanish Catholic Church, Madre Castillo faced the necessity of writing without retaining authorship. That is, her works were not written for publication in the conventional sense, but as a pious exercise for herself and a small audience of nuns and clergymen. None was published during her lifetime."[34] These writings were not supposed to be composed and polished as if they were going to be published, a circumstance that gives them distinctive textual features. In line with an ideal of humility and modesty, the nuns were only to make those emendations that their spiritual directors deemed necessary for theological and spiritual correctness. For Schlau, this sparse editing makes convent writing especially revealing: "We can read the sexual dynamics of power with which Sor Francisca [i.e., Madre Castillo] lived through the gaps not usually visible in more polished writing. . . . Madre Castillo exemplifies how some early modern Hispanic religious women found the means to express themselves through the discourses of orthodoxy."[35]

While scholars have recently learned much about the often vivid intellectual and imaginative lives of obscure Colonial nuns, the center of attraction for researchers continues to be the brilliant scholar and baroque poet

Sor Juana Inés de la Cruz. This seventeenth-century Mexico City nun, noted for her defense of women's entitlement to learning, cannot be called a feminist discovery. Even before women's studies brought new attention to female writers, Sor Juana enjoyed general recognition as the leading intellectual light of Colonial Mexico. While many nuns' writings were archived and only later reencountered, two volumes of Sor Juana's creative work were published during her lifetime (1689 and 1692). It may seem odd to speak of a resurgence of interest in a national heroine whose features have been kept familiar through her frequently reproduced portrait and who is honored as "The Tenth Muse of Mexico."

Nonetheless, as the topic of women's writing was reexamined, critics began to wonder whether Sor Juana was being fully taken into account as a writer, as opposed to an emblem or icon. While there was an abundance of commentary on Sor Juana, a good deal of it centered on her life and personality rather than on her poetry, plays, and other writings. For example, one of the best-known studies of Sor Juana was a psychoanalytic study by Ludwig Pfandl. It attributed the nun's exceptional intellectual and creative accomplishments to confusion over her sexual identity.[36] Speculation ran high as to why the beautiful and witty Sor Juana would commit herself to a convent, even though she had plainly stated that she was seeking a quiet place to study. Sor Juana's personal traits, especially her beauty and markedly feminine features, preoccupy such writers as Amado Nervo. There has also been a tendency to compare Sor Juana with contemporary male writers, often emphasizing her debt to the foremost baroque poets. Feminist critics were not being overly suspicious when they asserted that Sor Juana was treated less seriously than comparable men.[37]

Since women writers came newly into focus in the 1970s, research on Sor Juana has become a much more substantial field of study. Not very surprisingly, much attention has gone to her self-defense, "Response to Sor Filotea de la Cruz." In this letter, which is really addressed to the Bishop of Puebla, Sor Juana argues in favor of the education of women. She was writing from a vulnerable position, responding to the bishop's accusation that she was unduly preoccupied with displaying her intellect and had neglected the piety to which nuns were held. One may judge the importance currently given to the "Response" by the frequency with which it is cited in the 1990 collection *Feminist Perspectives on Sor Juana Inés de la Cruz*.[38] Though it is a letter to an individual, it has merited the same analytical scrutiny given to works intended for the literary public.

The new critical attention to the "Response" brings to the fore a difficult issue for feminist critics. Existing commentary on Sor Juana was seen as unsatisfactory in part because critics made too much of her being a woman. At the same time, the new analyses of Sor Juana's writing often took into account her situation as a woman in what was then called New Spain. What, then, had changed?

One important difference is that the longtime critical tendency had been to view Sor Juana as an anomaly among women. She appeared as the exception among her sex, endowed with a greater spiritual life or with traits normally found among men. More-recent researchers certainly recognized that Sor Juana's career had been unusual for her time and place, yet they avoided the suggestion that only a woman unlike other women could achieve her success. Instead, the society in which Sor Juana and contemporary nuns lived appears as the factor that made such a success a rarity. Sor Juana, though she possesses special talents, typifies women in having to deal with a society that hinders women's efforts to develop their intellect and creativity.

One of the best new essays on Sor Juana is "Tretas del débil" (Strategies of the weak) by Josefina Ludmer.[39] Though the "Response" is not a literary work, Ludmer recognizes it as an outstandingly subtle text deserving close analysis. As well as a reply to an accuser, it is an intellectual autobiography. The letter is also an exercise in Biblical exegesis designed to strengthen women's role in the church.[40] Ludmer analyzes ways in which Sor Juana compensates for her powerless position vis-à-vis male authority backed by the Church. She offers her analysis of the "Response" as an example of the complexity and significance that critics may discover in women's nonliterary writing. Ludmer is like many feminist critics in believing that women placed in their correspondence, autobiographies, personal journals, and notebooks the ideas and sentiments they could not express by more public means.

Feminist critics of Latin American writing frequently cite Ludmer's essay. Castillo gives a clue why this article is treated as if it were a guidepost. In Castillo's analysis, "Tretas del débil" provides clues to the puzzle of how to devise a feminist criticism for Latin American writing. When Ludmer details Sor Juana's strategies for transmitting her ideas, she is also suggesting a way in which feminist criticism may be built up within Latin American literary studies: "The weak (woman) strategically refers not only to the colonial nun but also to Ludmer, the postcolonial critic."[41] Castillo notes that Ludmer discovers Sor Juana building the case for her ideas with what-ever source materials suit her purposes: "In divining Sor Juana's tactics, Ludmer hints at her own: to take from tradition whatever is salvageable and useful, to borrow from other writers what is needful and helpful, to fill in the gaps with her own meditations."[42]

In summing up the field of feminist studies of Latin American literature, some generalizations are possible. To a certain extent, the difficulties in building up a feminist approach to Latin American writing are common to gender studies in all fields and worldwide. Virtually nowhere has there been general agreement on the direction that feminist scholars should pursue, and the entire interdisciplinary area of gender studies has been marked by controversies over what type of research would be beneficial both to the field and to the status of real-life women. This lack of consensus inescap-ably affects Latin American literary studies. Yet, the polarization of feminist criticism between a "French" school, heavy on theory, and an "Anglo-American" one has not been a feature of Latin American literary studies. While there has been interest in theorizing about a feminine form of writ-ing, drawing concepts from French thinkers, there has also been a strong concern with reencountering actual texts composed by women who have lived under different historical circumstances. If there is one common be-lief among feminist critics of Latin American literature, it is a general con-viction that its women writers have not received enough careful and sub-stantive attention from either researchers or nonspecialist readers.

At the same time, there are other dilemmas and special circumstances involved in the development of feminist criticism suitable to Latin America. As has been noted, the growth of women's studies in Latin American uni-versity circles has lagged behind the spread of feminist thought and action in public life, policy formation, and social activism. This difference would seem to reflect more on the resources and environments of Latin American universities than on scholars, since Latin American critics based at foreign universities have often been especially active both in theorizing and con-ceptualizing in a feminist vein and in carrying out feminist analyses.

While many distinctive features of Latin American feminism could be enumerated, the most significant for the present discussion is the need, faced by both critics from Latin America and international students of the region's literary production, to construct a suitable body of theory for their research. Feminist literary critics confront an unusually marked case of a problem that is almost inescapable in scholarly inquiries into Latin

American phenomena. This perennial dilemma is the struggle to adapt and transform concepts and terms that were originally developed in Western Europe and the United States. Witness to the extreme difficulty of carrying out this adaptation is the detailed and painstaking discussion of the issue by such critics as Castro-Klarén, Mora, Castillo, and Lucía Guerra-Cunningham.[43] These analyses of the problem suggest that it will never be fully resolved and that critical self-vigilance, beyond that required in all literary criticism, will always be called for in applying feminist concepts in the analysis of Latin American writing.

As noted in the opening to this chapter, the concern with gender awakened by feminist criticism has given rise to an even more recent area of research, gay and lesbian studies. This scholarly inquiry, as such, only in the latter part of the 1980s became any sizable part of Latin American literary criticism, though same-sex attraction has always been at least an implicit theme of certain literary works. Since classical antiquity, literary and historical works have included allusions to sexual activity between partners of the same sex. With some notable exceptions, such as the often-noted poetry of Sappho, these references appear either in works considered ribald or risqué or in underground writings such as exposés and secret histories. These premodern works are valuable sources of information about attitudes toward homoerotic phenomena in different eras, but few of them provide information about what today would be considered the gay or lesbian experience. In modern fiction and theater, audiences find a greater number of characters who are, are reputed to be, or vaguely seem to be gay men or lesbians. Homoerotic desire is, or certainly appears to be, a theme of many poems, although until the 1960s it generally appears in coded form.

In addition to the evidence that texts provide, the lives of authors give some clues to a gay and lesbian presence in the literary world. In Latin America, as elsewhere, some writers have been privately known for their same-sex orientation. Written references to these individuals, though, allude only in the most veiled terms to this aspect of their existences. Late-twentieth-century researchers have been both fascinated and frustrated by the difficulty of culling, from authors' personal correspondence and the cryptic hints of their contemporaries, evidence of past writers' sexual orientations.

Homosexuality, whether viewed as forms of sexual activity or as a characteristic of particular individuals, can hardly be considered a new or previously undiscovered topic. Nonetheless, fresh attention, including that of literary scholars, has been focused on gay and lesbian themes, in large part as an outgrowth of the gay and lesbian rights movement and community organizations that came out of the social activism of the late 1960s to mid 1970s. In Latin American cities, gay and lesbian organizations began to come to the attention of the general public during this period of accelerated social change. Yet there was some delay before the impetus was transferred from activism to literature, and from literature to literary studies.

During the immediate prehistory of what may be called gay and lesbian writing—widely recognized as such—by Latin American writers, many literary figures were generally perceived as being gay men and lesbians, and related topics were certainly not absent from the region's literature. An outstanding example is the 1966 *Paradiso* (which bears the same title in English), the respected novel by the Cuban poet and fiction writer José Lezama Lima (1910–1976). The novel's references to sex between men, though presented in somewhat oblique fashion, have been evident to readers since the book's publication and have often been remarked upon by both critics and nonspecialist readers. Nonetheless, *Paradiso* cannot be called a novel of gay life. This complex, allegorical novel exhibits many concerns, but they do not include the effort to convey to readers the experience of being gay in contemporary society. The Cuban novelist Reinaldo Arenas (1943–1990), who established himself with his 1969 novel *El mundo alucinante* (*Hallucinations*), drew a good deal of attention for the difficulties he experienced as a gay man in Cuba. Still, it was not until later in his career that Arenas fully emerged as a novelist concerned with the problems of gay people. Manuel Mujica Láinez (Argentina, 1910–1984) had enjoyed a *succès de scandale* with his 1962 novel *Bomarzo*. The Uruguayan poet and fiction writer Cristina Peri Rossi (b. 1941), now a resident of Spain, has long been noted for her lesbian themes as well as for her concern with promoting democracy and human rights through literature. Alejandra Pizarnik (Argentina, 1936–1972) is another writer whose lesbian topics predate any sizable emergence of Latin American gay and lesbian writing. The Cuban Severo Sarduy (1937–1993) was generally perceived as a representative of gay culture; such topics as cross-dressing appear in both his fiction and his essays. Luis Rafael Sánchez (Puerto Rico, b. 1936) began publishing his critical and often satirical fiction in the 1960s; one of his recurring themes was gay men and the absurd reactions that male homosexuality provoked in society.

While more antecedents could always be identified, it is fundamentally during the 1970s and 1980s that Latin American writers produced a sizable body of literary works in which gay and lesbian protagonists are prominent. The Argentine Manuel Puig, whose *Betrayed by Rita Hayworth* was discussed in Chapter One on autonomy and dependency, was important in establishing gay subject matter as part of Latin American fiction. Readers of *Rita Hayworth* had many clues that its protagonist was growing up to be a gay man. Even so, this novel was not as explicit in its gay themes as some of Puig's later work. His 1976 *El beso de la mujer araña* (*Kiss of the Spider Woman*), an international success, had as its central narrative line the development of an affair between two men sharing a jail cell. Such novels as the 1979 *Las aventuras, desventuras y sueños de Adonis García, el vampiro de la Colonia Roma* (published in English as *Adonis Garcia: A Picaresque Novel*) by the Mexican novelist Luis Zapata (b. 1951), the 1979 *No país das sombras* (In the land of shadows) by the Brazilian Aguinaldo Silva (b. 1944), *Nivaldo e Jerônimo* (Nivaldo and Jerônimo, 1981) by Darcy Penteado (1926–1987), also of Brazil, and the 1983 *La brasa en la mano* (A burning coal in his hand) by the Argentine Oscar Hermes Villordo (b. 1928) all attracted enormous attention when they first appeared. Gustavo Alvarez Gardeazábal (b. 1945) of Colombia also assumed the role of gay novelist.

During the late 1970s and early 1980s, for the first time there was talk, both nationally and in some cases internationally, of a gay novel or gay writing from Latin America. It was at this moment, when the public eye was riveted on this emerging writing, that Winston Leyland brought two samplings of this writing to an English-language public: *Now the Volcano: An Anthology of Latin American Gay Literature* (1979) and *My Deep Dark Pain is Love: A Collection of Latin American Gay Fiction* (1983).[44]

Novels with lesbian subject matter, such as the 1986 *Diana caçadora* (The huntress Diana) by Márcia Denser of Brazil (b. 1949), also drew wide attention during this period. In Mexico, Rosa María Roffiel (b. 1945), known for her lesbian poetry, gained wide notice with the 1989 novel *Amora*, as did Sara Levi Calderón (b. 1941) with *Dos mujeres* (1990), which the author revised for its English version *The Two Mujeres* (1991). *Las andariegas* (The wandering women), the highly experimental 1983 novel by the Colombian Albalucía Angel (b. 1939), is at times referred to as a lesbian narrative; however, it might better be characterized as an outgrowth of radical feminism and, in particular, the quest for a distinctively female expression. The above list of names and novels is far from exhausting the authors who have won prominence as part of gay and lesbian writing. Rather than seek comprehensive coverage, it is more important to move on to some of the issues facing gay and lesbian studies of Latin American writing.

The texts that earned such attention from the 1970s forward were, for the most part, narrative accounts of the lives of gay men and lesbians, written from a sympathetic and knowledgeable perspective. A number of novels from the late 1970s through the mid 1980s were narratives of social repression as well as gay writing. This circumstance reflects the rise of military regimes in the southernmost Latin American countries and Brazil, and the singling out of gay men as special targets of repressive measures. Though the focus on the experience of gay people in society seemed to distinguish these novels from earlier fiction in which gay characters appeared, it would be difficult to draw a sharp distinction between these novels and writing on similar themes from previous decades. The gay writing of the 1970s, 1980s, and 1990s stood out as such in part because it appeared at a time when gay and lesbian issues were in the public consciousness. The authors' unguarded identification as gay and lesbian writers fascinated a public that had grown accustomed to the notion that, even in the creative arts, discretion had to be exercised concerning sexual orientation. It should be noted that not all gay and lesbian writers who made their names during this period did so by offering realistic accounts of the difficulties faced by gay men and lesbians. Alvarez Gardeazábal, for example, has a fantastic and ribald streak that runs through his fiction.

A new awareness of gay and lesbian issues continued to become generalized throughout the late twentieth century. Conference sessions on gay and lesbian topics in Latin American literature were fairly common during the 1980s, although this phenomenon spread more rapidly among critics working at U.S. universities than those based in Latin America.

By the 1990s, book-length studies were appearing. David William Foster's 1991 *Gay and Lesbian Themes in Latin American Writing* is a pioneering study.[45] Foster's book includes textual analyses of Spanish American and Brazilian literary texts from the late nineteenth and twentieth centuries. He examines only literary texts that overtly treat gay and lesbian themes; the sexual orientations of the authors, in real life, are not part of the discussion. In compiling the multi-authored reference work, *Latin American Writers on Gay and Lesbian Themes: A Bio-critical Sourcebook* (1994), Foster has followed the same principle in selecting the authors to be covered. Foster's research concern extends to authors who cannot be said to represent gays or lesbians but who offer interpretations of sexuality in their writing. This 1994 *Sourcebook* presents brief summaries of the careers and writings of Latin American authors who treated gay and lesbian issues as themes, rather than those who were known as gay men or lesbians. However, with some sixty contributors to the volume, not required to pursue a uniform approach, many critical methods are represented. Some contributors interpret the authors' work with reference to their lives, while others avoid making such direct connections.

As well as these books, Foster has published a number of articles in which he develops a critical approach to gay and lesbian issues in Latin American literature and other cultural forms. In "Some Proposals for the Study of Latin American Gay Culture," included in his 1994 *Cultural Diversity in Latin American Literature*, Foster offers suggestions to other researchers seeking to explore this relatively new subject matter.[46]

Emilie L. Bergmann and Paul Julian Smith co-edited *¿Entiendes? Queer Readings, Hispanic Writings* (1995), a multi-authored compilation of essays that includes articles on Spanish peninsular, Latin American, and Chicano cultures. The interrogative in the book's title would generally convey "Do you understand?" or "Are you in on it?" but the authors convey a secondary meaning via the translation "Are you queer?".[47] While the bulk of the book concerns literature, the essays range beyond creative writing to examine such forms as turn-of-the-century essays on social hygiene and late-twentieth-century performance art. *¿Entiendes?* is limited to a time frame starting in the late 1880s. By the end of the nineteenth century, the educated public was adopting concepts of homosexuality that, even if they may seem outmoded, at least are recognizable and comprehensible to current-day readers. Its essays go beyond analysis of scenes in literary works to include information, reports, and conjecture about the real-world lives of the authors; indeed, a segment of the book is dedicated to biographical research. Two essays deal with Spanish American writers whose lesbian attachments were known to their personal circles but were long hidden from the general public: Teresa de la Parra of Venezuela, known for her 1924 novel *Ifigenia* (*Iphigenia*), and the Nobel Prize-winning Chilean poet Gabriela Mistral.[48] In addition, one article treats the sexual preoccupations and desires of Jorge Luis Borges (1899–1986), whose sexuality has long been the focus of speculation and rumor in his native Argentina.[49]

¿Entiendes? also showcases new research into late-nineteenth-century discourse about social pathology and hygiene.[50] As noted above, the abun-

dant treatises produced around this time to diagnose social ills distinguish homosexuals as unlike other members of society. However, this is not the only reason that critics of Latin American literature study these efforts to take a scientific approach to alternative sexualities. Students of gay and lesbian issues in literature are often stymied by the extremely meager or coded information that literary writings provide until fairly recent times; what is missing from literature appears in supposedly scientific discourse. Oscar Montero points out that the same phenomenon described by scientific writers as homosexuality is characterized by the Cuban poet and essayist Julián del Casal as companionship and camaraderie. Montero concludes that literary writers' reticence about sexual acts between males "confirms the transgressive nature of such practices and the need to keep them secret, that is to say unwritten about except in sociomedical treatises. It is important to point out that the dominant strategy of suppression is to keep homosexuality out of written texts not classified as legal or medical, which is to say to keep it out of literature."[51]

A 1996 volume, *Bodies and Biases: The Representation of Sexualities in Hispanic Cultures and Literatures,* was edited by Foster and Roberto Reis. Though this compilation includes many articles on gay and lesbian issues, it has a broader scope; as its title notes, it potentially covers the many alternative expressions of sexuality. No doubt many other volumes with similar research concerns will appear in print before long. One looks forward to book-length studies of Latin American gay and lesbian writing published by Latin American publishing houses. It should be noted that presses based in Latin American studies have brought out many titles on gay and lesbian topics in society and culture generally, if not specifically in Latin American writing. These range from informative works for a general audience to specialized research studies.

Gay and lesbian studies of Spanish American and Brazilian literature face difficult issues. One of the most intricate is the approach that should be taken to works from earlier eras. For example, Latin American narratives composed in previous centuries at times contain characters that, by current-day criteria, would be regarded as gay men and lesbians. But it is not always clear how these fictional phenomena were viewed at the time the works appeared. Some students of these issues would contend that the public did not, until roughly the late years of the nineteenth century, possess a sharply delineated conceptual category for homosexuals. According to this view, sexual activity between partners of the same sex was deemed a vice or a decadent pleasure into which anyone might potentially fall if overcome by temptation or isolated from the opposite sex. Others would argue that in all eras certain individuals have stood out as exceptions to the general rule because of their sexual attraction to people of the same sex.

The debate between these two views is quite extensive and complex. Its roots appear to be in the unresolved question of whether homosexuality is inherent in the individual, or whether social and cultural forces create or *construct* the category of gay or lesbian. The latter view, in which gays and lesbians inhabit a constructed category, has taken strong hold among students of literature. Proponents of this outlook generally owe an intellectual debt to the French theorist Michel Foucault. They trace the emergence of "the homosexual" to the treatises on social hygiene that proliferated toward the end of the nineteenth century. (Latin American physicians and other experts were prolific contributors to the turn-of-the-century scientific, or at least scientific-sounding, characterization of deviance.) The emergence of a sector of society designated *homosexual* allows gay men and lesbians to make their sexual orientation part of their identities and also to be recognized by others as an exceptional segment of the population.

The lack of unanimity in literary critics' view of same-sex attraction and sexual activity reflects the more general lack of a single, well-agreed-upon theory and characterization of the phenomenon. The outlook of the cultural or social constructionists described above, while many find it extremely convincing, is not the only view currently held by scholars. One should remember, for example, the lively research interest in the hypothesis that a child may be born with a genetic predisposition to become a gay man or a lesbian. In addition, some researchers and essayists continue to pursue the idea of a gay sensibility, which would go against the idea that gayness was purely a social construct. Smith and Bergmann express some concern over the transfer of Anglo-American concepts of same-sex preference to the Spanish-speaking world. They observe that the "social-constructionist bias dominant in English-language" conceptualizations of sexual orientation may not be the most useful outlook for Spanish-speaking researchers seeking to develop theory suited to their societies.[52]

In addition to divided opinion over whether a gay and lesbian segment of the population was sharply differentiated before the late nineteenth century, there is uncertainty over how certain expressions and behaviors were understood in their time. Current-day readers are struck by the affection with which people of the same sex, until fairly recently, often addressed one another in their correspondence. In particular, passionate or romantic friendships between women often seem to later observers to be simply liaisons whose lesbian nature has been denied. In the case of Spanish American letters, the poetry of the seventeenth-century Mexican nun Sor Juana Inés de la Cruz, discussed earlier, has perplexed modern readers. The effusive affection with which she addresses her patroness to congratulate her on special occasions has caught the attention of many subsequent readers. Mainstream scholarship maintains that Sor Juana was merely following seventeenth-century convention. Rhetorical standards of the time allowed for displays of sentiment that today would betoken an amorous or erotic relation. Yet many readers still perceive in Sor Juana's poetry the expression of a sexual attraction toward other women. Despite warnings that such a reading reflects an ignorance of the customs of Sor Juana's time and place, speculation about the nun's sexuality has grown rather than diminished. The association of Sor Juana with lesbianism is so strong that, as Smith and Bergmann note, her name "has become a code word for lesbian poetry." [53]

In gay and lesbian studies of Spanish American and Brazilian writing, interest is widespread, but the number of publications on the topic has just recently begun to be sizable, with book-length studies only appearing in the 1990s. In this case, the development of the field appears to have been slowed by a reticence on the part of potential scholars, apprehensive of negative consequences if they publish the results of their research. Now that the field has begun to establish itself, it is reasonable to predict its rapid expansion.

Conclusion

All the issues examined in this survey of social questions in Latin American writing have come in for consideration by many observers, from many points of view, and, in most cases, over a significant stretch of time. Some of these debates have been running for decades; for example, the discussion of Latin America's cultural autonomy arose during the time when the Latin American countries were colonies of Spain and Portugal. Others have only recently begun to be openly discussed. For instance, gay and lesbian studies of Latin American writing and culture only in the 1970s began to appear in print with enough consistency to constitute a research field. Despite the late date at which it began to surface in notable quantities, the examination of gay and lesbian aspects of Latin American literature has a much lengthier history in informal discussion. On the other hand, the wide-ranging *postmodern* is a recently developed term, but its application to Latin American culture has already generated a large number of studies and polemical essays.

However long-standing the debate and however numerous and dedicated the participants, none of the critical questions examined in the chapters of this book has been resolved. As is often the case with important issues in literary theory and criticism, all of them constitute perennial problems which can always sustain inquiry and debate. Even when a fairly wide consensus is reached concerning any given issue, it does not hold for long.

While inquiry into these issues will never be brought to a completely satisfactory resolution, the terms continue to be debated and to evolve. Here a reader may quite reasonably wonder why, if no permanent answers are ever forthcoming, cultural critics still pursue these debates and continually change the way that the principal questions are posed. Why does the discussion continue, with no hope of a permanent solution in sight?

It should be kept in mind that the central questions concern real-world phenomena that intellectuals are strongly motivated to understand, even if their grasp of them will remain imperfect. The difficulties of obtaining first-person accounts of life in non-mainstream groups, the inequalities between national cultures, and the effects of mass media are matters thinkers would like to know more about even if they cannot exhaust their changing complexities.

While the most perplexing questions concerning Latin American writing and culture are never fully laid to rest, scholars are able to sharpen and refine their insights into them. One era's grasp of social and cultural problems is never entirely adequate to the needs of later generations of intellectuals. Dependency theory, for instance, as it was originally formulated quickly came to appear simplistic in the stark distinctions it made between the controlling metropolitan nations and the exploited periphery. Virtually since its inception, the theory has been undergoing revisions intended to take into account subtleties and contradictions that were previously overlooked. Dependency theory offers a clear instance of a type of thought that continues to be debated although it is clear that no revised version of the theory will satisfy all participants in the discussion. While complaints about the shortcomings of the theory are often severe, they have never caused the concepts of dependency and autonomy to be abandoned.

In some regards, social change itself is the reason for adaptations in the way issues are formulated and discussed by literary and cultural critics. Accelerated globalization and the recently revealed vulnerability of some long-industrialized economies forced a reworking of certain aspects of dependency theory. Here, scholars working with the theory had to account for new phenomena, as well as to refine a theory whose generalizations were too stark.

Often a particular argument will be voiced so frequently, or come to seem so simple, that it loses its interest. For example, when *postmodern* spread worldwide and began to be applied to Latin American social and cultural realities, many commentators simply refused to recognize it as relevant, considering the term useful only with reference to such societies as those of Western Europe, the United States, and Japan. While no doubt many observers continue to reject the term as a foreign imposition, this overworked judgment has largely dropped out of current research, which has had to move on to fresher insights.

Readers of this book will no doubt have noticed a considerable degree of overlap among the issues surveyed in the various chapters. Researchers inquiring into mass media and their effects often draw upon concepts of cultural dependency. This book separates the two, however, by restricting the chapter on mass media to literary intellectuals' participation in this phenomenon. In this chapter, Latin American creative writers and literary critics are seen to take an active role in utilizing mass-media techniques for their own purposes. They seek to bring a new complexity to mass-media production. A number of these literary intellectuals strive to naturalize mass-media entertainments, which often betray their foreign origins even when they are locally produced. The goal in this case is to create a popular culture better suited to the outlook and needs of audiences in the region where these cultural products will be distributed and utilized.

In turn, the long-standing debate over cultural autonomy and the critical inquiry into testimonial literature have certain major themes in common. Both discussions arise in large part from a concern over the relations between materially and technically advantaged cultures and those that lack the resources and expertise to distribute and publicize their creative production on any massive scale.

In the discussion of autonomy and dependency, attention is most typically focused on the interaction among entire regions or nations, where one side has the upper hand through its greater control of production, marketing, and distribution systems. A major issue in testimonial literature is the entry of members of technically less sophisticated groups into the literary marketplace, which can only be negotiated with the assistance of technically more expert collaborators and advisers. In both cases, though, a fundamental problem is the tendency of wealthy and technically skilled groups to spread their culture at the expense of all others. The concept of transculturation, which in this book has been associated with the issue of autonomy, examines the often creative responses of cultures to the imposition of a dominant culture from a wealthier group.

Another pattern that should be observed is that discussion of a given set of issues often has already been going on for many years before one specific term or phrase becomes attached to the debate. The word *feminism* came into general usage only around the mid 1910s, and the phrase *gender studies* began to gain acceptance in the 1970s. Yet one can scarcely set a beginning date on readers' and critics' desire to know more about women writers and to understand how femininity and masculinity are presented in literature. With the resurgence of feminism in the late 1960s and 1970s, readers became aware that even specialists in Latin American literature were often poorly informed about women writers and gender issues. Since then, there has been a drive to make both the works of and studies and information about women authors more available. At the same time, critics have struggled to adapt international feminist theory to the historical specifics of Latin American literary cultures.

A problem that has given rise to many polemics is the difficulty of applying theory and methods of study developed in Europe and the United States to the study of Latin American culture. The discussion brought about by every issue surveyed in this book includes consideration of this problem. (Of all the terms and issues reviewed, only *transculturation* was originated by a Latin American thinker, the Cuban anthropologist Fernando Ortiz.) As readers will have noted, one possible response to the problem is a rejection of such concepts as *postmodernism*. The idea of the *postmodern* clearly arose to characterize phenomena in long-industrialized, technically advanced societies. Yet it undeniably has at least enough applicability to the Latin American cultural scene to sustain widespread debate, which would be impossible if the concept were simply irrelevant. Occasionally, not simply particular concepts but an entire tendency of thought, such as feminism, will be challenged as a potentially foreign imposition.

Still, at least among scholarly participants in these debates, there is relatively little complete rejection of foreign terms, concepts, and theories to the point of closing off consideration of them. More typical is a situation exemplified by the interchange over the application of *postmodernism* to Latin American culture. Even those scholars who exhibit the greatest resistance to the term are still willing to take part in discussions of its general validity and relevance to the Latin American scene. A greater number of those engaged in the debate, though, are at least disposed to develop and revise the concept in order to adapt it to the Latin American scene. The continued participation in the debate, even by scholars who seem reluctant to accept the term, shows that *postmodernism* has become too significant to ignore.

At times there is such an uneven correspondence between a term of European or U.S. origin and Latin American social and cultural realities that critics feel the urge to discard these ill-fitting terms and invent fresh ones. On the whole, though, it has proven more productive to examine the differences for what they reveal about the distinctive historical path taken by

Latin American cultures, and to transform terms and ideas to make them useful in Latin American contexts.

Critics frequently assert that terms and concepts devised to characterize European and U.S. literature require adaptation to apply to Latin American phenomena. What should also be remembered is that the phrases and ideas used in the discussion of culture also need to be revised with the passage of time. With the inevitability of social change, it is virtually certain that all the discussions and debates surveyed in this book will need to be reframed continually.

Notes

Introduction

1. Rama, 12.
2. Ibid., 30.
3. Ibid.
4. Stanley Fish, "Being Interdisciplinary Is So Very Hard to Do," *Profession 89* (New York: Modern Language Association, 1989), 16. Fish pursues this argument throughout his article, 15–22.
5. Gayatri Chakravorty Spivak, "Can the Subaltern Speak?" in Cary Nelson and Lawrence Grossman, eds., *Marxism and the Interpretation of Culture* (Urbana: University of Illinois Press, 1988), 271–313.

Chapter 1

1. This is not to say that there was never direct communication between the economists responsible for dependency theory and literary critics working with concepts derived from this tendency. An unusual case is the participation of the Chilean economist Osvaldo Sunkel, an important figure in the development of dependency theory, in a conference on "Contemporary Latin American Literature and the Ideology of Dependency" held at the University of Minnesota, Twin Cities, in March 1975. While literary critics presented the papers, Sunkel served as a consultant and gave his reactions. The conference resulted in the special issue of *Hispamérica* 4.1 (1975), *Literatura latinoamericana e ideología de la dependencia*, guest-edited by the conference organizer, Hernán Vidal. Joseph Sommers, one of the contributors to the conference and volume, credits Sunkel with identifying, in the novel that Sommers was discussing, "a satire of neo-capitalist penetration"; see his "Literatura e ideología: la evaluación novelística del militarismo en Vargas Llosa" (Literature and ideology: the novelistic evaluation of militarism in Vargas Llosa), 104 of the issue cited above.
2. Lienhard, 47.

3. Ibid.

4. Pedro Henríquez Ureña, *Ensayos en busca de nuestra expresión* [Essays in search of our expression] (Buenos Aires: Editorial Raigal, 1952), 42–44.

5. Rama, 78.

6. Henríquez Ureña, 44.

7. Juan José Arrom, *Certidumbre de América* [Certainty of America] (Havana: Letras Cubanas, 1980).

8. See, particularly, Rolena Adorno, *Guaman Poma: Writing and Resistance in Colonial Peru* (Austin: University of Texas Press/Institute of Latin American Studies, 1986).

9. Lienhard, 59.

10. Jean Franco, "Dependency Theory and Literary History: The Case of Latin America," *Minnesota Review* 5 (1975): 69.

11. Ibid., 66.

12. Lienhard, 66.

13. Paz, 23.

14. A celebrated example is the 1825 poem *La victoria de Junín: Canto a Bolívar* (The victory at Junín: Song to Bolívar) by the Ecuadorian poet José Joaquín Olmedo (1780–1874). In Olmedo's commemorative and didactic text, Huayna Cápac, the last Incan emperor to rule over the undivided empire, makes a supernatural appearance at one of the last great battles of the Independence war. Huayna Cápac appears as an idealized figure of the native past. The advice and prophecies that he offers the nearly independent Latin Americans correspond closely with the social vision of the Latin American intellectual elite of the Independence era.

15. Enrique Anderson Imbert, *Spanish-American Literature: A History*, trans. John V. Falconieri (Detroit: Wayne State University Press, 1963), 137. Anderson Imbert is commenting on the specific case of Olmedo's *La victoria de Junín: Canto a Bolívar*, cited in the previous note, and the appearance in this poem of the emperor Huayna Cápac.

16. Henríquez Ureña, 42.

17. For example, Rama, in his posthumous *Las máscaras democráticas del modernismo* [The democratic masks of *modernismo*] (Montevideo: Fundación Angel Rama, 1985), 109, starts a discussion of literary modernism by reminding readers that "The incorporation of Latin America into the world economy became more intense from 1870 on." Paz's essays treat economic issues only in passing. Nonetheless, his work on *modernismo* also stresses that modernist writers, who encouraged an image of themselves as detached esthetes, were involved participants in the rapid modernization and increased closeness to Europe of late-nineteenth-century Latin America. See, in particular, the essays in his *The Siren and the Seashell*.

18. Joseph Sommers, "Comentario I," *Hispamérica* 4.1 (1975): 118.

19. Paz, 23. Franco, in "Dependency Theory," gives baroque poets and modernist writers as her examples of Latin American authors who, in striving to par-

ticipate in a European-style "universal culture," produce a uniquely Latin American variant.

20. Rama, *Las máscaras democráticas*, 62. Rama recognizes that he is not entirely new in seeing *modernismo*'s originality in its "tenacious and unabashed" (71), yet highly heterodox, imitation. He particularly singles out Federico de Onís as an earlier critic who had identified the paradox. Rama suggests that the modernists themselves were conscious that an eclectic fusion of diverse European tendencies was one source of their American originality; their encouragement of the extremely flexible term *modernist* for their efforts reflects such an awareness (63). Franco also suggests that the modernists' very eagerness to appropriate European novelties may have been what led to their creation of a literature unlike those of Europe (66).

21. Angel Rama, *Los poetas modernistas en el mercado económico* (Montevideo: Facultad de Humanidades y Ciencias, Universidad de la República, 1967); collected in *Rubén Darío y el modernismo* (*Circunstancias socioeconómicas de un arte americano*) (Caracas: Universidad Central de Venezuela, 1970).

22. Rama, 18.

23. Ibid., 15–16.

24. Theotônio dos Santos, *Imperialismo y dependencia* [Imperialism and dependency] (Mexico City: Era, 1980), 305.

25. V. I. Lenin, *Imperialism: The Highest Stage of Capitalism* (New York: International Publishers, 1966), orig. 1916. See also N. I. Bukharin, *Imperialism and World Economy*, Introduction by V. I. Lenin (New York: Howard Fertig, 1966), orig. 1929.

26. Emile G. McAnany, "Television and Cultural Discourses: Latin American and United States Comparisons," *Studies in Latin American Popular Culture* 8 (1989): 1–21.

27. Robert Buckman, "Cultural Agenda of Latin American Newspapers and Magazines: Is U.S. Domination a Myth?" *Latin American Research Review* 25.2 (1990): 134–155.

28. Herbert I. Schiller, *Mass Communications and American Empire* (New York: A. M. Kelley, 1969).

29. An English-language sampling of Dorfman's analyses of mass-culture texts is *The Empire's Old Clothes: What the Lone Ranger, Babar, and Other Innocent Heroes Do to Our Minds*.

30. Fábio Lucas, "Dependência ideológica e vanguarda" (Ideological dependency and the avant-garde), *Hispamérica* 4.1 (1975): 33–44.

31. Henríquez Ureña, 55.

32. Franco, 66.

33. Sommers, "Comentario I," 118, considering the practices that he deems betray a "colonial" outlook in U.S. academic research on Latin American literature, cites an excessively narrow focus on stylistic and structural features of specific works.

34. For a discussion of 1920s–1930s avant-gardism and regionalism that analyzes the problem of reliance on European influence, see Rama, 20–32. Since the 1970s, research into the avant-garde period is increasingly likely to take into account the peripheral situation of Latin American literary capitals vis-à-vis those of Europe. An excellent example is Beatriz Sarlo, *Una modernidad periférica, Buenos Aires 1920 y 1930* [A peripheral modernity, Buenos Aires in the 1920s and 1930s] (Buenos Aires: Ediciones Nueva Visión, 1988).

35. Hernán Vidal, *Literatura hispanoamerica e ideología liberal: surgimiento y crisis, una problemática en torno a la narrativa del Boom* (Buenos Aires: Hispamérica, 1971).

36. Hernán Vidal, "Introducción" to his special issue of *Hispamérica*, 7.

37. Sommers, "Literatura e ideología," 102.

38. Ibid., 100.

39. Examples include Beatriz Sarlo, *Jorge Luis Borges: A Writer at the Edge* (London: Verso, 1993) and *Una modernidad periférica: Buenos Aires 1920 y 1930;* George Yúdice, Jean Franco, and Juan Flores, eds., *On Edge: The Crisis of Contemporary Latin American Culture* (1992); and Desiderio Navarro, ed., *Postmodernism: Center and Periphery*, special issue of *South Atlantic Quarterly* 92.3 (Summer 1993).

40. For a summary of Puig's career before he became known as a novelist, one may see Angela Dellepiane, "Manuel Puig," in Angel Flores, ed., *Spanish American Authors: The Twentieth Century* (New York: H. W. Wilson, 1992), 706–707.

41. Elías Miguel Muñoz, "Manuel Puig," in Foster, ed., *Latin American Writers on Gay and Lesbian Themes*, 340. Muñoz's account of the author's early years, 339–340, stresses his admiration for the highly imaginative qualities of U.S. sound films of the 1930s and 1940s.

42. Ibid., 340.

43. Pamela Bacarisse, *The Necessary Dream: A Study of the Novels of Manuel Puig* (Cardiff: University of Wales Press, 1988), and *Impossible Choices: The Implications of the Cultural References in the Novels of Manuel Puig* (Calgary: University of Calgary Press, 1993).

44. Manuel Puig, *La traición de Rita Hayworth* (Buenos Aires: Jorge Alvarez, 1968; Sudamericana 1972), 297. An exceptionally readable translation of this novel exists: *Betrayed by Rita Hayworth*, trans. Suzanne Jill Levine (New York: Dutton, 1971). This version can certainly be recommended to readers who require an English edition, but I have preferred to quote using my translations from the original text. Page numbers in the text refer to the 1972 Sudamericana edition.

45. On page 158 of the novel, Mita reveals that she is reading the novelized biographies of Emil Ludwig; 157, she refers to weeping over Jorge Isaacs's romantic novel of 1867, *María*. She is also known to be an exceptionally dedicated reader of newspapers.

46. René Alberto Campos, *Espejos: la textura cinemática en La traición de Rita Hayworth* [Reflections: the cinematic texture in Betrayed by Rita Hayworth] (Madrid: Pliegos, 1985), 93.

47. Ibid.: "Toto carries out a reading that is easy to recognize as a psychological one."

48. Rama, 38.

49. Ibid.

Chapter 2

1. Fredric Jameson, *Postmodernism, or, The Cultural Logic of Late Capitalism* (Durham: Duke University Press, 1991), 2.

2. Ibid., 10.

3. Ibid., 15–16.

4. Marcel Cornis-Pope, "Postmodernism," in George Perkins, Barbara Perkins, and Phillip Leininger, eds., *Benét's Reader's Encyclopedia of American Literature* (New York: Harper Collins, 1991), 874. Cornis-Pope also finds the term *postmodernism* in Charles Olson's poetic essays published in the 1950s.

5. "Post-Modernists," in Jack Myers and Michael Simms, eds., *Longman Dictionary and Handbook of Poetry* (White Plains, N.Y.: Longman, 1985), 240.

6. Charles Altieri discusses 1940s–1950s postmodernism in "Modernism and Postmodernism," in Alex Preminger and T. V. F. Brogan, eds., *The New Princeton Encyclopedia of Poetry and Poetics* (Princeton: Princeton University Press, 1993), 794. Altieri distinguishes this postmodernism from the later tendency on two counts. In his analysis, the initial phase was a "confident postmodernism," characterized by a sanguine belief in the imminence of radical change. By the 1970s, artists and thinkers, "embarrassed by the failure of projected spiritual revolutions," had taken up a skeptical, relativistic outlook. Altieri observes that when postmodernism began to flourish anew in the late 1970s, it was "this time with an intellectual base," 794.

7. Cornis-Pope, 874, says: "Reacting against the aesthetic foundation of high modernism with its emphasis on transcendent reason and its separation of art from history and mass culture, the early postmodernists encouraged an eclectic, anti-elitist poetics concerned with sensuous immediacy and performance." Cornis-Pope notes that *postmodern* was "limited initially to discussions of poetry and architecture," though from the 1970s forward it was frequently identified in prose fiction, as well as in popular culture.

8. Santiago Colás, *Postmodernity in Latin America: The Argentine Paradigm* (Durham: Duke University Press, 1994), ix.

9. Néstor García Canclini, "Cultural Reconversion," trans. Holly Staver, in Yúdice, Franco, and Flores, 30–31.

10. Jameson, 18.

11. Colás, 6.

12. Innovations in microprocessing and telecommunications could be referred to as aspects of a postmodern society, beginning with such 1950s novelties as television and transistor radios and moving on to calculators, digital clocks, personal computers, fax machines, lasers and holograms, computer simulations, broadcasting

via satellite and cable, interactive video, the Internet and other computer network-ing services, electronic mail, cellular phones, and the entering of information via touch-tone.

13. C. Wright Mills, *The Sociological Imagination* (New York: Oxford University Press, 1959), 166. Robert Fiala, in researching the term and concept *postindustrial society*, of necessity dealt with the closely related *postmodern society*. Indeed, he dis-covered that social scientists had employed a number of competing and overlapping categories for what was in large part the same phenomenon: "An array of terms emerged to characterize the social milieu of advanced industrial societies, including *technocratic era* (Brzezinski 1970), *service class society* (Dahrendorf 1967), *personal ser-vice society* (Halmos 1970), *post-scarcity society* (Bookchin 1971), *post-economic society* (Kahn and Wiener 1967), *knowledge society* (Drucker 1969), *postmodern society* (Et-zioni 1968), and *postindustrial society* (Touraine 1971; Richta et al., 1969)"; "Postin-dustrial Society," in Edgar F. Borgatta and Marie L. Borgatta, eds., *Encyclopedia of Sociology*, Volume 3, 1513. The scholars and works to whom Fiala refers are: Zbig-niew Brzezinski, *Between Two Ages: America's Role in the Technocratic Era* (1970); Ralf Dahrendorf, *Society and Democracy in Germany* (English version 1967); P. Halmos, *The Personal Service Society* (1970); Murray Bookchin, *Post-Scarcity Anarchism* (1971); Herman Kahn and Anthony Wiener, *The Year 2000* (1967); Peter Drucker, *The Age of Discontinuity: Guidelines to Our Changing Society* (1969); Amatai Etzioni, *The Active Society* (1968); Alain Touraine, *The Post-Industrial Society* (1971); and Radovan Richta et al., *Civilization at the Crossroads: Social and Human Implications of the Scien-tific and Technological Revolution* (3rd. rev. ed. 1969). All allude to an era in which dominance is exercised less through the possession of manufacturing plants than through skill in applying scientific research to communications and information systems. A larger percent of the population is in service occupations and professions concerned with information; researchers, engineers, and technicians who can make commercial applications of research are highly prized in postmodern society.

These terms cannot be taken as marking a new era that breaks sharply with the age of industry. Obviously, industry continues into the postindustrial age, although it requires fewer workers. The terms *knowledge* or *information society* point to the current-day opportunities to exert economic and political power by being one of the possessors of advanced technical expertise. Still, the use of manu-facturing know-how to achieve dominance goes back to the Industrial Revolution. To argue that the newer technical expertise is valued in an unprecedented way, Fiala must make a subtle distinction: "In the postindustrial society major innova-tions are more a product of the application of theoretical knowledge (e.g., Albert Einstein's discussion of the photoelectric effect for the development of lasers, ho-lography, photonics) than the product of persons skilled in the use of equipment (e.g., Alexander Graham Bell and Thomas Edison)," 1513.

14. Jürgen Habermas, *Legitimationsprobleme im Spätkapitalismus* (Frankfurt am Main: Suhrkamp, 1973). *Legitimation Crisis*, trans. Thomas McCarthy (Boston: Beacon Press, 1975).

15. For Lyotard, modernity was marked by a belief that information—whether

that of science or that of art—moved society forward. Knowledge was seen as contributing to the overall growth of understanding of humankind's progress toward enlightened rationalism. However, a participant in modern culture was not necessarily an enthusiast of one of these sweeping projects or "metanarratives." For example, the early-twentieth-century avant-gardes are forms of modernism that propose to liberate readers and art viewers from the grip of such programs as the quest for rational living. Nonetheless, such anticonventional endeavors derive their legitimacy from the existence of metanarratives, and recognize them as powerful forces, worthy adversaries against which art can strike an opposing stance. Even when a movement proclaims itself "anti-art," as did Dada, it is still defined by art. It adds one more episode to a long-running narrative about establishment art and its rebellious young challengers.

16. Jean Baudrillard, *In the Shadow of the Silent Majorities . . . or the End of the Social,* trans. Paul Foss, John Johnston, and Paul Patton (New York: Jean Baudrillard and Semiotext(e), 1983). See also his *Selected Writings,* ed. Mark Poster (Palo Alto: Stanford University Press, 1988).

17. García Canclini, *Culturas híbridas,* 20.

18. George Yúdice, "¿Puede hablarse de postmodernidad en América Latina?" *Revista de Crítica Literaria Latinoamericana* (Review of Latin American literary criticism) 15.29 (1989): 105–120.

19. Yúdice, unpublished essay cited in Beverley, *Against Literature,* 110.

20. Colás, 6.

21. Nelson Osorio, transcribed commentary from a public discussion, *Revista de Crítica Literaria Latinoamericana* 29 (1989): 146–148.

22. Colás, ix.

23. An example of Jameson's commentary specifically on Latin American postmodernism appears in his "Introduction" to *South Atlantic Quarterly* 92.3 (Summer 1993): 417–422. Jameson identifies a postmodern, Latin American variant of autobiography in "De la sustitución de importaciones literarias y culturales en el tercer mundo: el caso del testimonio" (On the substitution of literary and cultural imports in the Third World: the case of testimony), trans. Ana María del Río and John Beverley, *Revista de Crítica Literaria Latinoamericana* 36 (1992): 128–130.

24. José Joaquín Brunner, "Notas sobre la modernidad y lo postmoderno en la cultura latinoamericana" (Notes about modernity and the postmodern in Latin American culture), *David y Goliat* 17.52 (September 1987): 33.

25. Ibid., 34. The entire text runs 30–39; in it, Brunner goes on to argue that progressive social thought and planning in Latin America need to take into account this exceptional capacity for multiplicity and heterogeneity.

26. Nicolás Casullo, "Posmodernidad de los orígenes" (Postmodernity of the origins), *Nuevo Texto Crítico* 3.6 (1990): 94.

27. Ibid.

28. Jean Franco, "Mapping Cultures," *Latin American Literary Review* 20.40 (1992): 40.

29. Yúdice, researching the apparently sudden flourishing of the notion that

Latin America was postmodern before the United States and Europe, finds such an assertion appearing almost simultaneously (1987–1988) in the work of such diverse scholars as José Joaquín Brunner, Nelly Richard of Chile, and the Brazilian José Miguel Wisnik; see his "Postmodernity and Transnational Capitalism," in Yúdice, Franco, and Flores, 24. Rather than attempt to single out one 1980s commentator as the source of this concept, Yúdice locates it further back in the history of Latin American thought, as noted in the text of this chapter.

30. Although Octavio Paz has only occasionally written directly on the concept of postmodernism, he has followed with keen interest the debate over postmodernism both worldwide and in Latin America. One may see the June 1987 issue of his much-noted journal *Vuelta* (11.127), which includes a special section on postmodernism, to which he contributed a brief introduction and an article that treats postmodernism along with other topics more within his usual thematic repertory. Over the years, Paz has at times mentioned modernity, but generally in the course of discussing his long-preferred themes; readers should not expect him to contribute to formulating a working definition of postmodernism.

31. Yúdice, "¿Puede hablarse?" 107.

32. Yúdice, "Postmodernity and Transnational Capitalism," 15.

33. Ibid., 9.

34. Yúdice, "¿Puede hablarse?" 106–107.

35. Yúdice, "Postmodernism in the Periphery," *South Atlantic Quarterly* 92.3 (Summer 1993): 543–556.

36. Beverley, 107.

37. Edited by Fernando Calderón, 17.52 (September 1987) of *David y Goliat* was entitled *Identidad latinoamericana, premodernidad, modernidad y postmodernidad, o, ¿Le queda chico el corsé a la gorda?* The subtitle, which translates "Is the corset too tight for the fat girl?" reflects the general apprehension that the term and concept might be applied to Latin American cases without being transformed to correspond to the region's special historical situation.

38. Antonio Benítez Rojo enjoyed an international success with *La isla que se repite*. In all fairness, though, Benítez's highly original study is not principally a contribution to postmodern studies, though it draws on this concept among many others.

39. For a sampling of the heated discussion generated when the concept of postmodernity began to be applied to Latin American history and culture, presented in English translation, see *Boundary II* 20.3 (Fall 1993), special issue "The Postmodernism Debate in Latin America," eds. John Beverley and José Miguel Oviedo, trans. Michael Aronna, subsequently expanded and published in book form by Duke University Press; and *South Atlantic Quarterly* 93.3 (Summer 1993), special issue "Postmodernism: Center and Periphery," guest editor Desiderio Navarro. Among Spanish-language collections of essays on the issues are Nicolás Casullo, ed., *El debate modernidad-postmodernidad* [The modernity-postmodernity debate] (Buenos Aires: Puntosur, 1989); and Jorge Ruffinelli, ed., *Modernidad y posmodernidad en*

América Latina (I) (Modernity and postmodernity in Latin America), a special thematic issue of *Nuevo Texto Crítico* 3.6 (1990).

40. García Canclini, *Culturas híbridas*, 55.

41. García Canclini, "Cultural Reconversion," 40.

42. García Canclini's *Culturas híbridas*, which gives an international set of examples to critique the situation of present-day creators, appeared in English as *Hybrid Cultures: Strategies for Entering and Leaving Modernity*.

43. García Canclini, "Cultural Reconversion," 33.

44. García Canclini, "Memory and Innovation in the Theory of Art," *South Atlantic Quarterly* 92.3 (Summer 1993): 434.

45. García Canclini, *Transforming Modernity*, 71.

46. Ibid., 40.

47. Yúdice, "Postmodernism in the Periphery," 551.

48. García Canclini, *Transforming Modernity*, 38.

49. Ibid., 113.

50. Ibid., 56.

51. Colás, 3.

52. Williams, 6.

53. Ibid., 14.

54. Ibid.

55. Ibid.

56. Ibid., 33.

57. Williams, "Colombia," in Foster, 213. Williams is here explaining why the novels of Marco Tulio Aguilera Garramuño are "postmodernist texts."

58. Williams, *The Postmodern Novel in Latin America*, 16. He observes that, while the boom novelists came to prominence as modernists, they began to move toward a postmodern outlook and writing as they sensed the cultural climate changing. Williams, in "Colombia," 212, traces such a change in the work of Gabriel García Márquez, who in his writing of the 1960s "used [a modernist form of narrative] in what is an identifiable modernist project—the seeking of order and the expression of the ineffable in a world lacking order and waiting to be named. García Márquez, like certain other Latin American writers (e.g., [Mario] Vargas Llosa and [Carlos] Fuentes), is rooted in the moderns, but not consistently so. He has also read the postmoderns and in his later work participates in some of their subversive and self-conscious practices."

59. Colás, 92. Colás's discussion of the postmodern writer's outlook on truth claims runs 92–93.

60. Donald L. Shaw, "The Post-Boom in Spanish American Literature," *Studies in Twentieth Century Literature* 19.1 (Winter 1995): 20. This article is the lead essay in a special issue of the journal devoted to the postboom.

61. Colás, 75.

62. Ibid., 94–95.

63. Yúdice, "¿Puede hablarse?" 127. In a similar move, Yúdice concludes "Post-

modernism in the Periphery," 555–556, by urging that the debate over this topic should include a questioning of the current significance of high-art forms. The closing paragraphs of the essay suggest, to those who would analyze postmodernism, other types of phenomena that should be examined. These are principally new developments in popular social thought and activist movements.

64. Ibid., 128.

65. John Beverley, in his "Introducción" to *Revista de Crítica Literaria Latinoamericana* 36 (1992): 16, pursues this idea and cites others who have also considered testimonial literature in some senses postmodern. Among these are Yúdice, Jameson, and the author of one of the most famous testimonial narratives, the Guatemalan Quiché Indian Rigoberta Menchú.

Chapter 3

1. Jean Franco, "Si me permiten hablar: la lucha por el poder interpretativo" (Let me speak: the struggle for interpretative power), *Revista de Crítica Literaria Latinoamericana* 18.36 (1992): 114. This special issue, *La voz del otro: testimonio, subalternidad y verdad narrativa* (The voice of the other: testimony, subordination, and narrative truth), is co-edited by John Beverley and Hugo Achugar.

2. Beverley and Zimmerman, "Testimonial Narrative," in their *Literature and Politics in the Central American Revolutions*, 173.

3. Ibid., 172–211.

4. David William Foster, "Latin American Documentary Narrative," *PMLA* 99 (1984): 41–55.

5. René Jara and Hernán Vidal, eds., *Testimonio y literatura* (Minneapolis: Institute for the Study of Ideologies and Literature, 1986).

6. Beverley and Zimmerman, 173.

7. Joseph Sommers, "Changing View of the Indian in Mexican Literature," *Hispania* 47 (1964): 47–55, and "The Indian-Oriented Novel in Latin America: New Spirit, New Forms, New Scope," *Journal of Inter-American Studies* 6 (1964): 249–265.

8. Ricardo Pozas, "Introducción" to his *Juan Pérez Jolote* (Havana: Editorial de Ciencias Sociales, 1972), 2.

9. Oscar Lewis, "Introduction" to his *The Children of Sánchez: Autobiography of a Mexican Family* (New York: Random House, 1961), xi.

10. Ibid., xii.

11. Franco, "Si me permiten hablar," 114, observes that in *The Children of Sánchez* Lewis "edits out his own questions" and is the one to structure the book "according to anthropological rites of passage." She states that while "What guarantees the authenticity of the narration is precisely 'the voice' . . . that authenticity is subverted not only by [Lewis's] process of editing the recordings but also . . . by the fact that [one Sánchez daughter] wrote her own autobiography and contributed

with written essays that Lewis later incorporated into the text without mentioning this non-oral source."

12. Lewis, *The Children of Sánchez:* "I dedicate this book with profound affection and gratitude to the Sánchez family, whose identity must remain anonymous," unnumbered dedication page.

13. Lewis, "Acknowledgments" to his *Pedro Martínez: A Mexican Peasant and His Family* (New York: Random House/Vintage, 1967), x.

14. Robert M. Levine, "The Cautionary Tale of Carolina Maria de Jesus," *Latin American Research Review* 29.1 (1994): 55–83.

15. González Echevarría, *"Biografía de un cimarrón* and the Novel of the Cuban Revolution," in his *The Voice of the Masters,* 118; entire essay, 110–123.

16. Ibid.

17. Ibid., 120.

18. Elzbieta Sklodowska, "Aproximaciones a la forma testimonial: novelística de Miguel Barnet" (Approximations to the testimonial form: the fiction of Miguel Barnet), *Hispamérica* 14.40 (1985): 28. Throughout her work on testimonial narrative, Sklodowska encourages skepticism toward the idea that such texts offer the direct, first-hand testimony of witnesses to history; she emphasizes the many mediating factors, including those that may be called literary. See her *Testimonio hispanoamericano: historia, teoría, poética* [Spanish American testimony: history, theory, poetics] (New York: Peter Lang, 1992).

19. Ibid.

20. Miguel Barnet, "Introducción" to his *Biografía de un cimarrón* (Havana: Instituto de Etnología y Folklore, 1966), 8.

21. Ibid., 9.

22. Ibid., 8.

23. Ibid., 6.

24. Sklodowska, "Testimonio mediatizado: ¿ventriloquia o heteroglosia? (Barnet/Montejo Burgos/Menchú)" [Mediated testimony: ventriloquism or heteroglossia?], *Revista de Crítica Literaria Latinoamericana* 19.38 (1993): 81–90.

25. Barnet, "La novela testimonio: Socio-literatura," *Revista Unión* [Havana] 6.4 (1969): 99–122. Also in Barnet, *La canción de Rachel* [The song of Rachel] (Barcelona: Estela, 1970), 125–150.

26. Barnet, comment in interview with Emilio F. Bejel, cited in Angel Flores, ed., *Spanish American Authors: The Twentieth Century* (New York: H. W. Wilson Co., 1992), 85.

27. For example, Monike Walter, "El cimarrón en una cimarronada: nuevos motivos para rechazar un texto y la forma como éste se nos impone" (The runaway slave in a herd of wild horses: new reasons to reject a text and the way it has been imposed on us), *Revista de Crítica Literaria Latinoamericana* 36 (1992): 201–205, is enthusiastic about Barnet's work, yet criticizes him for using traditional European literary terms to elaborate it.

28. Moema Viezzer, "To the Reader," introduction to Domitila Barrios de Chungara with Viezzer, *Let Me Speak! Testimony of Domitila, a Woman of the Bolivian Mines* (London: Monthly Review Press, 1978), 9–10.

29. José Carlos Mariátegui, *Siete ensayos de interpretación de la realidad peruana* [*Seven Interpretive Essays on Peruvian Reality*] (1928; reprint Caracas: Biblioteca Ayacucho, 1979), 335 (page citation is to the reprint edition).

30. Following the conquest, a number of Indian communities employed "a secretary charged with transcribing the memory of the community," so as "not to allow collective memory, which was now so imperiled, to be lost"; Lienhard, 55. Lienhard emphasizes that the Mayan-Quiché *Popol-Vuh* is only the most widely known of numerous compilations of native communities' most important lore. Angel Rama mentions that, in the years following Mariátegui's much-quoted wish for an Indian literature, several writers published literary works in native languages and Indians authored Spanish-language works on the debated issues of the day; see his *Transculturación narrativa en América Latina*, 78–79. Of the Indian-authored works he reviews, Rama singles out, 83–85, the 1980 *Antes o mundo não existia* (Earlier, the world did not exist) by two Brazilian Desâna Indians, Umúsin Panlõn Kumu and Tomalãn Kenhíri. He is struck by the ways in which the book goes beyond the preservation of narratives typical of folklore studies and shows an awareness of the situation of the Desânas in the twentieth century.

31. Beverley, "The Margin at the Center: On *Testimonio*," *Modern Fiction Studies* 35.1 (1989): 11–28. Beverley has also suggested that Menchú developed her arrestingly vivid mode of narration while giving Bible classes, which requires one to "dramatize the events he or she narrates": "Introducción" to *Revista de Crítica Literaria Latinoamericana* 18.36 (1992): 15.

32. Doris Sommer, "Sin secretos" (Without secrets), *Revista de Crítica Literaria Latinoamericana* 18.36 (1992): 135.

33. Beverley, "Introducción," 16, says " . . . we are face to face [in the analysis of testimonial writing, with specific reference to *I, Rigoberta Menchú*] with the problem of postmodernity. . . . It is not surprising that [George] Yúdice also thinks that it 'forms part of the cultural practices that today signal the decline of the "order of things" that correspond to modernity.'"

34. Ibid.

35. Ibid.

36. Ibid., 15.

37. George Yúdice, "Postmodernity and Transnational Capitalism," in Yúdice, Franco, and Flores, 23–24. Yúdice, in "¿Puede hablarse de postmodernidad en América Latina?" *Revista de Crítica Literaria Latinoamericana* 29 (1989), 128, suggests that researchers of Latin American postmodernism turn their attention to Burgos's *I, Rigoberta Menchú*, Poniatowska's *Until We Meet Again*, and a less noted work, *No me agarran viva: la mujer salvadoreña en la lucha* (They won't catch me alive: Salvadoran woman in the revolutionary struggle) by Claribel Alegría and Eugenia.

In his outlook, such writing "works to make it possible for experience to become, not empty spectacle or terrorist spectacle, as repressive regimes would like, but *articulation* and *transformation*," "¿Puede hablarse?" 128.

38. Elizabeth Burgos Debray, "Prólogo" to her *Me llamo Rigoberta Menchú* (Havana: Casa de las Américas, 1983), 19–20.

39. Ibid., 18.

40. See, for example, Franco, "Si me permiten hablar," especially 114, and Sklodowska, "Aproximaciones," as well as Fredric Jameson, "De la sustitución de importaciones literarias y culturales en el tercer mundo: el caso del testimonio" (On the substitution of literary and cultural imports in the Third World: the case of testimony), trans. Ana María del Río and John Beverley, *Revista de Crítica Literaria Latinoamericana* 18.36 (1992): 128.

41. Jameson, "De la sustitución," 129.

42. Ibid., 128–129.

43. Ibid., 129.

44. Ibid.

45. Sklodowska, "Testimonio mediatizado," 81–90.

46. Yúdice, "¿Puede hablarse?" 128, provides a dual attribution for each work. He refers to the authors as "Burgos/Menchú," "Alegría/Eugenia," and "Poniatowska/Jesusa."

47. González Echevarría, 123.

48. Sklodowska, "Aproximaciones," 33.

49. Franco, "Si me permiten hablar," 114.

Chapter 4

1. García Canclini, *Transforming Modernity*, 22.

2. Ibid. García Canclini's critical reformulation of concepts of popular cultures is summarized in Chapter 2, "Introduction to the Study of Popular Cultures," 21–35.

3. Emile G. McAnany, "Television and Cultural Discourses: Latin American and United States Comparisons," *Studies in Latin American Popular Culture* 8 (1989): 9, notes: "We need to recognize that the term popular culture as commonly used in North American writing, the term mass culture, and *cultura popular* in Latin American discourse have diverse meanings. In common United States usage, the term has, at least until recently, been one referring to popular response to mass-produced culture in purely market terms; in the Frankfurt school sense, it represents the industrialized cultural production that symbolizes all that is wrong with modern capitalist society; in the Latin American sense (and there is disagreement by authors on exact definitions), it stands generally for the culture of everyday lived experience of the subaltern classes."

4. Vicente Huidobro's script for *Cagliostro* earned an award from the League for Better Pictures (New York). According to Marcelo Coddou, *Cagliostro* "was never filmed, however, because the introduction of 'talkies' that same year [1927] made it anachronistic"; Coddou, "Vicente Huidobro," in Angel Flores, ed., *Spanish American Authors: The Twentieth Century* (New York: Wilson, 1992), 426.

5. René de Costa, the most noted Huidobro scholar, discusses Huidobro's involvement with silent film, and its effects on his innovative narrative, in *En pos de Huidobro: siete ensayos de aproximación* [In search of Huidobro: seven studies of his work] (Santiago, Chile: Editorial Universitaria, 1980), 71–93. In his invented genre of the *novela-film*, Huidobro also published the 1929 *Mío Cid Campeador*, translated into English as *Portrait of a Paladin*.

6. A collection of Villaurrutia's work in this form is Miguel Capistrán, ed., *Crítica cinematográfica* [Cinematographic criticism] (Mexico City: Universidad Nacional Autónoma de México, 1970).

7. Merlin H. Forster, "Xavier Villaurrutia," in Carlos A. Solé and Maria Isabel Abreu, eds., *Latin American Writers,* Volume 3 (New York: Scribner's, 1989), 975, remarks on Villaurrutia's skill at functioning in different cultural registers: "He was cultured and widely read, but at the same time had a passion for popular music and dance that led him to write romantic song lyrics, which were published anonymously."

8. J. Patrick Duffey, *De la pantalla al texto: La influencia del cine en la narrativa mexicana del siglo veinte* [From screen to text: the influence of film on twentieth-century Mexican fiction] (Mexico City: Universidad Nacional Autónoma de México, 1996).

9. Dwight B. Billings, "Critical Theory," in Edgar F. Borgatta and Marie L. Borgatta, eds., *Encyclopedia of Sociology,* Volume 1 (New York: Macmillan, 1992), 386.

10. The first segment in Cortázar's *Ultimo round* is "Teodoro W. Adorno gets religion"; see *Ultimo round,* Volume 1 (Madrid: Siglo XXI, 1974), 9–16. Cortázar's photograph of the celebrated cat appears early in *La vuelta al día en ochenta mundos,* Volume 1 (Madrid: Siglo XXI, 1974), 15, with a caption identifying the subject of the portrait as "Teodoro W. Adorno." Though neither text is available in its entirety in English, Cortázar and his long-time translator Thomas Christensen made a selection of texts from both volumes for the latter to turn into English. The resulting anthology appeared in 1986 as *Around the Day in Eighty Worlds* (San Francisco: North Point Press). Here, the Spanish versions will be cited because they include the texts in full.

11. Umberto Eco, *Apocalípticos e integrados ante la cultura de masas* (Apocalyptic and integrated ones in the face of mass culture), trans. Andrés Boglar (Barcelona: Lumen, 1968); *Apocalíticos e integrados* (São Paulo: Editora Perspectiva, 1970).

12. Cortázar, *Ultimo round,* Volume 1, 101, includes a citation from Marcuse surrounded by statements and slogans of the student protesters of 1968.

13. Cortázar, "What Happens, Minerva?" *La vuelta al día,* Volume 2, 5–11.

14. Ibid., 5.

15. Cortázar, *Ultimo round*, Volume 2, 265–280.

16. Ibid., Volume 1, 17.

17. Cortázar, "Una voce poco fa," *Ultimo round*, Volume 2, 178–180.

18. Cortázar, *Ultimo round*, Volume 2, 176.

19. Ibid.

20. Cortázar, "Gardel," *La vuelta al día*, Volume 1, 136.

21. Ibid.

22. David Viñas, interview with Mario Szichman, in *Hispamérica* 1 (1972), 66.

23. Following a reprinting of the 1969 version of *Ultimo round* in 1970, all subsequent editions to the present have utilized a simplified format that eliminates the division of the pages. The German edition, *Letzte Runde*, trans. Rudolf Wittkopf (Frankfurt: Suhrkamp, 1984), simplifies production yet further, reducing the number of different fonts and typefaces. The original, double-storied edition is now a collector's item.

24. Exemplary of cultural studies' upward reevaluation of popular culture is Janice A. Radway, *Reading the Romance: Women, Patriarchy, and Popular Culture* (Chapel Hill: University of North Carolina Press, 1984). Radway astonished many researchers with her finding that many readers of these romance narratives resourcefully derive from them a strengthening of women's role in society. This conclusion at first struck many observers as counterintuitive; yet many subsequent researchers have discovered among consumers a skill for transforming cultural items to generate new meanings and, in some cases, to resist the dominant values in their society. For reflections on the adoption of a cultural-studies approach to the analysis and teaching of Spanish American writing, see Beverley, *Against Literature.*

25. Fernando Ortiz explicates the term and concept *transculturación* in his *Contrapunteo cubano del tabaco y el azúcar.* This work has had many editions, including the English-language *Cuban Counterpoint: Tobacco and Sugar.*

26. McAnany, in "Television and Cultural Discourses," 9, observes that Néstor García Canclini and his collaborator Jesús Martín Barbero encourage greater attention to the adaptive strategies of less educated populations, yet "Canclini and Barbero argue that there was little evidence for an independent and liberating resistance on the part of audiences in the face of the massive presence of dominant media," and that scholars should not "assert the resistance of popular classes too strongly."

27. Cortázar, *Fantomas contra los vampiros multinacionales (una utopía realizable)* (Mexico City: Excélsior, 1975).

28. Wolfgang A. Luchting, "Julio Cortázar as a Strip-Teaser," *Chasqui* 6.2 (February 1977): 74–79.

29. One may see, especially, Ariel Dorfman's lengthy study "La última aventura del llanero solitario" (The last adventure of the Lone Ranger), in Dorfman and Manuel Jofré, *Superman y sus amigos del alma* [Superman and his bosom buddies] (Buenos Aires: Galerna, 1974), 11–92, for a critique of the individualistic and an-

ticommunal values embodied in action heroes. An English version, "The Lone Ranger's Last Ride," appears in Dorfman, *The Empire's Old Clothes*, 67–131. The critique of the solitary hero is amusingly encapsulated in "El llanero sin antifaz (Entrevista exclusiva de Ariel Dorfman)" (The ranger without his mask: an exclusive interview with Ariel Dorfman), in Dorfman's *Ensayos quemados en Chile: inocencia y neocolonialismo* [Essays burned in Chile: innocence and neocolonialism] (Buenos Aires: Ediciones de la Flor), 89–93.

30. One may see, for example, Carlos Montalvo, Jorge Vergara, Fernando Pérez, René Rebetez, and Ludolfo Paramio, *Ensayos marxistas sobre los 'comics'* [Marxist essays on comics] (Bogota: Ediciones Los Comuneros, 1976). Irene Herner's *Mitos y monitos: historietas y fotonovelas en México* [Myths and cartoon characters: comic books and photonovels in Mexico] (Mexico City: Editorial Nueva Imagen/Universidad Nacional Autónoma de México, 1979) is similar to Dorfman and Mattelart in its content analysis, but differs in devoting attention to the layout and graphic shorthand typical of comics, as well as the production, distribution, and marketing of the popular publications studied.

31. The original, French, Fantômas appeared in February 1911. The creation of Pierre Souvestre and Marcel Allain, the elegant "king of the night" was featured in a series of short novels, as well as in five films by Louis Feuillade. Fantômas narratives gained a cult following that included such avant-garde writers as Guillaume Apollinaire and Jean Cocteau. English-language reissues of the 1910s Fantômas adventures were published by Morrow (New York) under the titles *Fantomas* (1986) and *The Silent Executioner: Fantomas Adventures 2* (1987). These two volumes include appreciative introductions to Fantomas by, respectively, the distinguished poet John Ashbery and the neo-Gothic illustrator Edward Gorey. Fantomas is well known in Spanish-speaking countries through a comic book, which would appear to be the direct antecedent of Cortázar's *Fantomas*.

32. Cortázar, *Fantomas* (1989 edition), 42.

33. Luchting, 74.

34. Rubén Sánchez, *Fantomas, la amenaza elegante* (Fantomas, the elegant menace), artwork executed in the Estudio Martínez and published by Editorial Novaro, Mexico City, in 1983.

35. Rius (Eduardo del Río), *Marx for Beginners* (New York: Pantheon, 1979).

36. Karl Marx, Friedrich Engels, and Rius, *The Communist Manifesto Illustrated and Explicated to Fit Your Brain, Schooled, Fooled, Learned, or Burned* (Madison: Quixote Press, 1977?).

37. Rius, *The Chicanos* (New York: National Congress on Latin America, 1973).

38. See, for example, Charles M. Tatum, "Ruis [sic]: der Comics-Autor als Sozialkritiker und politischer Unruhestifter" (The comic author as social critic and political agitator), *Iberoamericana* 13/14 (1982), 78–91; and Paula K. Speck, "Rius for Beginners: A Study in Comicbook Satire," *Studies in Latin American Popular Culture* 1 (1982), 113–124. Phyllis Ann Proctor's 1972 dissertation from the University of Texas at Austin, *Mexico's "Supermachos": Satire and Social Revolution in*

Comics by Rius, focuses on Rius's early work mocking the Mexican ruling party and political system.

39. Rius's most successful U.S. disciple has been Richard Appignanesi, who interested the Pantheon house in producing Rius comics in translation and Rius-inspired sequels. An example of the former is *Marx for Beginners* (cited above), while the latter is represented by A. & Z. (i.e., Appignanesi and Oscar Zarate), *Lenin for Beginners* (New York: Pantheon, 1978) and *Freud for Beginners* (New York: Pantheon, 1979). An effort to win a U.S. public for Rius's teaching is the translation of his *Cuba para principiantes*, issued under the new title *Cuba for Beginners: An Illustrated Guide for Americans (and Their Government) to Socialist Cuba* (New York: Pathfinder Press, 1970).

40. For example, Harold E. Hinds, Jr., while recognizing *How to Read Donald Duck* as "the single most influential work on comics written in Latin America . . . without doubt," says of Dorfman and Mattelart: "Their approach essentially ignores semiology or the idea that comics are composed of a system of signs to convey meanings and focuses instead on narrative more than visual elements"; see his chapter "Comics" in Hinds and Charles M. Tatum, eds., *Handbook of Latin American Popular Culture* (Westport, CT: Greenwood Press, 1985), 90.

41. Jofré, "Las historietas y su cambio: experiencias prácticas para la transformación de los medios en el Proceso Chileno" (Comic books and changing them: practical experiments in the transformation of the media during the Chilean Process), in Jofré and Dorfman, 95–201.

42. Frank Gerace Larufa with Hernando Lázaro, *Comunicación horizontal* (Lima: Studium, 1973).

43. Cortázar in *Nicaragua tan violentamente dulce* [Nicaragua, so violently sweet] (Managua, Nicaragua: Editorial Nueva Nicaragua/Ediciones Monimbo, 1983), admires the campaign by the Nicaraguan revolutionary government to involve workers in the creative arts.

44. Jofré, "Las historietas y su cambio," 131–134, offers an illustration of how *cotidianización* is carried out in reworking the plot of a comic.

45. Ibid., 131–132.

46. Ibid., 185.

47. Ibid., 190.

48. Ibid., 186.

49. Ibid., 187.

Chapter 5

1. Gabriela Mora, "Un diálogo entre feministas hispanoamericanas," in Vidal, *Cultural and Historical Grounding*, 53–77. Amy K. Kaminsky's "Lesbian Cartographies: Body, Text, and Geography," 223–256 of the same volume, also makes the point that Latin American intellectuals are more hesitant to be identified as feminists and more apprehensive about being perceived as lesbians. She notes that the

growth of feminist research from Latin America was for a long time slowed by "women scholars' fear of having their sexuality impugned" (225).

2. Castillo, 33.

3. Ibid.

4. Ibid., 36.

5. Ibid., 30.

6. Following her own recommendation, Castillo opens *Talking Back* with a four-page, unpaginated "Recetario" (recipe collection) of citations; the majority of these are from Spanish American women writers.

7. Mary Wollstonecraft's 1792 treatise continues to be reissued; see *A Vindication of the Rights of Woman* (Buffalo, N.Y.: Prometheus Books, 1989).

8. Flora Tristán, *Perigrinations of a Pariah, 1833–1834*, trans., ed., and intro. Jean Hawkes (London: Virago, 1986).

9. The new interest in this nineteenth-century feminist has led to fresh editions of her work. English-language readers may see *Flora Tristán, Utopian Feminist: Her Travel Diaries and Personal Crusade*, selected, translated, and with an introduction to her life by Doris and Paul Baik (Bloomington: Indiana University Press, 1993).

10. Rosario Ferré, "La cocina de la escritura," in González and Ortega, 139–141, refers jokingly to her early efforts to follow the advice of Simone de Beauvoir and Virginia Woolf. An English version, "The Writer's Kitchen," appears in Doris Meyer, ed., *Lives on the Line: The Testimony of Contemporary Latin American Authors* (Berkeley: University of California Press, 1988), 212–227.

11. Gwen Kirkpatrick, "El feminismo en los tiempos del cólera" (Feminism in the time of cholera), *Revista de Crítica Literaria Latinoamericana* 42 (1995): 45.

12. For example, Elaine Marks and Isabelle de Courtivron entitle their extremely useful collection of essays by French theorists *New French Feminisms: An Anthology* (Amherst: University of Massachusetts Press, 1980), although some of its contributors reject the term *feminist* to describe their work. This title reflects the perception of most observers that the ideas and concerns represented in the anthology are feminist in character.

13. Lillian S. Robinson, *Sex, Class, and Culture* (Bloomington: Indiana University Press, 1978).

14. Domitila Barrios de Chungara, statements made during the Encuentro de Mujeres in Mexico City, 1975; cited in Kirkpatrick, 48.

15. Sara Castro-Klarén, "A Possible Poetics for Women," in Vidal, *Cultural and Historical Grounding*, 103.

16. Vidal, "Introducción" to *Cultural and Historical Grounding*, 13. Vidal draws his examples from an actual debate over the Spanish translation of *gender*. This discussion took place over the course of a conference held at the University of Minnesota, 31 March–2 April 1988, which produced the original versions of the papers Vidal includes in his volume.

17. Ibid., 14.

18. Mora, 55.

19. Ibid., 74. Mora draws attention to the difficulty of translating such terms as *femaleness* and *nurturing being*. She notes (75) that her reflections on the difficulty of translating terms were prompted by the debates at the 1988 conference at the University of Minnesota noted above.

20. Patricia Ann Meyer Spacks, *The Female Imagination* (New York: Knopf, 1975).

21. Patricia M. Spacks, *La imaginación femenina*, trans. Paloma Albarca and Soledad Puértolas (Madrid: Editorial Debate, 1980).

22. Elaine Showalter, *A Literature of Their Own: British Women Novelists from Brontë to Lessing* (Princeton: Princeton University Press, 1977); Sandra Gilbert and Susan Gubar, *The Madwoman in the Attic: The Woman Writer and the Nineteenth-Century Literary Imagination* (New Haven: Yale University Press, 1979).

23. Castro-Klarén, "A Possible Poetics," 98.

24. Marta Traba, "Hipótesis de una escritura diferente," in González and Ortega, *La sartén por el mango*, 23; entire article, 21–26.

25. Ibid.

26. Ibid.

27. Ibid., 24.

28. Castro-Klarén, "La crítica literaria feminista y la escritora en América Latina," in González and Ortega, *La sartén por el mango*, 27–44.

29. Ibid., 31.

30. Ibid.

31. Ibid.

32. Emir Rodríguez Monegal, *Sexo y poesía en el 900 uruguayo: los extraños destinos de Roberto y Delmira* [Sex and poetry in twentieth-century Uruguay: the strange fates of Roberto and Delmira] (Montevideo, Uruguay: Alfa, 1969), 35–43, gives many examples of the way in which Agustini was written about as if she were a child. (The number 900 in this title refers to the twentieth century; dates are occasionally styled in this manner in Spanish.)

33. Electa Arenal and Stacey Schlau, *Untold Sisters: Hispanic Nuns in Their Own Works*, trans. Amanda Powell (Albuquerque: University of New Mexico Press, 1989).

34. Schlau, "Madre Castillo (1671–1742), Colombia," in Diane E. Marting, ed., *Spanish American Women Writers* (Westport, Conn.: Greenwood Press, 1990), 160.

35. Ibid., 158–159.

36. Ludwig Pfandl, *Sor Juana Inés de la Cruz, la décima musa de México: su vida, su poesía, su psique* (Sister Juana Inés de la Cruz, the tenth muse of Mexico: her life, her poetry, her psyche), trans. Juan Antonio Ortega y Medina (Mexico City: Instituto de Investigaciones Estéticas, Universidad Autónoma de México, 1963). The original edition appeared in Munich in 1946.

37. For a summary of the dissatisfaction with traditional Sor Juana criticism,

see Julie Greer Johnson, "Sor Juana Inés de la Cruz (1648?–1695) Mexico," in Marting, 278–279.

38. Stephanie Merrim, ed., *Feminist Perspectives on Sor Juana Inés de la Cruz* (Detroit: Wayne State University Press, 1990).

39. Josefina Ludmer, "Tretas del débil," in González and Ortega, *La sartén por el mango*, 47–54.

40. Ibid., 49.

41. Castillo, 36.

42. Ibid.

43. Castro-Klarén, Mora, and Castillo, in the studies discussed in this chapter, all exhibit this outlook. Worth noting is Castillo's accurate subtitle, *Toward a Latin American Feminist Criticism*; Lucía Guerra-Cunningham, "Las sombras de la escritura: hacia una teoría de la producción literaria de la mujer latinoamericana" (The shadows of writing: toward a theory of the literary production of the Latin American woman), in Vidal's edited collection, 129–164. In addition to individual articles in Vidal's volume, its overall title, *Cultural and Historical Grounding for Hispanic and Luso-Brazilian Feminist Literary Criticism*, reflects the struggle to make feminist criticism correspond to historical circumstances often unlike those under which it was originally generated. A somewhat different aspect of the same perennial problem is explored by Kaminsky, noted above for her research on lesbianism. In her 1993 *Reading the Body Politic: Feminist Criticism and Latin American Women Writers*, Kaminsky repeatedly draws attention to her own position as a U.S. feminist carrying out analyses of Latin American texts. Her goal is to make herself and readers who are either North American or educated in Anglo-American feminism self-critically aware of the biases that they may bring to their readings.

44. Winston Leyland, ed., *Now the Volcano: An Anthology of Latin American Gay Literature*, trans. Erskine Lane, Franklin D. Blanton, and Simon Karlinsky (San Francisco: Gay Sunshine Press, 1979); *My Deep Dark Pain Is Love: A Collection of Latin American Gay Fiction* (San Francisco: Gay Sunshine Press, 1983).

45. A second volume of Foster's analyses of gay and lesbian issues in Latin American texts is forthcoming from the University of Texas Press; its working title is *Sexual Textualities: Essays on Queer/ing Latin American Writing*.

46. One may see also Foster's *Producción cultural e identidades homoeróticas: teoría y aplicaciones* (Cultural production and homoerotic identities: theory and applied studies). A desktop publication available from the author at the Department of Languages and Literatures, Arizona State University, Tempe, AZ 85782-0202, *Producción cultural* gives an overview of current-day "queer theory," a discussion of gay and lesbian themes in Spanish American, Mexican American, and Brazilian texts, and, in an appendix, sample analyses.

47. Paul Julian Smith and Emilie L. Bergmann, "Introduction" to Bergmann and Smith, 1.

48. Licia Fiol-Matta, "The 'Schoolteacher of America': Gender, Sexuality, and Nation in Gabriela Mistral," and Sylvia Molloy, "Disappearing Acts: Reading Les-

bian in Teresa de la Parra," Bergmann and Smith, 201–229 and 230–256 respectively.

49. Daniel Balderston, "The 'Fecal Dialectic': Homosexual Panic and the Origins of Writing in Borges," in Bergmann and Smith, 29–45.

50. The section of *¿Entiendes?* subtitled "(Neo)historical retrievals" contains Jorge Salessi, "The Argentine Dissemination of Homosexuality," 49–91; and Oscar Montero, "Julián del Casal and the Queers of Havana," 92–112, both of which draw on late-nineteenth-century treatises and reportage concerned with social hygiene.

51. Montero, 101.

52. Bergmann and Smith, "Introduction" to their jointly edited *¿Entiendes?*, 9.

53. Ibid., 8.

Selected Bibliography

This bibliography is of works of scholarship and more-popular cultural and social criticism. It does not include any narrative texts, focusing instead on critical discussion of the issues discussed in this book. It is fundamentally a list of suggested readings for those who would like to pursue further the questions and debates that have been surveyed here.

In the selection of works for inclusion, preference has gone to works available in English translation. Special attention has also gone to books that, though they have not been translated into English as of this writing, would inherently seem to be of potential interest to an English-language readership. The hope is that drawing attention to them here will increase their likelihood of appearing in English.

Benítez Rojo, Antonio. *La isla que se repite: el Caribe y la perspectiva posmoderna*. Hanover, N.H.: Ediciones del Norte, 1989. *The Repeating Island: The Caribbean and the Postmodern Perspective*. Trans. James E. Maraniss. Durham: Duke University Press, 1992.

Bergmann, Emilie L., and Paul Julian Smith. *¿Entiendes? Queer Readings, Hispanic Writings*. Durham: Duke University Press, 1995.

Beverley, John. *Against Literature*. Minneapolis: University of Minnesota Press, 1993.

Beverley, John, and Marc Zimmerman. *Literature and Politics in the Central American Revolutions*. Austin: University of Texas Press, 1990.

Castillo, Debra A. *Talking Back: Toward a Latin American Feminist Criticism*. Ithaca, N.Y.: Cornell University Press, 1992.

Dorfman, Ariel. *The Empire's Old Clothes: What the Lone Ranger, Babar, and Other Innocent Heroes Do to Our Minds*. With translations by Clark Hansen. New York: Pantheon, 1983.

Dorfman, Ariel, and Armand Mattelart. *Para leer al Pato Donald*. Valparaíso, Chile: Ediciones Universitarias de Valparaíso, Universidad Católica de Valparaíso, 1971. *How to Read Donald Duck: Imperialist Ideology in the Disney Comic*. Trans. and intro. David Kunzle. New York: International General, 1975.

Fernández Moreno, César, ed. *Latin America in Its Literature.* Asst. ed. Julio Ortega. Ed. for the English edition, Ivan A. Schulman. Trans. Mary G. Berg. New York: Holmes and Meier, 1980.

Fernández Retamar, Roberto. *Caliban and Other Essays.* Original date of *Calibán,* 1973. Trans. Edward Baker. Minneapolis: University of Minnesota Press, 1989.

Foster, David William. *Gay and Lesbian Themes in Latin American Writing.* Austin: University of Texas Press, 1991.

———. "Some Proposals for the Study of Latin American Gay Culture." In his *Cultural Diversity in Latin American Literature.* Albuquerque: University of New Mexico Press, 1994, 25–71.

———, ed. *Handbook of Latin American Literature.* 2nd. rev. ed. New York: Garland, 1992.

———, ed. *Latin American Writers on Gay and Lesbian Themes: A Bio-critical Sourcebook.* Westport, Conn.: Greenwood Press, 1994.

Foster, David William, and Roberto Reis, eds. *Bodies and Biases: The Representation of Sexualities in Hispanic Cultures and Literatures.* Minnesota: University of Minnesota Press, 1996.

Franco, Jean. *Plotting Women: Gender and Representation in Mexico.* New York: Columbia University Press, 1989.

García Canclini, Néstor. *Culturas híbridas: Estrategias para entrar y salir de la modernidad.* Mexico: Grijalbo, 1989. *Hybrid Cultures: Strategies for Entering and Leaving Modernity.* Trans. Christopher L. Chiappori and Sylvia L. López. Minneapolis: University of Minnesota Press, 1995.

———. *Transforming Modernity: Popular Culture in Mexico* [Original title *Las culturas populares en el capitalismo,* 1982]. Trans. Lidia Lozano. Austin: University of Texas Press, 1993.

González, Patricia Elena, and Eliana Ortega, eds. *La sartén por el mango: encuentro de escritoras latinoamericanas* (The frying pan by the handle: meeting of Latin American women writers). Río Piedras, P.R.: Ediciones Huracán, 1984.

González Echevarría, Roberto. *The Voice of the Masters: Writing and Authority in Modern Latin American Literature.* Austin: University of Texas Press, 1985.

Kaminsky, Amy K. *Reading the Body Politic: Feminist Criticism and Latin American Women Writers.* Minneapolis: University of Minnesota Press, 1993.

Lienhard, Martin. *La voz y su huella: escritura y conflicto étnico-social en América Latina, 1492–1988* (The voice and its mark: writing and ethnic-social conflict in Latin America). 3rd. rev. ed. Lima: Editorial Horizonte, 1992.

Magnarelli, Sharon. *The Lost Rib: Female Characters in the Spanish American Novel.* Lewisburg, Penn.: Bucknell University Press/Associated University Presses, 1985.

Masiello, Francine. *Between Civilization and Barbarism: Women, Nation, and Literary Culture in Modern Argentina.* Lincoln: University of Nebraska Press, 1992.

Miller, Yvette, ed. *Latin American Women Writers: Yesterday and Today.* Pittsburgh: Latin American Literary Review Press, 1978.

Navarro, Desiderio, ed. *South Atlantic Quarterly* 93.3 (Summer 1993). Special issue "Postmodernism: Center and Periphery."

Ortiz [Fernández], Fernando. *Contrapunteo cubano del tabaco y el azúcar: advertencia de sus contrastes agrarios, económicos, históricos, y sociales, su etnografía y su transculturación.* Havana: J. Montero, 1940. *Cuban Counterpoint: Tobacco and Sugar.* Trans. Harriet de Onís. New York: Knopf, 1949; reissue, Durham: Duke University Press, 1995.

Paz, Octavio. *The Siren and the Seashell and Other Essays on Poets and Poetry* [Original title *Cuadrivio*, 1964]. Trans. Lysander Kemp and Margaret Sayers Peden. Austin: University of Texas Press, 1976.

Rama, Angel. *Transculturación narrativa en América Latina.* Mexico City: Siglo XXI, 1982.

Ruffinelli, Jorge, ed. *Modernidad y posmodernidad en América Latina (I)*, *Modernidad y posmodernidad en América Latina (II)*. Special thematic issues of *Nuevo Texto Crítico* 6 (1990) and 7 (1991).

Sarlo, Beatriz. *Escenas de la vida posmoderna: intelectuales, arte y videocultura en la Argentina* (Scenes of postmodern life: intellectuals, art, and videoculture in Argentina). Buenos Aires: Ariel, 1994.

Vidal, Hernán, ed. *Cultural and Historical Grounding for Hispanic and Luso-Brazilian Feminist Literary Criticism.* Minneapolis: Institute for the Study of Ideologies and Literature, 1989.

———, ed. *Literatura latinoamericana e ideología de la dependencia.* Special issue of *Hispamérica* 4.1 (1975).

Vuelta 11.127 (June 1987). This much-noted Mexican intellectual review contains a section on postmodernism.

Williams, Raymond L. *The Postmodern Novel in Latin America: Politics, Culture, and the Crisis of Truth.* New York: St. Martin's, 1995.

Yúdice, George, Jean Franco, and Juan Flores, eds. *On Edge: The Crisis of Contemporary Latin American Culture.* Minneapolis: University of Minnesota Press, 1992.

Index